Global Business and Corporate Governance

Global Business and Corporate Governance

Environment, Structure, and Challenges

John Thanopoulos

business**expert**
Press

Global Business and Corporate Governance:
Environment, Structure, and Challenges
Copyright © Business Expert Press, LLC, 2014.

First published in 2014 by
Business Expert Press, LLC
222 East 46th Street, New York, NY 10017
www.businessexpertpress.com

ISBN-13: 978-1-60649-864-4 (paperback)
ISBN-13: 978-1-60649-865-1 (e-book)

Business Expert Press International Business Collection

Collection ISSN: 1948-2752 (print)
Collection ISSN: 1948-2760 (electronic)

Cover and interior design by Exeter Premedia Services Private Ltd., Chennai, India

First edition: 2014

10 9 8 7 6 5 4 3 2 1

Printed in the United States of America.

To George and Sofia and to all my teachers
and students who made my life's trip so magnificent!

Abstract

This textbook presents, dear reader, a new era where the main force for social change, research, education, economic betterment, and even employee happiness is the global enterprise. From the outset it is assumed that today all business is global though often with conflicting priorities and potential civilization clashes. Also, it showcases that we operate in a practically borderless world seeking ideas and talents globally.

Therefore, this book aims to brief you on business-related issues ranging from historical matters to the realities of the 21st century, from local cultures to global organizations and from political, legal, and economic topics to accounting, finance, marketing, and management perspectives. It also aims to direct your attention to critical business challenges as well as to the need of corporate governance at all levels. These issues relate to the environment and the structure of the corporation.

However, these very issues may result in restating the organizational objectives since the corporate era parallels the roles and the responsibilities that countries had in the past. For that matter wise, prudent, knowledgeable, ethical, philosophically-oriented, and enlightened corporate leaders are needed.

From a practical side the material presented is better suited for upper-level undergraduate, graduate study, and executive education, and it provides a combination of how-to-do matters and philosophical perspectives of a new and challenging era.

Keywords

business challenges, business ethics, corporate governance, ethics, global business, global organizations, international accounting, international finance, international management, international marketing, philosophy, self-actualization

Contents

Preface

During my years of business and academic experience, I have collected hundreds of books on international business,[1] philosophy, history, sociology, and so on. It fascinates me that most of the international business concepts we perceive as brand new were discussed and challenged since the mid-1950s, or even earlier.

Therefore, in writing this book I aim not only to present the environment and structure of today's global business but also to address challenges that the globalization of business has brought. In the process, this book became a mix of the technocratic needs of the global enterprise, an economic theory, and a philosophical perspective of our era. These concepts are interconnected. In fact, I believe that the era of global business—an era that will propel the human enterprise to become the major societal player in the near future—is already taking shape in terms of research, significance, size, employee happiness, philosophy, and ethics.

At the outset, I would like to clarify a few essential definitions. This book deals with "business." I use all related nouns such as business, company, corporation, enterprise, firm, organization, or transnational interchangeably. In a parallel sense and although most businesses have a profit motive, to a great extent the material presented also applies to the not-for-profit entities, including governmental and nongovernmental ones. Business is now perceived as a societal player that takes on new roles and is responsible for economic growth and social betterment,[2] and operates within a practically borderless global environment.

National identities, symbols, and icons are milestones of the passage of civilizations: the Roman Empire, the British Empire, the Pyramids, the Great Wall of China, Alexander the Great, and Napoleon the Great are all indicative of past eras motivated by economic ambitions and personal glory.

In my opinion, the 21st century is also motivated by economic ambitions and personal glory. It will be established as the era of corporate identities and, to some extent, by personal icons. The geopolitical dynamics of the past are giving way to a new societal order that is rapidly changing to a corporate-driven status quo. Already we are witnessing hundreds of corporations with annual sales (as well as wealth portfolios of individuals) that are larger than the gross national product of entire nations. We are also witnessing corporate executives who are routinely rewarded salaries and bonuses that are a hundred times more than the average employee; and athletes, musicians, and politicians who may define, through their lifestyles, the *modus vivendi* of the future. Alas! Their ways of life are very different from those of the average individual. They are the pharaohs of a new era. Benchmarking should be realistic and achievable to be meaningful.

This is one side of the 21st century coin. The other?

Material motivation should be questioned; though, for most people a larger home, a yacht, or a private jet are still valid objectives for a better life. Nevertheless there is a trend toward self-actualization of the individual, simplicity of human desires, and a deeper understanding of existential reasoning. Wise people like Mahatma Gandhi taught us that "one must become as humble as dust before he can discover truth."[3] We shall revisit this statement at the end of this book. My proposition is that corporate governance in the near future will embrace these values and become more focused toward philosophy, truth, and ethics.

This book begins with an introductory chapter on historical perspectives and modern era corporate governance, and then transports the reader from topographical issues to cultural developments, to philosophy and ethics, to national and corporate cultures, to the environment of the global business village, and the functions of the contemporary enterprises. The business world has one constant: Change! Everywhere there are realities, risks, trends, and challenges. This book points to these business challenges, which are often opportunities for the daring and reasons for the demise of others. There are dozens of business challenges presented in this book. Some examples include: geopolitical and business dynamics; cultural adaptation; cultural imperialism; behavioral protocols; civilization clashes; perceptions of philosophy and truth; ethical concerns; corporate cultures; 21st century realities; societal changes; effects of technology, information technology, and media; international finance issues; global marketing trends; and different political, legal, and economic systems.

Business addresses these challenges as potential opportunities, not only to achieve business objectives but also to perform a defining societal role as *the* factor responsible for sustainable economic growth, production, equitable development, research, education, social balance, and human happiness. In my opinion, the minimum requirements for today's enterprise are that it must be creative, consumer-based, human resource-centered, ethical, and able to capitalize on the available information technologies.

Finally, I want to sincerely thank Rob Zwettler, Destiny Hadley, and Shyam Joseph for making this text available to a broader audience and for significantly improving its grammatical flow. Moreover, I want to express my gratitude to certain individuals, most of whom are deceased, whose example, mentoring, and assistance made it possible for my humble self to communicate concepts of social improvement. They include my parents, John Dorbis, Jim Dunlap, George Minettas, Lawrence Schkade, Evan Syrigos, Phil Taylor, Willis Wolf, and Panayiotis Ziridis.

John Thanopoulos
February 2014

Abbreviations

Note: In this book, acronyms that have been used extensively as corporate names, for example, GM or IBM, are also used.

AIB	Academy of International Business
ASEAN	Association of South East Asian Nations
DC	developed country
ECOWAS	Economic Community of West African States
ERP	enterprise resource planning
FASB	Financial Accounting Standards Board
FDI	foreign direct investment
GCC	Gulf Cooperation Council
GLOCAL	Combination of the words Global and Local
GNP	gross national product
IBRD	International Bank for Reconstruction and Development
IDA	International Development Association
IFC	International Financial Corporation
IMO	International Maritime Organization
ISM	International Safety Management (Code)
IT	information technology
LDC	less developed country
MARPOL	International Convention for the Prevention of Pollution from Ships
NAFTA	North America Free Trade Agreement
OPEC	Organization of Petroleum Exporting Countries
PPP	Purchasing Power Parity
RFID	radio frequency identification
SFAS	Statements of Financial Accounting Standards
SOLAS	International Convention for the Safety of Life at Sea
SRC	Self-Reference Criterion
UNCITRAL	United Nations Commission on International Trade
WTO	Word Trade Organization

CHAPTER 1

The Human Enterprise and Its Governance

In the 1960s, I had the first discussions focusing on the topic of this book. During those years these discussions were bordering on science fiction, though rapid social change was evident. The human enterprise, often directed by individual might and not by the power of the state, was already globalized though rarely following standardized game rules. The issue of corporate social responsibility and responsiveness was a major managerial concern, sound corporate governance was *sine qua non* of business success, and 25 U.S. academic programs have already a series of courses on business internationalization. Four decades does not seem a long time ago, however, at that time, most of the developed world had only a superficial understanding of global business.

This chapter aims to be an introduction to those that follow addressing historical perspectives of the enterprise and main issues surrounding its philosophy, ethical behavior, corporate culture, and its corporate governance.

Working Hypotheses

Although the main purpose of this book is to familiarize the reader with the conceptual framework of the modern enterprise, it is important from the outset to begin by repeating the relativity of our existence; the diameter of the known universe is measured in billions of light-years.[1] This is a system infinitely larger than our conception. Therefore, in our infinite cosmos, in itself systemic, we need to accept some initial working hypotheses:

1. The framework of analysis is a function of the knowledge we possess at a specific time; it constantly evolves.
2. The quality of data is critical. Without data we cannot draw conclusions.

3. Leaders' competence is questionable. Are the most competent persons chosen to lead? Thus, due to the leadership, its abilities and motivation, do we suboptimize our potential?
4. Have we studied the trends that will shape the decades to come? Who are (truly) listening—nations or corporations?

Therefore, it is important to repeat a statement made at the preface and to be reminded of the relative revenue size of the world's largest corporations as compared to the gross national product (GNP) of countries.[2] Thus, in a table where countries and large global companies are presented together, the largest global company may rank around the 25th position, whereas more than 80 countries have GNP smaller than the revenues of the 500th largest corporation.

Countries and corporations have leaders who are responsible for the well-being of the people as well as for any living organism on the planet, sustainable future of our tiny planet, and an equitable and fair management of the organizations it happened to govern.

Historical Perspectives

During all stages of human history, the individual is empowered through his or her family, tribe, society, and nation. The main factors of his or her social progress relate to the environment, resources, culture, philosophical tenets, scientific-technological achievements, and the entrepreneurial thinking of the era. Spatial perception is based on one's own observation. The existence of significant individuals relates to acceptable norms (e.g., Pharaohs being considered as deities) and power relationships (e.g., the losers of wars become slaves). The enterprise, as an institution, exists but not at the importance of the postindustrial revolution era.

The wars and significant structures left by our ancestors were enterprises that demanded vision, planning, factors of production, administration, and control procedures. At the end, ruling over other nations depended on military, economic, and cultural might. Achieving goals was teleological[3] in nature. However, the implementation force was human activity, mainly that of submissive slaves. The laws were in favor of the rulers and the perception of morality did not apply to most of the workers.

After the Second World War, major global corporations from the United States, Europe, and Japan, using breakthrough business practices undertook social roles, traditionally found only under governmental umbrellas. Serving the interests of the company stockholders was not enough, anymore. Management realized that company survival and growth depended on a corporate culture serving all its stakeholders needs, including employees, customers, and the environment, in general. Since the corporate mission invariably has a teleological character, its vision toward stockholders, employees, customers, and the environment, in general, can be described as a four-sided tunnel whose sides are flexible, depending on the deontology that the corporation has with respect to specific social practices.

Before and After the Industrial Revolution: Two Business Models

Business processes have been described with superb details for hundreds of years. From Sun Tzu to the Trojan War and from the Olympic Games to the Roman Empire bureaucracies, one can fathom with focused detail of the practices utilized. However, it is only during the past 50 to 100 years that the business *modus operandi* has been seen as the primary mechanism of societal evolution, and has been studied through functional modeling and scientifically acceptable methodologies.

We may visualize the before-and-after of the industrial revolution business realities through two "models." The first having at its center the people of power, the Pharaohs, the Kings, and the Emperors, whereas the second focuses on the individual, the everyday person.

Let's start with the before the industrial revolution era social model. As we said, for thousands of years of human evolution the individual is reinforced by the bonds and the social support structure of the family, the society, the race, the nation, and the state. The main factors of social progress depend on the environment, the resources it provides, the philosophy and principles of the culture, scientific-technological and cultural achievements of the times, and the business thinking of society. The perception of outer space is based on personal observation and senses. The existence of powerful and lesser people is linked to the prevailing behavioral codes and to the generally acceptable dynamics of relations.

During those years business, as an institution, did exist, but it had not gained the importance and momentum it has acquired in the past 200 years. Achieving (business) objectives was teleological in nature. For example, the hardships of the workers who built the Great Wall of China were not inhibitors of the progress of the project. Yet, ultimately, country-state might, trade opportunities, economic prosperity, and cultural recognition were the main elements of sovereignty of the people.

In essence, submission to the laws, religious constructs, and the concept of morality was instrumental in forming the societal fabric by limiting individual freedom. Business profits depended oftentimes on the painfully oppressed, human labor.

> Prophetic of future business mismanagement applications, the Revelation of John states "*Why your merchants (Babylon) were the rulers of the earth because of the spell you put on all nations.*"[4]

By extension, and for our era, the idea of "spell" could be partially seen as advertising and influence of the media, whereas the idea of "nation" appears to be analogous to modern internationalized corporations.

How did business operate before the industrial revolution? The environment and its topographical and geographical realities have always defined its unique character and adaptation needs. It had to operate in a different way in Alaska and a different way in the Sahara. Moreover, the geographical realities, to a great extent, defined the (then) social fabric (race, nation, and state) including elements such as laws, religions, procedures, science, technology, art, and so on.

It should also be mentioned that the systemic focus before the industrial revolution was the status quo of those in power, those who make the rules, lead the spiritual elite, and possess the means to suppress the rest. Notice that before the industrial revolution the focus was not toward the ordinary people who, for all practical purposes, were considered as slaves. In this model, everybody and every system were working for the benefit, wealth, and fame of the rulers and of those who control the laborers. We may visualize this model as three concentric circles, the outer being the environment, the middle one being the social fabric, and central one the people in power.

Let us now move to the realities of the postindustrial revolution era model[5], which effectively is the same as before but the attention, the center of it, is the everyday individual. In many ways the previous model still exists, especially in underdeveloped and developing regions of our planet. After the industrial revolution, the use of engines and energy exponentially multiplied the productive entrepreneurial potential of human creativity. To reach their destination people no longer needed human labor to propel vehicles and vessels. The machines, powered by coal or oil, assumed this work. Thus, former rowers began using their spare time and energy to build more and better machinery and processes. Over time, the abilities of the workers accelerated the rate of change and, now being managers, redefined systemic priorities. In redefining priorities earlier production systems were not satisfactory anymore.

After the industrial revolution individuals assumed their own rights, societal dynamics, and reason of being. They move away from home early, have social choices, divorce easily, and consider their perceived happiness and interests. They follow new and meritorious norms of employment, upgrade constantly their education, seek material wealth, adopt lifestyles suited to their own priorities, engage to ethical responsibility norms, and understand the importance of virtual environments.[6] Because the system enables the individual to be freer of restrictions imposed by family or country, dependence on them is much less pronounced than in the past.

Of course, beyond the individual and the family, the state and the political establishment continues to exist,[7] but it acquires regulatory roles, both in terms of the individual's social upbringing and institutional operation, standards, and controls. Moreover, the well-managed state offers a justice system that applies to all (no one is above the law), whereas previous such systems were biased in favor of persons with power.

One may ask: So, between before and after the industrial revolution what is the major systemic change? My answer is: The role of the large global corporation! It now has an enhanced social role. Although partially in agreement with those who believe in a strict hyper-capitalism of financial and corporate profitability,[8] the large global corporation is now responsible for social change, production, research, development, education, and even happiness of employees. Due to technological advances, for example, energy usage and robotized production, it is now feasible that on a global level corporate might can satisfy the material needs of all people. Corporate size is essential for it allows for cost advantages as well as for research and development potentialities, whereas the globalistic thinking leads toward multicultural organizations. This corporation is taking advantage of existing institutions, regulations, resources, national sovereignty, cultural diversity, science, technology, and so on to achieve a new social equilibrium. The corporation is, in relation to the states, much less vulnerable to cultural conflict, more flexible in social mutations of the global village, and given the system of transparent business ethics and governance; it is much more meritocratic and fair. Allow us to remind the reader that the largest 500 corporations, employing less than 1/100th of the planet's population, produce almost half of the equivalent of the global gross domestic product (GDP) and that these corporations have as annual turnover more than the GDP of most nations.[9] These global corporations seek "talent"; talented people are usually motivated through higher-order constructs!

Therefore, the center of the after industrial revolution model shows where the societal focus should lie: On the everyday man, whose talents, knowledge, skills, and attitudes assures the corporate competitive success and its constant improvement. Nevertheless, thousands of years of human slavery cannot change behavioral modes in just a generation. Business ethics has a pivotal role to play. A more modern understanding of the oppressed man at work is given to us by the socio-philosophical text of the Urantia Book, which states: "Involuntary slavery has given way to a new and improved form of modified industrial servitude."[10]

To most people, even 30 years ago, it was an oxymoron to use the terms business and ethics in the same phrase. Nowadays, terms like business ethics, ecology, or sustainability are necessary for social progress. They are also necessary conditions for the survival of human dignity, which is now independent from traditional bonds, such as family, tribe, or the nation.[11] In fact, the well-managed global corporation aims to recruit talented employees and to keep them by meeting their everyday needs and their concepts of progress, education, and even self-awareness.

This is not a theoretical construct. Let me offer as an example part of Canon's[12] corporate philosophy, which uses the Japanese word *kyosei*. A concise definition of this word would be "Living and working together for the common good." In fact, Canon's definition is broader: "All people, regardless of race, religion or culture, harmoniously living and working together into the future."

Moreover, the true era of global business, the era that will optimize the human enterprise and create the new socially responsible player, something that effectively started after the industrial revolution, in this writer's opinion, is *ante portas*. More on this issue will be addressed at the end of Chapter 4, while discussing the emergence of a new economic theory about the financial impact of the global large entities.

Managers, Self-Actualize!

Obviously, we are in a transitional stage between two periods separated by the industrial revolution. As it was implied before, the future enterprise will be the main institutional force of the social fabric. Moreover, corporate management philosophies, now oriented toward industry and region-specific needs, are rapidly changing to accommodate the merit-based, knowledgeable, and pro-social thinking of a new era. If they fail to do so, this might justify the George Orwell's *1984* prediction of a future terrorist state, which will be controlled by ignorant and unethical bureaucrats (big brother is watching). Moreover, during this transitional stage, do not expect that the people in power will give up their assumed fame, royal weddings, and mega yachts without a fight. For the time being, the laws are in their favor. Therefore, any major institutional change needs methodical steps and prudency.

It is hoped that soon the focus of all our business activity, the core of it, will be on the everyday individual—not only on the people in power; this focused change is already a viable societal objective but it can be sustained only if the human race acts with prudence, restraint from excessive spending, concern for the environmental balances, and return to self-actualization learning.

Thus, let us return to the beginning of this discussion and its working hypotheses, now working propositions:

1. The framework of analysis is a function of the knowledge we possess at a specific time; it constantly evolves. *Seize the moment! Forget enslaved behaviors! Free the man and his spirit!*

2. Without data we cannot draw conclusions. *The quality of data is critical.*
3. Leaders' competence is questionable. *Select meritorious leaders!*
4. Have we studied the trends that will shape the decades to come? *Presently corporations are most suited to lead the social change!*

Therefore, attention: In a future corporate-centered state, hopefully, citizenship equity will not be at stake. People's rights will be guarded through a system-wide information platform, capable to express not only group thinking, but also individual opinions and cutting-edge concepts. Since the beginning of the 1990s we have been witnessing a wave of such efforts; one may say that we are moving toward a social mutation, because of IT, blogs, and media.

However, the persons in charge should not be selected through the classical sense of a democratic process. Instead, the future business managers should be selected solely through constantly evolving merit-based selection systems—in themselves nondemocratic for there will be no room for voting of less capable individuals. Historically, democracies worked well for countries but will play insignificant roles when the best and the talented should lead the output, the research, the social upgrading, and the ethical behaviors of future corporations.

Therefore, the global education system becomes the main thrust of our attention. Obviously, it must meet the regional demands and peculiarities. A grand plan should illuminate focused learning activities that will require specialized labor, from haircuts to health. A gravely important concern is to identify the most suited individuals for the jobs at hand. This will enhance societal satisfaction by honing knowledge and skills according to the individual predispositions. Moreover, future global citizens will not only be superior production machines, but they should also be capable of seeking self-actualization in their daily quest. Thus, both the educational depth and width should be its objectives of the corporate-centered state which in itself will be an education-driven learning organization. The weight, therefore, lies on the shoulders of enlightened leaders who understand that a future corporate-centered state should be based on meritorious selection of the human resources and their continuous spiritual enhancement.

Knowledge, Corporate Engineering, the Modern Enterprise, and Its Governance

As we shall see in the section of Evolution of International Accounting, for thousands of years simple addition of records determined the value of an enterprise. This was a great help for the entrepreneur of those times, but it also had some risks. Past recording errors could not be found. Only during the 15th century, in Venice, traders found a more appropriate record keeping method. By having a double entry of the accounts, they had finally found a mechanism to check for possible recording errors. Computers brought speed and efficiency, and today's accounting processes can produce highly elaborate business records and offer a wealth of reports and statistics. Moreover, thousands of "doctors" in accounting, using very accurate methodologies, have analyzed all facets and processes of every aspect of record keeping of the modern enterprise. The depiction of the modern enterprise must be correct! Right? Maybe!

> ... able to maintain a remarkable amount of discreet anonymity about its widespread operations because of tight-lipped company policy and because it adheres to the auditing profession's ethical canons, which frown on "publicity."
>
> T. A. Wise (1966)[13]

Let's see an example,[14] which in my opinion, was a milestone in the change of business actions: In its January 17, 2001, news release, IBM had selling, general and administrative expenses (SG&A) at $15.5 billion, down 8% from 6 years, in spite of the fact that earlier it had added billions of additional annual revenue. To arrive at this number IBM used the questionable method of counting some revenue sources not as revenue but as a reduction of its SG&A. A patent fee having the effect of reducing overhead? "I've never heard of anyone doing it that way," says the editor of *High-Tech Strategist*. We are in front of another case of *financial engineering* and, naturally, very few will question the validity of the accounting actions of mega-multinationals who are also edited by prestigious accounting firms. But how can we be sure that the corporate financial picture is true, especially when it operates in a variety of legal environments and faces a multitude of pressures? The Chief Financial Officer of a corporation has to monitor all sorts of indices and compares them with the competitors' and the industry averages. He or she is responsible toward his or her stakeholders for corporate performance. He or she continuously must observe benchmarks,[15] which often can be seen as pressure elements. A true picture of the corporation maybe in jeopardy due to lack of knowledge, pressures, benchmarks, corporate ethical conduct, or a variety of other reasons.

The key mechanism for the modern era enterprise is its corporate governance principles. Its main parts refer to its board role and structure, facing risks and changes, control and auditing mechanisms, corporate structure, internal regulations, stockholders and shareholders rights and information flows, corporate social responsibility issues, executive reward system, and corporate remunerations. This is something like the constitution of a nation. Based on the constitution, laws are developed, and when changes are necessary, constitutional amendments affect all related laws. The same applies to the corporate governance principles. All operating manuals, wherever the enterprise operates, are based on its accepted practices. These principles are usually dictated by the corporate shareholders. Nevertheless, please remember (at the historical perspective discussion) that the corporate mission invariably has a teleological character, but also our previously mentioned concept of a four-sided tunnel whose sides are flexible, depending on the deontology that the corporation has with respect to specific social practices toward stockholders, employees, customers, and the environment. It is important to understand, and it appears to apply both at the teleological and deontological thinking, that recent research indicates unconscious processes influence much of our behavior and decision making.[16] What is missing? We have already used in this chapter some confusing wording like teleology or deontology. Those are philosophical concepts. The individuals and their societies lived in cultures having particular philosophical and ethical codes. Philosophies for the individuals and their societies were developed for thousands of years. They are embedded in their thinking and their daily actions. On the other hand, enterprises, major players of our global era, were intuitively developed, often without the preconditioning of a business philosophy, the adoption of rigid governance procedures, or the stock-holders' understanding of ethics and corporate social responsibility.

Therefore, we shall return to the corporate philosophical thinking in Chapter 3 but after we discuss geography and culture-related issues. These form the traditional springboard of most international business books; also, culture is the basis of philosophy and of corporate governance. Finally, at the epilogue, we shall summarize our beliefs about this challenging era of the human enterprise and its governance.

CHAPTER 2

From Geography to Culture

Starting Our Global Travels

> By not knowing the topography of mountain, forests, obstacles, and swamps, one cannot conduct maneuvers
>
> Sun-Tzu[1]

You lived all your life in this big city and you plan to go from your home to visit a friend in a new subdivision at the other side of the city. You get directions and study your map. As you go there, signs are familiar, people speak the same language you do, and the symbolisms are known to you.

The same applies to your global travels. You need to get directions and study your maps before you venture traveling. However, as the signs, languages, symbolisms, cultures, institutions, laws, and ethical norms are different, you need to familiarize yourself with them before you depart. As you move through time zones you face jet lags. As you go from north to south you realize that climate changes. As you go through your travels you understand that *large mountains, substantial bodies of water, tropical forests, and deserts separate and isolate civilizations and cultures, whereas plains, small mountains, and rivers allow more cultural communication.*

> At the China's Gobi Alashan Plateau, an immense desert, you can meet today, "... an aging population still living a tradition that stretches back to before Genghis Khan."[2]

In this chapter, we will learn certain things about geography, focusing more into business-related aspects, and use it as a platform to discuss cultural issues. Culture is of major concern in international business. Chapter 3 will take you a step further, discussing beyond culture issues of philosophy, and how changes of the past 100 years has affected societal overall thinking, given the emergence of technologies and the new player, global corporation.

Geographic Position and Physical Resources

Open your map again and find what the Romans call *mare nostrum*, the Mediterranean Sea. The Greeks, the Egyptians, the Babylonians, and so many other people used this sea for over 5,000 years for trade and moving people and armies. Go to the North of Europe. The ports of Amsterdam and Rotterdam are huge, effectively shipping products to Central Europe through waterways. Geography has always played a critical role in human growth and geopolitical realities. Let's see some examples:

- For decades now we refer to an area in which three nations, Belgium, Netherlands, and Luxemburg that share similar topography landscape and cultures as Benelux.
- Since 1994 we call the North American Free Trade Agreement, which is the trade union between Canada, the United States, and Mexico, effectively covering the North American continent as NAFTA.
- In a similar way we refer to the Association of South East Asian Nations, namely Brunei, Cambodia, Indonesia, Laos, Malaysia, Myanmar, the Philippines, Singapore, Thailand, and Vietnam as ASEAN.
- We also refer to the Asia Pacific Economic Cooperation— comprising of more than 20 countries that border the Pacific Rim, both in Asia as well as in the Americas—as APEC.

Geographic and cultural conditions brought together these nations to achieve common social, economic, trade, and investment objectives. For most of the human history, *the combination of geographic position, resources, and climate gave these nations economic power and assisted in the development of their people.* Studies of the World Bank show that nations in the tropics could not develop, mainly due to their climate.

Physical resources are another advantage the countries have going for them. Forests in Canada or Russia and strategic minerals, like cobalt, in Indonesia or Zambia are examples of resources. Moreover, *energy resources dearly needed by the developed countries to keep their economic prominence give strategic might to the countries that possess them.* After the industrial revolution, petroleum, water, coal, electricity, uranium, and many other forms of energy have given nations that possess them significant means and global prominence. At the same time, the energy resources have mobilized many industries and created new business opportunities, related risks, and necessitated the development of suitable legal frameworks.

Oil is a case in point: Two hundred years ago the Middle East nations had lots of sand and deserts, but their petroleum was not needed, thus, their economic development was minimal. Today, the picture is different. There are skyscrapers, airports, universities, hospitals, roads, and luxury hotels everywhere. Petroleum offered these nations the economic means to grow and, at the same time, mobilize sector-specific industrial growth, from refineries to shipping.[3] However, transporting oil can create huge ecological problems, as in the case of the *Exxon Valdez* in Alaska in 1989, where 11,000,000 gallons of crude oil spilled over an area of 800 kilometers, or of the *Prestige,* which sank in 2002 in North Atlantic, 130 miles out of Portugal, gradually leaking 80,000 tons of oil. Obviously, incidents of this sort necessitate total reassessment of transporting regulations, at a global level.

Another example is of nuclear energy. The Chernobyl nuclear accident in April 1986, necessitated total reassessment of using this type of energy. What about populations who elected to live far from the Chernobyl plant, but eventually were in danger of the radioactive fallout? People in at least 1,000 square miles area around were forced to evacuate. Twenty years later, "a new wave of ailments may be striking the 240,000 men and women who worked on the front lines of the disaster."[4] Today, we project that dozens of new nuclear plants will appear in the next 10 years. It is a great energy solution and a superb business opportunity. However, regulating their construction and monitoring their operation will be a formidable task. Their potential risks are global.

Geopolitical[5] Dynamics and the Role of Business

In the past the geographic position of a country was also a determining factor of its political power. However, in today's reality, the established status quo of nations is challenged by unions of nations (e.g., NAFTA or ASEAN) and major global corporations. National geopolitical influence is shifting because of the global village. Company sales of large business entities are often greater than the gross national product (GNP) of most nations. These companies' R&D, product characteristics, customer influence, employee recruitment, resource utilization, and so many other corporate dimensions are defined in our era beyond national borders. It follows that *companies, acting usually within their local legal constraints, may operate at will everywhere in the world and may establish, through their own governance rules, a new elite of rulers: their managers.*[6]

At the same time, established venues of influence, like OPEC—the Organization of Petroleum Exporting Countries—continue to exist and supply their products worldwide at top prices! Are we in for major changes to come?

Let's further analyze the examples of energy resources. Ethanol, produced from starchy grains like corn, for example, can be less polluting and costs half the price of oil. Brazil is leading the world, where one-fourth of all gasoline used is ethanol. Even Brazilian factories work on ethanol, not to mention that Brazilian-made Embraer planes fly on ethanol. It is estimated that, without too much effort, producing ethanol from sugarcanes in Brazil and India could replace 10% of global gasoline fuel.[7] Ethanol is not the only solution for cheaper and better energy.

Biofuels, solar energy, wind energy, and so forth, are increasingly playing a role and eventually will *create a new map of "business dynamics" similar to what geopolitics were in the past for nations.* States even propose tax incentives to introduce alternative energy resources and unions of nations (as in the case of the European Union) have directives converting their energy dependence from traditional to alternative resources.[8] To a greater extent, geopolitics in the past was based on topographical advantages, whereas *today the status quo of business dynamics is established on the basis of consumer-orientation, knowledge, and creativity of the contemporary enterprise.*[9] Naturally, businesses will also build the necessary energy-related facilities and use their output.

What about nuclear energy facilities? France, for example, has dozens of reactors providing at least three-fourths of its needs in electric power.[10] It seems that dozens more of reactors, especially in Asia, are scheduled to operate during the next 15 years, though people are very skeptical seeing huge nuclear plants in their backyards.[11] Alternative venues in the field of nuclear fusion have been proposed, ever since 1985, when Mikhail Gorbachev proposed a project to build an international thermonuclear experimental reactor (ITER). After many years of negotiations, leading nations, from China to the European Union, agreed to foot the bill of 12 billion dollars to build the 500-megawatt reactor.[12] The project, finally agreed upon in 2006 and which, from a managerial perspective, resembles the International Space Station, will use as fuel a heavy isotope of hydrogen called deuterium, which is present in ordinary water. The international thermonuclear experimental reactor, with an implementation horizon of a commercial reactor of at least 30 years, plans to use seawater—safely producing power with renewable resources.

Most probably, ITER will be run by businesses—not by governments. Business, being a very basic premise of this book, will follow ethical rules of conduct and will be socially minded. Geopolitical dynamics will be replaced by business dynamics and *business will be responsible for meeting humanity's needs without harming future generations of human and nonhuman life.* It is not anymore a token issue for preservation of physical resources, "greening," "growth sustainability," or ecological thinking. Deforestation, in great numbers, naturally, will continue. However, expect the European Union and the United States, two very strong global voices that have not yet did so in the past, will soon take leadership roles in favor of ecological issues. Moreover, it is proven recently, over and over again, that often "business is doing well by doing good."[13] We will revisit physical resources sustainability and the role of business issues in forthcoming chapters.

The Human Footprint

On our precious planet, with its billions of years' of history, the "human footprint" is very recent, less than 10,000 years old. One can see great achievements like the Great Wall of China or Egyptian Pyramids, however, only after the industrial revolution did the human footprint become evident in 83% of the land mass of this planet.[14]

Using the most advanced satellite and mapping technologies, and capitalizing on population data, roads, land usage, city lights, and so forth, scientists from the *National Geographic,* the Wildlife Conservation Society, and the Earth Institute (Columbia University) composed an index, the "human-influence score," for each square kilometer of our planet. Thus, through the Human Footprint Project they created a world map, which presents the changes of the planet because of man's influence. *It is impressive to see the world's map in this light. Huge areas, such as Europe, Far East, or North America (with the exception of Alaska and Canada) have clear human footprints, which can be related to human enterprising.* Even continents like Africa have intense signs of human footprint.

> Stephen Hawking's[15] observation merits special attention, which states that if today's population and energy growth rates continue, by the year 2600 humans will stand on the planet's land mass side by side, and the Earth will glow as red-hot iron.

We see that the human footprint is evident only after the industrial revolution. What, then, if, as Professor Vassilis Doukakis states, the industrial revolution had started in antiquity[16]? It could have happened since all necessary means were available. Of course, this is a hypothetical question for the purpose of this text. However, the responsibility and challenge for solving the predicament lies with the corporation and its future role.

What Is Culture?

Previously we discussed that large mountains, substantial bodies of water, tropical forests, and deserts separated and isolated civilizations and cultures, whereas plains, small mountains, and rivers allowed more cultural communication. Humans who ended up in certain parts of the world, given their environment and climate, developed their own cultures. Anthropologists and sociologists alike define *culture* as "the total of human behavior patterns and technology communicated from generation to generation."[17] An operative definition of the previous statement is "the sum of elements that characterize a human population a certain time."[18] We may classify these elements at least under the following categories: aesthetics and art, beliefs–attitudes–lifestyles, religion and philosophical tenants, education, language, history, institutional framework and laws, and material culture.

Each population, confined by topography and climate, developed these elements in a different way than the adjacent population, as abstract constructs, intellectual creations, or technological achievements. Slowly, the evolution of these elements further separated populations who now were facing national borders, different philosophies, religions, and languages. *Individuals from each society see the world outside their culture in their own way, and since they get limited information of the details of other cultures, we often observe ethnocentric behaviors, where an individual perceives that what his culture and his history tells him is the right one and is applicable everywhere.* In general, it is accepted that (a) culture(s)

- can be learned. We are not born knowing its elements;
- is comprised of elements that are interrelated. For example, people tending to their agricultural occupation may develop their art around the same themes;
- defines populations;
- is common to the people who share it.

Note, that within cultures there are subcultures. We do not have a single American culture, for example, Polish Americans share the same elements with other Americans, but do have some very strong beliefs and ways of their own. The same applies to other subcultures, from a ghetto in Chicago to truckers, or those living in Ohio versus in Southern California.

From the start, people had to cross cultural borders. In doing so, they had to adjust in the new culture, a process called acculturation. Furthermore, and according to the context, we can anchor cultures in two opposite directions. We refer to *low-context cultures* where the parties involved express in words their intentions—and this suffices for their behavioral understanding. We refer to *high-context cultures* where the parties involved need to understand the context, the meaning, the substance of the culture, not only to what actually has been said in words. The Egyptian or

Greek cultures are considered high-context ones, whereas the American or the German are considered of low context.

> In a more academic sense, people will say ... "Our analysis highlights the more differential effects of cultural practices on entrepreneurial entry and growth aspirations ..."
>
> Professors Erkko Autio, Saurav Pathak, and Karl Wennberg[19]

Elements of Culture

Let's discuss some of the cultural elements we previously stated.

Aesthetics and Art

In this subsection, we include all types of art, color, shapes, symbolisms, music, dance, tales, or whatever refers to people's artistic predisposition. We need to have in-depth understanding of these elements as we move across cultures. For example, for some cultures the black color is for mourning, whereas for others, it is the white. Similarly, a successful advertising tune in one culture may not be as good in another.

Beliefs–Attitudes–Lifestyles

The conditions people face shape their attitudes. Because topography and climate conditions do not change overnight, attitudinal changes should not be expected to change easily.

Justification toward work and success is an example. We say that "Mexicans work to live, whereas Americans live to work." We should not easily generalize that Mexicans have "siestas" because it is too hot to work in the afternoon. This does not make them less productive when they work. It simply indicates that the climate conditions, in a way, affect their work ethic. We can find the concept of the work ethic everywhere in the world, usually related to religious tenants. For example, we find Protestant work ethics in Europe or in North America and Confucian work ethics in Asia. Also, work provides the means for life's comforts and the jobs' prestige with different manifestations, according to local beliefs. In North America, for example, a manager's prestigious corner office at the 40th floor of a New York skyscraper signifies that she has reached a top-level position. On the other hand, the CEO of a large pharmaceutical company in Switzerland may continue to work from his smaller office where he was heading the company's legal department; he will not see his office size as indicative to his job prestige.

Another example refers to culture's acceptance of change.[20] Usually, given the existing cultural norms, a culture faces a reason for change after a novice concept enters into focus; let's say a technological innovation coming from abroad. At this point there is an evaluation of the reason for change using existing cultural yardsticks. Older cultures change much more slowly than newer ones. The novice concept affects the status quo of the local culture which is modified accordingly. We observe all sorts of such influences that have changed societal thinking in most societies—television and Internet are classic examples.

A third example refers to the concept of time. Time is money is a usual American saying. However, in an Islamic reality, trying to predict future events may be considered as being disrespectful to religious teachings and, in Hong Kong, with customary traffic delays, to be on time signifies that you might need to leave significantly earlier from your home or to risk not to be on time.

Religion

> The strength of a country is the strength of its religious convictions.
> Calvin Coolidge[21]

Maybe the most profound element of culture is religion. In religions one may find the basic principles and beliefs of a culture. About one-third of the people are Christians, 20% Muslims, and 15% Hindus. Being effective businesspersons in international travels, we need to understand that we cannot use general labels to cover religious aspects. There are important religious sectors and belief divisions within the Sunnis or Shiites as there are within the Christian Orthodox or Catholics.

As we travel the world we have to be very observant about religious, philosophical similarities and dogmatic differences because of religions.

There are similarities in the basic philosophical ideals and ethics of religions. For example, we learn that the Koran's underlying message is "a prescription for harmony in the everyday life," and that "God commands us to be merciful to one another, to live an ethical life."[22] However, it is within the human nature to build religious walls, to torture others, or to start wars based on religious premises and dogmas. Therefore, give attention to strong-held convictions. Friedrich Wilhelm Nietzsche said that "convictions are more dangerous enemies of truth than lies."[23]

> The 265th Pope's decision to give up earthly power offers the world an unusual-and needed-spiritual lesson.
>
> Jon Meacham[24]

Education

> The direction in which education starts a man will determine his future life.
>
> Plato[25]

Education is another element of culture, and it is offered only in schools. Family, church, peer groups, and so many other influencing factors also affect the individual's development, social adjustment, and productivity. Formal and informal educational experiences provide different educational yardsticks and produce different educational mixes. Local cultures may dictate their own priorities, but may not educate their people for the global business arena. The local cultures will affect people's abilities, skills, and attitudes. They will affect their attitudes toward management, acceptance of innovation, adjustability, priorities, sense of belonging, national pride, and so many more.

But, as we will see later, in today's global realities, the competition for executive positions may come from people who have the appropriate content knowledge and attitudes, these people may come from Argentina, Belgium, Canada, Denmark, or wherever. They come from different cultures, where the individuals have traveled beyond their cultural barriers and have understood the needs of the global corporation.

To a great extent today's business education follows global patterns, is dictated by specific functional needs, and has been evaluated and standardized through major accrediting associations, like the Association to Advance Collegiate Schools of Business.[26] Related to the previous discussion is that of brain drain. *We should expect that the better individuals will gravitate toward the better opportunities.*

> I am not an Athenian or a Greek, but a citizen of the world.
>
> Socrates[27]

Language

It is estimated that there exists hundreds of languages, from which about 10 represent the 50% of native users. The languages, which started as an element of culture, in the continuation became a definite communication barrier, as that of a tall mountain or a sea. Some observations are in order:

- Colonial powers needed to bridge the communication barriers within and among their colonies. Therefore, they established a common language from Latin, known as *lingua franca*. For today's reality, English has become the lingua franca for trade.
- A common problem with languages is their translation. Let's assume we want to translate an advertising message. Ideally, we use two translators. One translates the message in the local language, and the other takes the translated message and translates it back to the original language. We call this approach a double translation or backtranslation. The case needs specific attention because if the message is translated on the basis of Webster-type definitions, it might miss the contextual essence of the message.

> England and America are two countries separated by the same language.
> George Bernard Shaw.[28]

- Translations of technical or scientific documents may not have a lot of problems if the terms needed have the same meaning in both languages. The formula for an aspirin is the same in every country. However, if we need to translate terms of social sciences, we may face more difficulties as the term appears in other language but its interpretation may be slightly different from our intended use. The word marketing, for example, may not have the same meaning everywhere.

- Humor: As a general rule, a positive individual with a sense of humor, is better suited for an international assignment than a strict, humorless one. If you must use a joke, use neutral ones and avoid those of political, religious, sexual, or cultural orientation. You can become a little more open when you know very well the other party and when conditions and cultural protocols permit this openness.

- Body language plays a great role in every communication. Observe not only what has been said but also the body language behind it. Edward T. Hall, a well-known anthropologist, believes that more than half of our daily communication is nonverbalized—we show through our body language. In high-context cultures body language, personal distance, and so forth, is of greater importance. For example, if in one culture a "close" distance is appropriate and expected and in another it is not, an individual from the first culture might feel rejected when he approaches a person from the other culture and the later steps back to accommodate what he believes is convenient to him.[29]

Material Culture

In this subsection we list all the technological means that a society uses for its social and economic survival and growth. These vary from number of hospital beds per 1,000 to cement production. The mass utilization of technology and machines has led to an era where common people enjoy conveniences that only emperors of the past could. Good use of technology leads to economic growth and, to a greater extent, determines the potential growth of a land. For example, machines need fuel, and oil is plentiful in the Middle East. When oil became a source of revenue, the poor nomads of the last century became among the richest people on earth. It is worth mentioning that cultures change very slowly. Although the economic advancements in the Middle East are everywhere and that cars, televisions, and hospitals have significantly impacted the people's daily lives, principles, religion, and language remain vastly unchanged. People from the Middle East are now traveling and studying in America and Europe. Therefore, *New concepts are forging new cultural norms. More, but gradual, changes will appear in the future resulting in cultural convergence with the rest of the world.*[30]

Furthermore, the existence of material means and technology advances people's cultural base and their abilities toward new and creative developments. For example, research on biotechnologies, DNA, or cloning emerged in areas where mature material cultures prevailed. Creativity is the operative word for high-quality R&D and in Chapter 9 a whole subsection addresses the role of the creative enterprise. As a general rule, creative technological developments are not produced in underdeveloped regions of the world. Two definitions are pertinent to this discussion:

- *Technological dualism*, which means finding in the same place the technologies of two different eras. For example, we see at the front of the picture a farmer with a traditional ox-driven plough and at the back a nuclear energy plant. Technological dualism maybe found in less developed parts of the world. India is a case in point: Over one-fourth of *Fortune* 500 companies have now R&D facilities in India,[31] a picture in total contrast with past stereotypes that may lead us to wrong assumptions.
- *Appropriate technology*, which refers to our obligation to bring in an area not necessarily the latest word in technology but the appropriate technology needed for the application at hand.

Changes in the material culture lead us to the basic model of social change. We start from the existing cultural state and lifestyle. Then, a new innovation, a change, is entering in the picture (let's say a simple black and white television). At the next stage society is called to evaluate the change, the good and bad elements of this innovation and the society's propensity to change. Finally, a new status quo is established and, if needed, the appropriate institutional framework is developed.

The innovation slowly will impact the everyday lives of people, and the cycle will get ready for the next innovation.

Social Organization

The social organization develops the fabric on which a culture is based. Here we refer to the family, the tribe, the school, the church, the organizations, and, yes, the business enterprises that exist in a human society. We also refer to the roles the individuals are asked to play and the respective institutional frameworks. For example, the social organization in a Bolivian village adopts and pronounces the role of a family patriarch or the framework of the village's administration.

After the discussion of elements of culture, we need to revisit the meaning of culture. Cultural dimensions cover a vast area of contrasting behaviors, from patriotic sentiments where millions of people died sacrificing themselves for their nation, to Calvinistic doctrines which, according to researchers, maybe the basis for today's capitalistic thinking. *The progress of certain people, as well as the economic stifling of others, may be related to cultural dimensions.* Mariano Grondova,[32] in his typology, defines certain contrasting cultural factors that have been defining the overall progress of people. Here are some of them:

- *Religion*: Some religions promote manifests that do not promote wealth (Buddhism) where others, as Christianity, accept the economic and social progress as a desirable objective.
- *Trust in the individual*: Accordingly, to have faith in the individual, is one of the elements of a value system that favors development.
- *The moral imperative*: The highest being altruistic and self-denying; the intermediate being called "reasonable egoism"; and the lowest being criminal attitude.
- Similarly, he defines other contrasting cultural factors, for example, wealth, competition, justice, value of work, education, utility, authority, virtue, and so on.

Culture change is often a prerequisite of progress. However, and before we affect any change, we need to fully understand cultural interpretations in every region that our enterprise applies its business affairs.[33] Moreover, although only 10% of the people on this planet are truly internationalized,[34] we are in front of an era where cultures converge toward a global culture, mostly with reference to the ways, values, and principles of Westerners as well as some of those from the upper strata of non-Westerners.[35] At the same time we are witnessing the presence of common folklore, with European and North American characteristics.

Acculturation and Behavioral Protocols

In 1945, G. P. Murdock wrote about cultural dimensions that can be found practically in any culture. Such example may be the interest in sports, home hygiene, or taboos around the idea of sex. We call these *cultural universals*. This typology may be useful, however, we need to adequately prepare the individual who will undertake international assignments, and to assist him or her to understand significantly more culture-related issues than the low-context versus high-context argument we examined in the definition of culture.

Cross-cultural adaptation is not easy and it is not for everyone. In general, it is easier to use for individuals in international assignments, who already have significant international exposure (have traveled extensively or speak foreign languages); they have behavioral flexibility, sensitivity, optimism, tolerance, self-discipline, stamina, ability to work without supervision, good project management and time management skills, maturity, and team-playing capacity. Given these, let's assume now that we have decided to send an individual as the manager of one of the host sites of our enterprise—far away from his or her familiar surroundings. What does he or her, have to observe?

- Acceptance of the idea of living in this new environment with others, who will go with him or her, especially his or her spouse.
- Extremely good technical knowledge of his or her field.
- Thorough knowledge about culture in general and specifically about geography, history, laws, religion, philosophy, political and daily issues, art, and literature of the new place.

- If possible, the language of the new country, at least a few words.
- Behavioral protocols of the new culture.

When we refer to behavioral protocols, usually we refer to the way knowledge, information, or communication takes place. There are significant differences in social behaviors, business etiquette, gestures, signs of respect, dress codes, and so forth. Awareness of these issues takes time and often requires the employment of suitable individuals or consultants, who assist in learning the peculiarities of cultures. There are, of course, books that assist us in our initial understanding of cultural differences. These books will aid a business person in specifics about business practices, cognitive styles, negotiation strategies, locus of decision making, and so on.[36]

One should understand that the issue of acculturation is ever present, even when we move within the same country. A classic book on the topic is Garreau's *The Nine Nations of North America*.[37] Politically, there are no nine nations in North America. However, if we see culture-related dimensions to the people that are in this land, maybe we can share the author's opinion, which divides this continent as Mexamericana, Breadbasket, Ecotopia, The Empty Quarter, Quebec, New England, The Foundry, Dixie, and The Islands.

Cultural Imperialism

With this term we refer to symbolisms and elements of one culture that are readily accepted and adopted by another culture. Such elements are often found in the areas of material culture, art, processes of social organizations, and business-related influences. Observe, for example, how well people around the world know Mickey (Disney), MTV, Coca-Cola, Microsoft, or Nike.

In terms of cultural imperialism, the impact of business and its related promotions are noteworthy. For thousands of years, cultural dimensions were defined within geographic realities. Wars and trade were giving a glimpse of the ways and products of a foreign land, but their influence and usage was limited. Only very few people were in a position to enjoy these products or learn from the foreign cultural developments.

Soldiers of Alexander the Great brought to Greece some "ways" of the Persians, and the "silk" road brought to Europe some precious materials, but the overall impact of these ways and products was minimal.

> I do not want my house to be walled in all sides and my windows to be stuffed. I want the cultures of all lands to be blown about my house as freely as possible. But I refuse to be blown off my feet by any.
>
> Mahatma Gandhi[38]

Electronic media, telecommunications, promotions, product distribution, and the availability of economic means have also changed this landscape. It is a clear case of cultural imperialism when someone, unrelated to the American culture, tattoos on his back the Harley-Davidson logo—his motorcycle. In terms of cultural imperialism, think what is going to happen 20 years from now, when a 4-year-old boy routinely plays on his PlayStation aggressive games of Japanese origin—decades away from what his forefathers knew, or when an 18-year-old young lady learns in her remote village, in Jordan, SAP software technologies, bypassing traditional educational institutions, where they are unable to provide cutting-edge professional training.

Self-Reference Criterion

One of the most important issues in the internationalization of the corporation is the self-reference criterion (SRC). *With SRC we subconsciously refer to our own culture, mores, history, value system, principles, ways, and symbolisms.* We tend to ignore that the "other" people have lived for centuries in their own lands and have developed very appropriate and efficient ways to deal with their environment. If we want to market our products to find good use with the foreign workforce, we need to avoid SRC. Other cultures see the world through their own eyes and have different managerial and consumption patterns. Avoiding SRC has four stages:

1. Define the issue according to the designs of the home market.
2. Define the issue according to the designs of the host market.
3. Find the differences between 1 and 2 (SRC).
4. Redefine the issue without the SRC.

Let's say that in the home market we sell an over-the-counter phar-maceutical in large bottles and that the host market is in need of this product, but in smaller bottles. Exporting it in family-size bottles (as in stage 1) is one solution, but not the best (since the host market wants one-fourth of this size, stage 2). We find the differences (stage 3) size, label, promotions, and so on. Therefore, we redefine our marketing strat-egy, taking into account these differences.

The previous example sounds very easy. Think, however, that SRC is the *subconscious* reference to our cultural predispositions. We often are unable to observe differences because of our own ways and beliefs.

Civilization Clashes and Business Repercussions

Many saw the terrorist attacks of September 11, 2001, in New York city as symptoms of a large-scale civilization clash that repeated itself in March 2004 in Madrid, July 2005, in London,[39] and often on a daily basis around the world. The repercussions from such civilization clashes are enormous both in human and nonhuman costs. Individuals identify themselves with tribes, nations, religious groups, and in a broader sense, civilizations. Traditional wars were estimated to be one-sixth the duration of cultural conflicts. In a global society, without the traditional barriers of the past, civilization clashes are very possible, especially, at the frontier line that once existed.

If we take Professor Samuel Huntington's ideas of the world order, we can see a global landscape in the 1920s, where the world can be classified into two parts: One is controlled by the "Western" thinking and one that is not. Then, 40 years later, there are three most dominant forces: the *free* world, the *communist* world, and the *other*, the independent, not-committed countries. In the 1990s, Huntington observed nine dif-ferent *civilizations* defining the identity of people, such as the Western, the Latin American, the African, and the Islamic.[40]

It's becoming increasingly difficult for China and the United States to mask profound differences in their approaches to the world. ... Could this be the real clash of civilizations?[41]

Because of multicultural realities of the 21st century, the challenge is civilizations' coexistence. The world does not need a single homogeneous culture. Cultural diversity promotes individualism, creativity, and social strength. Harmonious cultural coexistence is possible and leads to progress and peace. Bridges between civilizations are constantly built. For example, Turkey aims to achieve its European Union membership, following the practice of looking toward "the secular West rather than the more religious East." In fact, it is reported that Turkey's prime minister believes that a Turkish European Union membership leads to "world peace, fighting global terror and the clash of civilizations."[42] But which are the major forces that may control potential civilization clashes and shape future behaviors, further than the nations and the supranational unions? Businesses! There is a global acceptance of their might. Moreover, business globalization is happening without undue repercussions on the individual and his or her rights. Big business (and small business, too) are behaving according to prespecified codes of ethics based on their philosophy and corporate cultures.

Take, for example, the five largest U.S. companies whose sales revenue is about 10% of the United States' gross domestic product, and whose individual sales are more than most countries' GNP. *These companies understand their multicultural employee, customer, or investor. They have clear codes of ethics and governance processes, and they rapidly adjust to the changing environmental conditions. They study civilizations and cultures. They continuously adapt to the needs of the people they aim to serve.* If they do not do the above, they should!

In the previous sections we discussed how cultures develop and what elements are present. Cultures are the backbone of civilizations' philosophy and ethics, something we will address in the next chapter. As we will see, although the basic socially acceptable behavioral principles were established through an evolution that lasted thousands of years, the relatively recent technology revolution maybe forcing the modern man to rethink previous philosophical and ethical tenants.

CHAPTER 3

Philosophical Tenants and the 21st Century

Some Principle Thoughts

We studied in the previous chapter about culture. Given its location, neighboring influences, and geography characteristics, each culture develops its unique philosophy and ethics. The backbone of a culture is its philosophy. Study of philosophical and ethical predispositions allows us to better understand the reasons behind local developments and to smoothly function in an environment foreign to us.

This chapter addresses basic philosophy and ethical notions, which developed through thousands of years and are not necessarily similar all around the world. However, in the past 50 years we have been in front of phenomenal changes, which could not have been foreseen five centuries ago. Telecommunications, information technology, and mass media have changed in terms of philosophy, truth, and ethics, and the way we see the world, our principles, our motivation, and our overall thinking. In fact, because of communication and media changes, we maybe are facing social mutations that will necessitate very educated behaviors if we want to be successful global businesspeople.

Additionally, philosophy, truth, and ethics are not the exclusive domains of the individual, the tribe, or the nation. Given that the new global player is the business concern, and that its size, its technological base, and its economic might is of increasing social importance, this chapter also addresses corporate philosophy and corporate ethics.[1]

What Is Philosophy? What Is Truth?

People agree that the term philosophy is based on a similar Greek term (*philosophia*) meaning friend (*philos*) and wisdom (*sophia*). Some more definitions state philosophy as:[2]

- the love or pursuit of wisdom;
- the study or science of the truths or principles underlying all knowledge;
- the study or science of a particular branch of knowledge;
- a system of philosophical doctrine (as the philosophy of *Spinosa*);
- a system of principles for guidance in practical affairs.

Basically, philosophy is concerned with three areas: epistemology, the study of knowledge; metaphysics, the study of the nature of reality; and, ethics, the study of morality.[3] We may say that philosophy seeks to find truth at different levels and under different angles. Therefore, understanding of truth becomes the central component of philosophy.

But what is truth? Formal definitions specify it as a spiritual or philosophical verity; an accepted or verified fact; a concept that relates to reality, honesty, constancy, and veracity;[4] whatever is in agreement with a populations' general sentiment; and so forth. However, let's see what other contemporary writers and thinkers answer to the question "What is true?"[5]

- "Everything is changing, and change is good. Speed is the key to understanding information; speed changes the meaning of information. The speed of message is the message."
  —Michael Wolff
- "The truth can be elusive, or at least difficult to express in the business world. So I find myself turning to metaphors and analogies."—Scott McNealy
- "We live, writes a critic, in the 'Age of Falsification,' filled with surfaces we cannot understand."—Virginia Postrel
- "Within this new world of human, economic, and technological relationships, many people are struggling for a

metaphor to give us a sense of where we are right now."
—Stanley Crouch
- "Virtual reality has been with us for a good long time: We call it fiction."—T. C. Boyle
- "When there is a discrepancy between appearance and reality, we regard it as untrue."—Dalai Lama
- "A little learning is a dangerous thing. This has never struck me as a particularly profound or wise remark, but it comes into its own when that little learning is in philosophy."
—Richard Dawkins[6]

Traditionally, truth was based on personal understanding and the observation of natural phenomena. Seeing and sensing was believing. Today, we need to readjust our thinking when some people say that we live in the "Age of Falsification," when "the speed of message becomes the message," when holistically we can persuade the little boy that there is out there a real "Dinosaur Park," or the experienced businessman that the corporate accounting resource planning system is always correct.

At this point we should explain that business, too, has its own culture, philosophy, and ethics. *Each business concern operates within a broader cultural framework that defines the way owners, employees, customers, and the environment, in general, understand the societal roles and responsibilities of all players—one of them being the individual firm.* These roles and responsibilities, as well as the institutional framework that surrounds them, change over time. Emperors of the past, with their immense power over life, could not bring the latest information from a building site or a war field. They did not have the technology for that. We are in front of what we may call as *homo technologicus.* This person, via his or her technological capability, is the one who will persuade the young boy that there is a dinosaur at the nearby forest, falsify business truisms, change the DNA structure, mutate soybeans, present a global video conference, wear artificial members that can function even better than his or her original. Moreover, this person, mostly the product of the *generation Y,*[7] may be somehow dysfunctional for more traditional culture settings. She does not give the priority to interact with whatever routine objectives traditional cultures demand. She can choose what she likes. She does not learn to function well in social environments. It is possible that this person is a poor social player, learner, and a weak member of global workforce.

> Business students should be trained in understanding the responsibility of business to its larger social system.[8]

Each "age" had its technology and this technology defined the way of living of the people. The Egyptians built pyramids which represent top mathematical and engineering understanding, and affect, in different ways, the then individuals' concepts of culture, family, individualism, or deity. Five thousand years later, Marshal M. McLuhan[9] talks about social mutation, from a society of the group to a society of the individual, primarily because of technology. *We are in front of an era where philosophical and ethical trends that developed through hundreds of years possibly will change in a very short period, following the demands of our technological era.* We will address the issue later in the chapter. For the time being, it suffices to repeat that the moral evaluations of good and bad, true or untrue, are specified with location and time parameters.

> Hundreds of doctoral dissertations in accounting and ethics are produced and potentially redefine the way a stakeholder can evaluate a business. Still, the starting points are business philosophy, business ethics, and the picture(s) that accounting spreadsheets give about business performance. So, why no one observed that Enron was in danger when Sherron S. Watkins, on time, indicated that the company might "implode in a wave of accounting scandals?"[10]

The previous thoughts might have given the reader a changing sense of truth, logic, and philosophy. A central part of philosophy is ethics. The following section addresses some of our concerns.

Ethics and Business Ethics

For thousands of years civilizations based their philosophies on their cultural thinking. In almost the same way an individual learns his or her native language, the religious tenants or the whereabouts around his or her village, he or she learns about principle philosophical beliefs and ethics. A newborn in a strict Islamic community will learn different concepts of ethical conduct than another baby born in a wealthy suburb somewhere in California.

Civilizations developed their philosophical tenants based on the topographical realities they had to face. Through the ages, sociopolitical developments, historic necessities, wars, cross-country influences, and technological advancements further fine-tuned their philosophical thinking and legal frameworks. Since ethics directly relate to philosophy, we may say that ethical predispositions are closely related to the environment, the economy, the social realities, the technology, as well as the timing we wish to analyze a specific civilization. But what is the definition of ethics? The *Websters Lexicon* defines ethics as the principles of morality, or the field of study of morals or right conduct.[11] Similar definitions are static. They represent what is ethics at a particular moment of analysis.

Thiroux, in his effort to present a "working definition," states that:

> Morality deals basically with humans and how they relate to other beings, both human and nonhuman. It deals with how humans 'treat' other beings so as to promote mutual welfare, growth, creativity, and meaning and to strive for what is good over what is bad and what is right and what is wrong.[12]

Let's relate now ethics and business ethics.

Business and entrepreneurial thinking existed always. It was this thinking that organized states, wealth, wars, or built the Pyramids. The rule of survival of the fittest was in force. The benefits were tangible and significant. By today's standards unacceptable behaviors were practiced throughout human history. To some extent, the mentality of slavery was in place even during the industrial revolution. It was acceptable to have little concern about the surrounding environment or to have spillover benefits to the established manufacturer and spillover costs to the individual who had to live near the polluting factory. Given the then very simplistic legal frameworks, most business, from Far East to Central Europe and from Africa to South America, operated outside the borders of business ethics. Then, because of communications, human enterprising, media, and speed, "business" became the very important social player it is today. Effectively this happed only after World War II. The birth of business concerns with social responsibility and responsiveness was a reality.

Since then, we are in front of a new era of business ethics. Initially, business laws defined operating frameworks, and codes of conduct were established worldwide within the different industries for various matters. Legally correct behaviors were enforced—business survival depended on them. The corporate layers were at the very top of the enterprise advising before any major business decision. Sharing of wealth came under public and media scrutiny as well as human resource administration, production, marketing, innovation, sourcing, and technology. The legal framework of operation became of paramount importance. But then, it was realized that the legal framework was not sufficient for the demands of the new era of business ethics.[13] Beyond the legal framework was now human morality in force. The evolution of the human thinking (and well-being) necessitated new frameworks to protect the human and nonhuman forms of life. We were moving beyond the legal correctness to the ethical and to socially responsive business.

Let's illustrate the socially responsive business with an example: The tangible benefit, because of the innovation of a new biotechnology, may be given to the principle stakeholder of the enterprise in the form of "license fees."[14] Our stakeholder is now wealthy and a very successful businessman. He wants to give back something to the society, and decides to direct part of his wealth toward philanthropic causes. This is a decision within his own personal ethical system. For example, he feels that part of his wealth should be given to the African poor. He creates a philanthropic organization to meet this objective and continues to keep his initial business focused toward the research, development, and distribution of more medicines. However, in the process, he realizes that his initial enterprise might not have done everything in a socially responsible manner. He wants to take steps with respect to his, now very-very large, initial enterprise, to make it more socially responsive and, through his own philosophy, to affect the corporate philosophy and ethics and, maybe, to some extent, the world.

"Guided by the belief that every life has equal value, the Bill & Melinda Gates Foundation works to reduce inequalities and improve lives around the world."

Creed of one of the largest non-for-profit organization[15]

As in the past where a well-organized state continuously adapted its legal framework to the socially accepted philosophical and ethical principles, in the same way today business needs to operate within the accepted legal realities and define their philosophical tenants according to what their stakeholders believe. These philosophical tenants, extended to the perceived by the stakeholders' ethical behavior, become the foundation of the corporate governance principles and respective manuals.

Schools of Ethics and the Mission of Business

The concepts of ethics, developed within broader frameworks of philosophy, can be classified as teleological theories and deontological theories of morality.

We refer to the school of teleological thinking (or the consequentialist theory of morality) when ethics are based or are concerned with the consequences of our actions and deontological thinking (or the nonconsequentialist theory of morality) when ethics are not based or are not concerned with the consequences of our actions. *Telos* comes from a Greek word meaning "end result," whereas *deon* comes from a word meaning "should."

In business terms the above relate to the mission or the actions of a corporation. How? Business focuses to an end result. Therefore, by its nature, business mission is teleological in purpose. However, the way that the company achieves the end result, philosophically speaking, is deontological. This is why it is important to understand philosophy and ethics, before you venture into the business world: The term morality might be confusing, if you do not have a clear understanding of the concepts behind it. Morality is not the same for everyone. People will understand the essence of business mission but they might see under a different light how this should be achieved.

Usually, the objective, the business mission, is found at the end of tunnel that has four sides. These sides include the deontological thinking of the corporation with respect to

1. employees;
2. customers;
3. owners; and the
4. environment, in general.

For a moment, let's study the thinking of the businessman we saw at the previous section. He made his money because he invented some patents (innovation of new technologies) and developed the appropriate distribution channels to reach his markets. Now he wants to re-examine the philosophical tenants behind his very successful corporation. In his mind, he might have been very correct in focusing his business toward specific objectives. However, in the process, he realizes that he wanted to do differently a few things. For example, it would have been better if he had provided better tooling to some of his employees who dealt with dangerous substances or was more sensitive to using monkeys for his medical experiments. He now realizes the difference between the consequentialist and the nonconsequentialist theory of morality and wants to incorporate it into his overall corporate philosophy.

The Legal Versus the Ethical Framework of Business

The legal environment, which we will study in the next chapter, and the ethical one are like overlapping circles. In some cases the legal norms are first established at the cultural level, whereas in other cases the state, or the collective thinking of industries, defines them. Legal norms change over time, differ according to the countries of reference and, in our global world, follow the legal frameworks of the countries that have more experience on particular industry-wide regulations.

The legal environments for business have been developing for many years and, although there is an effort toward worldwide standardization through directives (e.g., from the European Union) and industry codes (e.g., in maritime industry MARPOL, SOLAS, ISM codes, etc.), we do not have as yet the equivalent of *lex mercatoria* (law merchant), an autonomous body of transnational commercial rules developed in the Middle Ages—some people tracing them back to the Roman Empire, even to the Ancient Greeks, Phoenicians, and Egyptians.

Legal environments define the norms acceptable by the society and the penalties for inappropriate actions. In contrast, ethical norms express personal moralities and philosophies. Only after the Enron's demise the U.S. Sarbannes–Oxley Act blended legal and ethical questions. However, by the time that there is a law, we need to revise our thinking terms of ethics. Ethics go beyond laws. We can say that ethics express trends that some people feel about certain behaviors. The same applies to corporations. Through their codes of ethics they define trends that, in the future, may become part of the legal business framework. Let's see the following example about bribing:

Bribing was (and is for many countries) a very acceptable way of doing business. However, only since 1977, the U.S. Foreign Corrupt Practices Act (FCPA) differentiated between a facilitating payment and a bribe. At a global level in 1997 OECD voted that "enterprises should not, directly or indirectly, offer, promise, give, or demand a bribe or other undue advantage to obtain or retain business."[16] *Today, through their internal policies, companies implement this concept and in fact, present an even more complete framework, as in the case of Shell that has "a no-bribe, fair competition policy." OECD cannot define national legal policies. However, its directive, which eventually is adopted and further modified at the corporate level, may eventually become part of the national business legal framework.*

Entering the 21st Century

Every era in the history of civilizations and philosophy has certain characteristics that differentiated it from the rest. For most part of human evolution the social survival of the fittest, a small minority, dominated the philosophical and ethical thinking of the times. However, only *in the past 300 years we have been in front of technological innovations that gave to the man the means to escape from the traditional social mold.* Only during this period we have witnessed the phenomenon of the industrial revolution and only very recently the man discovered the steam engine, the electronic communication media, robots, the computer, and so many more. The man traveled faster than the speed of sound, reached the stars, discovered biotechnologies, genetic mutations, information technologies, and extended his life and his life quality.

During that last period, which effectively covers only one century of human progress, the man freed himself from slavery, created new dimensions of living and working, became globalized, learned from the developments in other parts of the world, and gave to everyone the means to pursue happiness and liberty. This has very significant social implications. Let's take as an example divorce rates in the United States, which more than doubled in the past 75 years.[17] Let's take another example: The emergence of business as we know it today. Business existed always, however, only after World War II it reached the financial strength and social importance that it has today.[18]

Marshall M. McLuhan discussed 40 years ago, in his classic book *La Galaxie Gutenberg Face a l' Ere Electronique,* about the upcoming social mutation of the society of the unit to that of the society of the individual and the possibility of dramatic philosophical and ethical changes due to the demands of the technological era.

Today, if we compare national GNPs to corporate sales, we will find that, with the exception of the very large countries, large corporations have more sales than the GNPs of whole countries. In addition, we witness dramatic changes to the roles the state governments are playing. In the 21st century, corporations operating in an effective and productive manner are taking over traditional state domains ranging from supplying energy to supplying security and from transportation to mass media communications. The world is in a sensitive state. *Whereas the past empires and superpowers assured the rest of the world of relatively peaceful coexistence, the elimination of borders increased the possibility of civilization clashes.* The state defense controls are often incapable to face events as those of September 11, 2001, in New York, and the business motivation does not relate to political issues. Businesses produce mission statements driven by profitability and related reasoning. *Business is not in business to tackle political issues or civilization clashes. Actually, the same company that supplies needed items in one civilization supplies them to another, in spite of potential clashes between them.* A van, a refrigerator, a computer, medication, food, energy do not recognize nationalities or ethnic conflicts. *In some cases business see political actions or civilization clashes as parts of their environmental fabric and they lobby against or for them when they see that corporate lobbying is necessary for achieving the corporate missions.* But, in the today's world, and as Professor McLuhan foresaw (see previous box), the individual becomes central to the today's world, with all the benefits and risks that this transition contains. Let's see a few of the issues that define our era:[19]

- *Farewell to isolation.* Throughout history, national independence was based on defending borders, militarily or economically. In the age of globalization, mass media and information technology, this is not possible anymore. Speed and communication create new educational challenges and provoke competitiveness, adjustments, and commonality of personal objectives.
- *Civilization clashes.* As we discussed in Chapter 1, and following Huntington's typology, three different sociopolitical groupings defined the global civilization landscapes in the past 100 years. Future national cultural conflicts are very possible, whereas, in spite of well-defined corporate cultures, we will see corporate enterprising able to venture anywhere in the world and without significant handicaps due to possible civilization clashes.
- *Global security.* Traditional military might (armies, navies, air forces, nuclear bombs, and so on) can do very little to face the security needs of the today's world, that in most cases need to be able to surgically interfere and remove very well-prepared "enemies" whose aims, reasoning, means, tactics, preparation, size, or abilities are unknown variables. Even well-prepared military establishments facing more exact than the September 11, 2001 challenges, for example, the United States in Afghanistan or Iraq, have serious difficulties to survive political pressures after certain period of military actions.[20] In fact, given the complexities of our times,

philosophers and thinkers alike offer confused and often conflicting views about their solutions to the global secu- rity issues. For example, Wolfe says that "Intellectuals who opposed the Vietnam War appealed to universal values like human rights and world peace. Today's reactionaries offer a crabbed and confined view of the world."[21] So, are we in front of an era where traditional military is not needed anymore and, instead, we should protect other social players, including business enterprising?

- *Economic issues.* At this point it is well understood that conflicts usually do not happen between the "haves" and the "have-nots." The have-nots usually do not have the means to fight the haves. However, pointed differences exist and create political pressures and market opportunities. For example, if we say that the average world citizen has earnings equal to one (1), the citizen of developed nations will have about four times that, whereas the average Asian citizen about half, and the average African citizen even less.[22]

- *Unions of countries and agreements.* The League of Nations, and post-World War II, the United Nations, provided a much needed forum for global peace. Moreover, and as we will see in Chapter 4, with Global Organizations and Unions of Nations, starting in the 1950s, nations pulled together their individual weight in order to achieve regional dominance. By doing so they managed to unify legal codes and standardize actions. Most prominent among them is NAFTA and European Union. To those two unions, individuals, by the millions, continue to be highly attractive, this is known as the *magnet effect.*[23] With the exception of superpowers, individual nations realize that by themselves they are unable to dominate over resources, develop technological advantages, and so forth.[24]

Technology Shapes Philosophy

For a moment let's think about the scenario of a farm around 2,000 years ago. The slaves work hard, and if they don't, they should expect very severe penalties. The mores of the times accept these behaviors from the slaves' owners. After all, a slave is only *res,* a thing! Let's move in our times. The ultramodern facility assembles robots. The two supervising (the machines) engineers discuss about the merits of the 34-hour week, their educational possibilities, and their new cars. The productivity of our era has produced new conditions for everyone and new philosophical and ethical codes.

> Humans and robots will work elbow to elbow on the shop floor, but you will be surprised by who's giving the orders.
>
> David Bourne
> Carnegie Mellon University
> Author, *My Boss the Robot*[25]

We are in an era where millions of people are bringing in their lives all sorts of technologies and affect others to do the same. Humans now have the power to destroy everything, affect the ecological balance, modify the DNAs, and mutate the social fabric. They regulate techno-bureaucracies and, through them, affect millions. They dictate the capabilities of media. The list is endless. The industrial revolution brought productivity and changed technologies. A Pandora's box opened and past philosophical frameworks of analysis proved to be insufficient for the justifications needed in the 21st century. Because of technological advancements a number of issues radically affected the social fabric. Let's see some obvious cases:

> Thinkers of the past did not always see the emerging technological advancements, neither their repercussions.[26] Examples:
>
> 1899: U.S. Patent Office Commissioner proposes winding up the office because "everything that can be invented has been invented."
>
> 1943: IBM Chairman Thomas Watson Sr. estimates the worldwide market for computers to be "about five or six."
>
> 1972: The Club of Rome's report "The Limits of Growth" claims that civilization will soon collapse as natural resources dry up and populations explode.

The Death of the Family[27]

The traditional family is changing. According to Cooper there are at least four dimensions that characterized the family structure: (a) "there is a gluing together of people based on the sense of one's own incompleteness," (b) "the family specializes in the formation of roles for its members rather than lying down the conditions for the free assumption of identity," (c) "the family in its function as primary socializer of the child instills social controls in its children," (d) "there is an elaborate system of taboos that is instilled in each child by the family." The family bonding starts through submission of one's means, social time, and space into a "region of otherness," thus satisfying personal needs of completeness. It is very interesting that even almost 40 years ago, David Cooper was concluding: "The family form of social existence that characterizes all our institutions essentially destroys autonomous initiative(s) … The family over the last two centuries has mediated an invasiveness into the lives of individuals … The age of relatives is over because the relative invades the absolute center of ourselves …"

The above, as well as similar positions, indicate that we are in front of institutional social mutations[28] moving from a society of units to a society of the individual. Statistics already indicate that, in the so-called developed countries, more than half of the marriages will end up in divorces, something totally iconoclastic only 50 years ago. We are in front of an era that demands revisiting our philosophical and ethical base and redirection of roles and responsibilities of the individual man.

A World of Aging People

In Germany, for example, by 2030, almost half of the adult population will be over 65 years of age as compared to one out of five persons at present. Obviously, specialized products and services catering to the elders will be necessary. The same will apply to the rest of the developed countries, such as France, The Netherlands, or Japan, where human longevity will exceed 82 years, and where there will be a critical need to "import" younger working force from other nations.[29] Because of that, cultural conflicts should be expected.

The Emergence of the Global Enterprise

We have already made reference to this global new player which, because of its importance and size, needs new philosophical and operational frameworks to function. We are faced with the reality that all business is global and, due to IT developments, increasingly interactive, capable to feel, and react to global ripple effects. In the past 200 years the institution business mutated from locally centered and relatively small enterprises, where names such as Rockefellers, Rothschilds, and "industry captains" ruled, to globally functioning economic concerns with hundreds of billions of U.S. dollars in sales, such as Exxon Mobil, Wal-mart, or BP. After World War II, the world's business prima donna was the United States, effectively having the headquarters of the majority of the top 100 global corporations. Today, the business hegemonic rule is almost equally split between America, Europe, and Far East.

Today's global business plays critical social roles, balances very sensitive issues, and operates through advanced enterprise resource systems following nontraditional managerial configurations.[30] As it happened with the empires of the past, we should expect that business survival will follow the same rule, the survival of the fittest where information, knowledge, and creativity will determine successes and failures. At the same time the ethical, market-based focus toward the individual employee company certainly will have a competitive advantage, too.[31]

The New Media Society

> The era of mass media is giving way to one of personal and participatory media... That will profoundly change both the media industry and society as a whole.
>
> Andreas Kluth[32]

When in 1448 Johannes Gutenberg invented the "movable type," in effect he disrupted the mainstream media of that time where usually monks manually transcribed texts or curved entire pages into wood blocks for printing. This led to a mass media proliferation, until radio and television took over ... only 50 years ago. Printing, radio, and television became the sources of information and took over the task to transmit truth (or propaganda influence).

This was until (around) 1997 when Weblogs (later We Blog, blogs), in other words personal, online journals, appeared. Blogs allowed someone to add to his website something and start a conversation. In effect, this type of communication brought the era of participation—instead of lectures to the audiences we have conversation with the audiences ... individual talent contributes to creativity of the sum—though most publishing is useless and counterproductive. Therefore, this is not a publishing phenomenon, but a social phenomenon—it is a revolution in communication. The old media model was: There is only one source of truth. The new media model is: There are multiple sources of truth. This communication era may bring a new era of cultural richness and abundant choice. Peer production is an industrial force. It is a very democratic process, allowing to voice one's opinion, but also aristocracy and monarchy in some case. Journalism will not be a sermon anymore, will be, to a significant extent, a conversation.[33] From a societal point of view, the "quality of information" is bound to shape the thinking of future generations, which will partly continue to be influenced by mass media, print, radio, and television. Major issues will be eloquently presented to the masses. It will be up to them to select their perceived critical issues of the times, to review classic-important themes of the past, or to simply spend their precious little time absorbed in a naïve reality show. Education is both formal and informal. In the future, informal learning through the vast choices in the media society will be a driver for growth, expression of priorities, and compliance with systemic desires. This learning will be based on a modified Freudian model of id–ego–super ego.

In our opinion, (1) business interests and business influence on the media will dictate, according to business priorities, not necessarily according to national concerns, the future societal orientation, and (2) the messages that the average audience will process in the new media society will be shorter, more focused, and will be dominated by the intensity and recency of events with diminishing attention to past historic, philosophical, artistic, or literature references. For the population masses this may further isolate the individual from past cultural dependencies and self-actualization objectives. The last section of Chapter 9 "Concerns: Thinking of the Future of the Corporate Employee" is based on this thinking.

CHAPTER 4

Political, Legal, and Economic Issues

Introduction

In Chapter 2, we saw how topography affects elements of culture and how, within these elements, civilizations emerge. *Political ideologies*, usually driven by the needs of the people, rulers, and people of influence, express ideas, theories, and societal aims. Political ideologies tend to be region- and period-specific, and characterize the essence of *political systems*. Irrespective of the good intentions of the initial ideologies, quite often *political bureaucracies* emerge to deal with specific structural problems and implementation realities. The backbone of a country's political system is its *legal system*, which represents the collective wisdom of the nation and the acceptable operating norms. To a greater extent, the culture, the political, and legal systems are responsible for a country's economic advancement. In a broader sense these three *uncontrollable variables* are parts of the environment within which businesses operate.

In addition, the geographic position of a country offers specific strengths. For example, historic dominance over a large water basin allowed for trade and exchange of goods; its *geopolitical influence*[1] today extends also to the region's ability to command over energy and mineral resources. Prudent past use of its geopolitical influence resulted in social development and regional economic growth that attracted capital, technologies, and human resources.

We should also see that a global corporation operates in many different political, legal, and economic environments. Business should know about all of them and, wherever possible and if its ethical conduct permits, take advantage of them.

Finally, it is necessary to point out that major or strategically influential corporations have their own political, legal, and economic might.

One billion dollar investment from a sizeable corporation may bring to a small country significant employment, wealth, research, education, and so on; elements that most political systems will see favorable and promote appropriate legal actions to accommodate these investments.

In this chapter we discuss about the political, legal, and economic environment of business. In general, most of the individual *businesses, motivated by profit, acquisition of technology, markets, resources, and so on, are usually too small to affect or to change these environments, although through lobbying activities, they often influence industry-specific legislation.*

The following sections deal with various political systems, media in the political arena, political risk, privatization of public enterprises, legal systems, legal issues, arbitration, economic theories, main economic variables that affect the global businessperson, money, and exchange process.

Political Systems

Political ideologies shaped the main political systems, which, in turn, became the basis of their legal environment and propelled the countries' economic growth. As we discussed, businesses should not be affected by these uncontrollable (by them) variables. If a business feels that these variables conflict with its principles, profit expectations, business risk, or overall objectives, then it should get out of that particular country. After World War II, the world was primarily facing the political systems discussed in the following subsections.

Communism

Karl Marx's theory of a classless society was evolved by his successors as a doctrine that the government should own all the major factors of production. Therefore, government takes over private business and manages it. The quality of management by a single central bureaucracy is questionable. Often, allocation of resources is prioritized on a military basis. Consumer products and market-related concerns are not a priority. Another issue is the compensation of ex-private business, which is now owned and run by the government. The example of such communist country was Russia in 1917, after the Bolshevik Revolution. However, after the collapse of the USSR in the 1990s, very few countries (such as Cuba and North Korea) still embrace the concept of communism. Traditional communist countries, such as Russia and China, are transforming from command economies to market economies.

Socialism

Socialism born in an idealistic era advocates that government should own or control the basic means of production, distribution, and exchange. Socialism understands the concept of profit, but in itself, this is not an aim. Some less-developed countries are professing, practicing some degree of socialism, or doing both. In Europe strong socialist parties exist, such as in Britain, France, Germany, Greece, and Spain. In the past, industry nationalization was often an objective of socialist governments, for example, coal mining, railroads and shipbuilding in Britain. Today, socialists are strong proponents of people-oriented issues, such as ecology, health care, and education.

Capitalism

Capitalism is based on free enterprising and private ownership. Private entrepreneurs identify markets and use resources to satisfy consumer needs. Profit is a clear objective of the system. Governments are restricted to traditional roles of national defense, police or international relations, though, increasingly these roles are allocated to private concerns, as in the cases of private police, or even prisons. In a capitalistic system, however, the entrepreneur is free to direct his or her business within specific regulations. These regulations are usually based on nationwide initiatives, broader directives (e.g., from the European Union), or industry-specific rules.

Mixed Systems

In our global village political labels of the past have less and less applicability. Political systems are converging and identifying in the process the merits of other systems and molding operational frameworks suitable to the peoples' desires. There are often positive results when a political system promotes political rights, party freedoms, civil liberties, market-orientation, free education, free health care, privatization of business, and so on. It is a matter of maturity of a civilization to avoid specific political labels, to develop systems that fit the overall predisposition of people, to be fair and ethical. To that extent the key in shaping political systems is the *democratic principle*, allowing all citizens political equality, respect, freedom of belief, thought, opinion, and association. Moreover, in a well-run democracy people must be able, ready, and willing to voice their opinions. In our information technology era, the ability to create individual public forums, something parallel to standing in front of the ancient Agora[2] is very possible.[3]

Politics is a jungle—torn between doing the right thing and staying in office.

John F. Kennedy[4]

I have come to the conclusion that politics are too serious a matter to be left to politicians.

Charles de Gaulle[5]

The above theories sound good for a standard secondary level education 30 years ago. But what happens today, in an era where power of the country lessens, the political systems are converging and the new ruler of social power is called business. In fact, business has become the major financial benefactor of ex-state rulers who now, with their better knowledge of public relations, continue their assumed supremacy from elected, through democratic processes, offices. Mind you, as we say in this book, business does not follow democratic rules. Meritocracy is the basis of business!

And something else: If someone asks if there is a return to the power games and the world wars of the past, think twice before giving an answer. For a moment, please, bypass the historic knowledge of who lost World War II and consider newspaper findings of the recent past. Notice that banking rules have become the major tool that Germany uses to suppress a big part of Europe; or, notice that Japan in spite of having a pacifist constitution launched on August 6, 2013, the Izumo—its largest military vessel since the war.[6] Of course, one will notice that both banks and shipyards are business-controlled enterprises!

Politics and Media

Moreover, behind the political systems are individuals who, due to their own objectives, means, and traditions, manage the political scenes, balance seemingly opposing trends and power struggles. Throughout history, politicians mastered the public media of their times. Through them they persuaded their people. Through public speech skills, ancient Athens leaders skillfully addressed the agora, the forum of their times. Good writing skills were necessary when the dominant medium were papers and pamphlets. Franklin D. Roosevelt, in the 1930s, used the radio very successfully, and John F. Kennedy understood the power of television well.

> I find television very educating. Every time that somebody turns on the set I go into the other room and read a book.
>
> Groucho Marks[7]

Which will be the next public medium that will influence the masses? "Free media" shapes the outcome of presidential races, and the Internet is the freer of all, says Jonathan Alter.[8] It allows thousands of ideas to develop online which may be occasionally transcribed as risking information and data quality. Of course, the Internet will be more successful with people who were born in the past 40 years—that is, in the era of the information technology.

In the global business village, political influence maybe shifting from politicians to business leaders. Business political power is often manifested through the corporate ability to efficiently implement major projects, extensive networking, public relations departments, and the use of media and information technologies. At the same time we should observe that politics, media, and business interrelate—and this is consistent with the literature. Point of attention: In many regions of the world, "extensive family control of large corporate sectors could be an outcome of poor social, economic, and institutional development and low government quality. The oligarchies—a form of government in which power is vested in a few people—in turn use their economic might to reap political advantages and shape institutional development most favorable to their interests."[9]

Political Risk

In February 1994, Nelson Mandela was elected President of South Africa, the first Black leader of that country, emerging after 28 years of imprisonment as a political prisoner. In July 1997, Hong Kong formally was returned from Britain to China.[10] In February 2000, after national elections, major social reforms started in Iran. In September 2001, terrorist attacks destroyed the World Trade Center in New York and part of the U.S. Pentagon. These are cases of *political risk*, which *is any negative change of the value of an enterprise due to politically induced motivation.* If we examine all the previously mentioned cases, we can observe that 5 years later a different business status quo has been established. *There was a political risk that negatively affected some companies operating in those regions, but there were also business opportunities that others identified during the aftermath of the change.*

We have *macropolitical risk*, where due to the change of political factors in a region there are consequences to all international companies that operate there, as it was in Bosnia and Somalia in the 1990s. We also have *micropolitical* risk that affects only targeted corporations or industries, as we had in the Saudi Arabian oil industry during the 1970s.[11] Given the nature of the political risk, we can have *ownership risk* in cases of total or partial expropriation of the corporate assets, forced divestiture of the enterprise usually after a governmental initiative, or even property confiscation. We can also have *operating risk*, when there are direct repercussions in the operation of the enterprise, and *transfer risk* when international exchange matters are at risk.

Political risk does not always carry specific labels. It can cover areas, such as cancellation of performance bonds (unfair calling), control of business functions, exporting difficulties, loss of property or intellectual rights, price controls, tax-related changes, and so on. Some of these problems are known to any company that operates internationally. Elections, strikes, terrorists, wars, change of political thinking (ideology), foreign dangers, revolutions, and so on, are typical elements that can change the political risk ranking of a region.[12] To face this type of risks, international corporations try to operate in ways that do not separate themselves from the local entities. They create a local image, mind the community's interests and needs, recruit local personnel, utilize local facilities, use joint ventures and so on. However, prewarning of political risk and insuring against it, in certain cases, is a must,[13] especially while operating in less-developed countries. In general, corporations must follow the rule that *government stability, not its form, reduces the political risk.*

The Privatization of Public Corporations

Irrespective of political systems or ideologies, governments like to control public corporations. Often the reasons behind the creation and operation of public corporations by government bureaucrats were ideology, strategic significance, defense, and capital intensive enterprises that could not be funded by private initiatives (e.g., energy, transportation, health care, university education) or belief that similar services can be provided effectively, better, economically, or in a fair way by the public domain.

In practice, this did not prove to be always correct, easy, or efficient. For example, while performing central planning for the 11 time zones, the USSR could not focus on the specific needs of a region's ecosystem or on birth controls or on consumer desires. It became an impossible and often counterproductive task. Nevertheless, political systems tend to embrace some of their ideological tenants. Socialist governments tend to offer "free" health care and education to everyone, whereas capitalistic governments often employ, even for military-related services, private providers.

Since the 1980s major worldwide privatization efforts are evident. Such trends were observed irrespective of political beliefs. Public corporations usually do not show profit, do not undertake business risks, use cheaper capital, have low R&D levels, do not export, are not competitive, do not use modern management techniques, and do not observe changes in the marketplace.

> Globalization, aided by privatization and liberalization trends, is shaping the economic and sociocultural environments of the world economies.
>
> Ben Oumlil and C. P. Rao[14]

Additionally, public corporations command valuable resources. When sold they can be very desirable ventures for investors. The sale of public corporations give governments needed money, reduce the cost of running them, provide better service to the consumer, and creates a more competitive environment.

Privatizing a public corporation is not an easy task and often demands the use of specialized consultants. Existing status quos require specific treatment of employees and provide unique rights to regions or to other stakeholders (mining rights, waste management, etc.). The price of a public corporation is not market driven. The markets of public corporations are not well defined or managed. Geopolitical reasoning might hide further opportunities.

Legal Systems

> Laws are not invented; they grow out of circumstances.
>
> Azarias[15]

In Chapter 2, we discussed that we do not have as yet the equivalent of an international business law, what in previous centuries was known as *lex mercatoria*. In fact, in today's globalized society it is very difficult to process legal claims from one country to another as they often follow different legal systems. For the global businessperson understanding each individual legal system and the specific legislation in the country he or she is assigned to is critical, though the details will always be handled through specialized lawyers. The three main law systems are discussed in the following subsections.

Common Law

A common-law (or case-law) system is judge-made and based on tradition.[16] Although there are legal codes that guide him or her, the judge evaluates each specific case according to previous similar cases and customs in his or her area. Therefore, it is possible that for identical cases a different judgment may be pronounced in Florida versus Minnesota. Some of the countries engaging in common-law practices are Australia, Canada, England, and the United States.

Code Law

The code-law (or civil-law) system is based on a systematic codification of existing laws. These laws were created by the parliament of each country, and the judges are required to apply them in accordance with the spirit and letter of law. The code law has its roots in the Roman law and evolved differently according to the country that used it. Today, it is applied in most of Europe, Central and South America, the Far East, and elsewhere.

Theocratic Law

Many countries that followed the faith of Islam accepted a legal system that derives its principles from Islam's theological tenants. Whereas in countries with code or common legal systems, the law constantly and dynamically evolves by the people or their representatives, in theocratic legal systems, the legal environment assumes a divine base and has more permanency over time.[17]

The general principle is that the global businessperson should respect both the home and host legal tenants and the principles behind them. For example, doing business in Japan requires that the foreign visitor understands and accepts that legal-type implications should be minimized. Embedded in the Japanese thinking is the consensus decision making that operates harmonically even outside the business entity. Therefore, in-depth awareness of such principles greatly assists business growth, far more than problem-solving later through legalistic means.

Legal Issues

In each country the continuous and dynamic development of the legal environment presents formidable challenges to the companies, both domestic and foreign, which operate there. Knowledge of this environment is a must and should be addressed at the very top of the corporation. The legal department functions not only in an advisory capacity at the President–CEO level, but also at every line or staff level where its advice is needed. It does not only deal with legal disputes and corporate threats, but also is a vehicle toward achieving objectives and realize challenges. Awareness of the following issues has particular importance in international business.

International Agreements

In our global business village there are international agreements that facilitate the global trade. These agreements, some dating back more than 100 years, are in the areas of

- entry of persons, products, funding;
- acquisition of capital resources;
- protection of industrial property rights;[18]
- protection of trademarks;[19]
- tax matters;
- transportation matters;
- insurance;
- most favorite nations.

Due to similar worldwide agreements: tariffs, quotas, and nontariff regulations were significantly reduced during the 20th century. Additionally, gradual changes in the legal systems of individual countries allowed for faster growth of the international trade and expansion of the global corporations.

The reader should observe that international agreements may create unexpected conflicts. For example, in the fall of 2004, the judges of the World Trade Organization ruled that gambling regulations in Utah (and many other U.S. states) "conflict with America's obligation not to discriminate against foreigners providing 'recreational services.'"[20] One hundred and ten years ago, the people of Utah had decided that gambling was a vice that the state did not need. Nevertheless, probably without too much thought, the Federal government signed an international agreement that conflicts with statewide desires. This agreement assumes obligations that all states should follow. Violation of these obligations potentially brings millions of dollars in penalties. Moreover, this shows a classic case where traditional state or regional thinking conflicts with an overall positive pre-disposition toward a borderless global society.

Industry-Specific Arrangements

On a global level, industry associations are joining forces to improve their offerings, reduce costs, deal with fragile ecosystems, avoid unnecessary risks, and so on. Many industries, from coffee to oil and from insurance to maritime, have created forums and specialized organizations to han-dle issues all around the world. These arrangements represent usually the collective wisdom of an industry, and they merit attention at the national and international levels.

Let's see the role of industry-wide organizations through an example from the maritime industry.

Representatives of the ship owners, the shipbuilders, and organiza-tions like International Maritime Organization (IMO) and International Association of Classification Societies (IACS) often discussed standards, roles, relationships, and information exchange needs with respect to "fit-for-purpose" ships.[21] Maritime, of course, is the epitome of a global business industry and the fit-for-purpose ships are specially made vessels that require worldwide strict standardization codes. Here is where IMO comes to focus. International Maritime Organization operates under the umbrella of the United Nations, was born in 1982, and continues to exist since 1948 as International Maritime Consultative Organization (IMCO), and is highly specialized in the maritime field. The IMO has issued hundreds of "recommendations" and "codes," some of them extremely valuable, as in the case of the Civil Liability Convention (CLC), which is globally enforceable.[22] Similar industry-specific arrangements, in practice in most fields, define the ways to do business at a global level.

Arbitration in International Situations

Irrespective of good intentions in business transactions, occasional dis-putes always arise. These disputes become extremely complex, expensive, and time-consuming when business deals across national borders. Going to courts to solve a dispute is not necessarily an efficient solution. A much better proposition is to include an arbitration clause within the terms of the contractual obligation between the parties involved. Arbitration has been proved to be

- faster;
- more economical;
- avoiding formalities and bureaucracies;
- able to keep business continuity;
- not revealing business secrets;

The arbitration decision usually is enforceable through the preagreed processes. An arbitration clause should include the following:[23]

- The chosen legal environment enforcing the arbitration deci-sion. For example, if the issue is of an international loan, it is better to choose an international finance center, like London or New York, than Amalfi or Aruba.
- The choice of the arbitration forum to avoid ex-post surprises. The United Nations, in their effort to provide an arbitration platform, since 1976 have created the UNCITRAL (United Nations Commission on International Trade Law). Known arbitration mediators are the London Court of Arbitration, the Stockholm Chamber of Commerce, and so forth.
- The process of choosing arbitrators.

Economic Theory and Related Notions

Till now we have studied culture, philosophy, political, and legal systems. They are part of the business environment. In the following sections, we analyze aspects of the economic environment addressing (1) a theory framework, (2) economic variables, and (3) practical matters, for exam-ple, what is money and how we exchange it among countries.

Mercantilism

Just a few hundred years ago, the socioeconomic basis for managing a country's economy was mercantilism. Simply put, it was collecting wealth in the form of precious metals, like gold and silver, and, using this power, to buy things that the society needed but could not produce. Accumulation of wealth was the ultimate goal and manifestation of a powerful nation. In order to accumulate wealth a positive balance of payments was necessary, meaning that more was coming in the country than going out of it. The philosophy behind this dogmatic position dictated that nations had to put barriers in importing, motivation to export, a strong army to keep colonies, and so on.

The Absolute and the Comparative Advantage

In 1776, however, Adam Smith in his classic book the *Wealth of Nations* reversed the previous thinking. He suggested that *the forces of production and trade should lead the international commerce—not the accumulation of wealth or the protectionist attitudes*. Specialization should lead to higher productivity. According to the theory, country A should export to country B the good X as it produces it at an absolute cost advantage over the same product produced by country B; also, country A should import from country B the product Y that has there an absolute cost advantage over the same product when product Y is produced at country A. In order, however, to implement this exchange, *the preassumption of no trade barriers of any type was necessary.*

Then, a question arose: What will happen if a country has an absolute cost advantage for both products over another country? Is trade possible? The affirmative answer was given in 1817 by David Ricardo, who proved that this is possible in so far that the product exchange between the two countries had different input ratios.[24]

More than a century passed for this academic thinking to be politically acceptable. The first serious recognition that tariff barriers can be counterproductive was through the signing of the Smoot–Hawley Act by President Hoover in 1930. The reader should not be astonished on finding that the era of the global business village started only after World War II.

International Product Life Cycle

In the 1960s, Raymond Vernon presented his concept about how the business world moves in an international trade pattern. Although his idea appears to be ethnocentric, it merits attention and, conceptually and to some extent, repeats in many instances. It follows four stages:

1. Assume that we start with after the post–World War II United States. As the country's infrastructure was not destroyed by the war and as the rest of the world's production facilities were extensively damaged, the United States was in a position to export everywhere—to developed and to less-developed countries alike.

2. Developed countries, such as Germany and Japan, having the know-how of industrial production, slowly began their own production of goods that were previously imported. Through their own production, they satisfied their domestic demand and, therefore, reduced their imports dependency from the United States.

3. Now the developed countries had their own production facilities efficiently working. Slowly they started exporting to countries where the United States exported previously, thus further reducing the need of U.S.-made products.

4. Finally, the same countries start exporting to the United States and even building plants there to satisfy the American demand. In fact, Honda America, which built its plants in the United States, was in the 1990s exporting more "made in America" cars to Japan than any other automobile manufacturer.

We should also observe that factories and facilities built later are more advanced than those built 10 to 20 years ago. Germany and Japan have newer production facilities than the United States. The production at later stages of the international product life cycle is more efficient and the products produced meet the consumer demands better.

Porter's Theory on the Competitive Advantage

Professor M. E. Porter in his book *The Competitive Advantage of Nations,*[25] discusses four variables that affect global competitiveness of a region or an industry. They are as follows:

1. *Factor conditions:* There exist regionally available resources, such as physical, human, knowledge-based, capital, technology, and so on, allowing for business success.

2. *Demand conditions:* There is a local demand for products and services produced, sufficient to sustain initial business activity.

3. *Existence of related industries:* For a business to function efficiently, one must be able to find support-related businesses in their immediate environment.

4. *Business thinking:* Business strategy and overall managerial thinking follows high standards and promises cutting-edge performance.

> We should point out that the United States and Europe are steadily converging in terms of technology, business values, corporate mergers, finance practices, and so on. To that extent we may be in front of what will be termed as *The Atlantic Century.*[26]

The above appear in today's thinking commonsensical. It is, however, noteworthy that only 100 years ago the business world had not embraced such ideas neither had it embraced the importance for a global free trade principle, without trade barriers.

Concerns Against Global Trade

From the previous discussion it appears that free trade on a global level benefits everyone. Cheaper goods will be produced wherever this is possible thus allowing more people to enjoy them. However, we need to examine cases where free trade may not be very advisable. Such as the following:

- Military products give a unique advantage to countries that produce them. Therefore, they are often unwilling to share with others their military technologies for political reasons. In the opinion of politicians who lead the world, it might not be wise to offer to all the countries (that have the financial means to acquire them) long-range missiles or nuclear capacity. By the same token, any strategic-type capability is often questionable, including telecommunications. This is particularly important in an era where traditional military conflicts are facing untraditional "terrorist" challenges.

- Countries that develop new markets in other (host) countries, initially can cover their demand through exports from and production at the home country. This translates to more employment in the home market. Eventually, however, and as we will see later,[27] the home countries establish production facilities in the host countries, in order to cater better to the host countries' needs. This practice, which business-wise is a necessary step and shows forward thinking, may cost employment positions to the home country, and therefore, initiate political reactions, strikes, and so on.

- It is natural, as we saw in Chapter 2, that corporations entering into new markets bring with them their culture, logos, and products. It is natural that to some extent these corporations will affect the local cultures through what is known as cultural imperialism. This type of change is not always welcomed by the elders of the host cultures.

- New ventures often are like small babies. They need support. They are promising and, if allowed to grow, one expects that they be competitive and provide exciting products both for the domestic and export markets. This is called the *infant industry argument* and assumes that the states will protect such companies at least during their initial steps.

- A country's balance of payments account is another issue, often protected through trade barriers. In order to import goods a country needs enough means to pay for them.

Barriers in Global Trade

The General Agreement on Tariffs and Trade reduced significantly the existing post–World War II trade barriers. There are two types of them: tariff barriers and nontariff barriers.

There are three types of tariff barriers: On the value (*ad valorem*), which is usually a percentage of the declared value of the product; specific duty, which is calculated usually on a measurement base; and compound duty, which adds the two previous ones. An arithmetic example may illustrate the respective concepts. Let's assume that we import $2,000,000 of chemicals in 20,000 containers and we pay 10% *ad valorem* and $3 per container. This makes for *ad valorem* of $200,000 (10% × 2,000,000), specific duty of $60,000 (20,000 × 3$) and compound $260,000 ($200,000 + $60,000).

Quotas are the most important nontariff barriers determining a specific number of units that are permitted to be imported within a period. There are many other types of nontariff barriers that range from industry standards to the existence of a minimum of local content and from required documentation to bureaucratic difficulties.

Economic Systems

The economic systems often follow the political thinking of the region. Pure economic systems, described in the post–World War II literature, do not exist anymore. They tend to converge and adopt processes and practices that were proven successful in other economic environments. The main systems are classified in the following.[28]

Capitalist or Market Economies

These systems are characterized by private ownership of the means of production and distribution, existence of free and competitive markets, entrepreneurialism, and profit motivation. Theoretically, in these systems, there exist very little governmental intervention, although this can be debatable as standards, safety, legal, and business ethical conduct and accepted procedures should be upheld and the respective regulatory processes are usually governmentally controlled. Also, supranational union directives, like those of the European Union, and industry-driven codes affect business behaviors and practices.

Command Economies

In the international political compass these systems are at the opposite position of the capitalist or market economies. The state owns all means of production and distribution of goods and services and a central governmental agency is responsible for the state's overall economic planning. Therefore, governmental thinking, often far away from the daily consumer needs, define what is to be produced, how, or when. Military might or specific projects, like space exploration, have priority over the simplest of the desires of the everyday citizen. The pre-1991 USSR was a prime example of a command economy. Today, only Cuba and North Korea approach the "pure" command economy ideal.

Mixed Economies

Most of the world's economies have taken elements from both sides of the political spectrum. Self-interest has been the economic motivation for personal and social growth, for new inventions, better products, and market understanding. Individual businesspersons, being more flexible, adaptive, risk taking, and profit-motivated than their governments, seek new opportunities—especially in a globalized world. At the same time governments continue to play a determining role in many areas, such as defense, security, transportation, telecommunications, health care, and education. This role, in many cases has gone too far, and as the section on the privatization of public corporations discusses, there is a definite trend toward the sale of many of those publicly run businesses.

Traditional Economies

In many economies, which in fact represent a great number of people, the traditional economic model predominates. In countries like Africa, Central and South America, or Southeast Asia, people take a more fatalistic attitude toward their economic realities. "Religious and cultural values frequently dictate the societal norms as well as economic aspirations, and the status quo is self-perpetuated."[29] By Western standards these economies are poor, and, to a great extent are moving within the same vicious cycle of production–distribution. In these economies only outside support can guide leading economic sectors into a better future, social growth, and prosperity.

Population

The population of a country is a variable that allows an initial evaluation of its economic size. For example, one can compare the Canadian and U.S. economies as a multiple of their populations. Characteristics of the population, such as distribution by age, sex, education, and so on, determine economic growth patterns and market peculiarities of a region. However, we should not see populations only as variables determining the size of an economy or its market potential. Increasingly, policy makers and businesspersons alike are responsible for the quality of life and for sustaining the human and nonhuman growth and balance.

We should also examine trends that affect populations worldwide. Here are some:

- The growth of population will result in population density issues. This should determine new "design for living" ways and culture-related challenges.
- Another trend refers to people's desire to live in cities, usually due to employment, opportunities, quality of life, socialization, education, and so on. The megacities of the future exist now. Mumbai, for example, which in 1970 had only 6 million inhabitants, in 10 years from now will have more than 30.
- We should also observe the global dependency on talented immigrants, who provide to developed nations needed production means and a good human resource base. These, usually political or economic immigrants, are changing the national societal fabrics, providing a glimpse of their own practices and customs.

Gross National Product

Irrespective of the economic system, one of the most important variables in the economy of a country is the gross national product (GNP). With that we mean the *market value of all final*[30] *goods and services produced in the economy in a given period*. The GNP is a variable that gives us a measure of the total production of the economy during the specific period. Let's see a couple of issues that relate to this definition.

What Is Money?

Societies in the past used a variety of things to measure value, like precious metals, feathers, teeth of whales, slaves, barter items to exchange goods. Obviously, in a modern society we had to come up with something more convenient to measure value. So, thousands of years ago,[31] people invented money, which became the *acceptable and legal tender to repay all debts, public or private.* But how can we be sure that this coin or paper has real value? Why are we sure that this 100 euros[32] bill can be exchanged with two shirts and a pair of slacks?

Because we believe that the European countries behind the euro tell us the truth about its value. Therefore, this paper becomes a trade-able commodity of a specific value. Actually, in 1717 Sir Isaac Newton established for the first time an exact equation between an ounce of gold and sterling pounds, which was termed as the gold standard. Then, for many years, people either accepted this rule or the traders, through demand and supply, established a different value. In the continuation, in 1971, President Richard Nixon, "closed the gold window" effectively allowing the global currencies to float. Finally, floating currencies became the rule through the Jamaica Agreement and the market was to determine the value between currencies.

It is worth mentioning that the Frenchman Jacques Rueff started a school of thought of governmental "discipline," effectively indicating that bureaucrats should not "create" money for political necessities. Today, prudence is the operative word in any national bank having the responsibility to issue money.

Market Value

We said before that the market determines the value of currencies as they are commodities. The market also determines the value of goods that a society produces.

Somewhere in South China, Mrs. Zhang finishes a handmade tablecloth that will be sold at the local tourist store for about $300. Mrs. Zhang learned her craft from her mother and is very good at it. The tablecloth took her about two months to finish. In Brugge, Belgium, Mrs. De Witt, following the old art of "kant klossen" just finished her tablecloth, which will be sold at the local market for $1,500. An expert can say that both ladies are equally gifted in their crafts and worked about the same hours to produce their final product which are of the same dimensions and of the same quality material. However, why is this huge difference in price? Here is the market factor. We include in the GNP a product at the price in its own market.

Moreover, we observe that GNP is not the only indicator of the value of a country's production. If we *adjust a nation's GNP according to its purchasing power, we have what is known as PPP (Purchasing Power Parity index)*. From the perspective of the economic size, this might change the rankings of the countries. Obviously, what is produced in a country becomes its citizens' income. The largest component will be spent by its citizens as consumption. A smaller component will be kept for their savings, which is invested further and becomes a propelling power for the economy's future growth.

Balance of Payments

Most economies in our modern world greatly depend on imports from other countries. As we discussed, it is not anymore an era of mercantilism, where countries build barriers, but, in our epoch, free trade and production specialization are the operative words. To pay for its desired imports a country must accumulate the necessary financial means. *The balance of payments equation represents the accounting position of a country with respect to the rest of the world.* There are three main subaccounts of the balance of payments account:

1. *Current account,* that includes all receipts and payments (inflows or outflows) for goods, merchandising, services, and unilateral transfers that are coming in or going out of the country. If a car is imported in our country, we need to pay for the value of the car. This amount goes into the current account. Also, with respect to unilateral services, a certain amount is paid (or received) because of an assumed obligation or desire, but, in this case, no exchange takes place. Examples of unilateral transfers are pension payments to nonresidents, educational expenses to our son who studies in another country, monetary gift to our niece for her wedding, aid from one country to another, and so on.

2. The *capital account* includes inflows and outflows for financial assets and liabilities, such as stocks and bonds. Short-term capital flows are also classified under this heading. Attention should be paid to the volatility of these transactions as exchange rate fluctuations (see following section) may result in many (and costly) hedging activities.

3. The *official reserves account* includes inflows and outflows like (1) gold reserves, (2) foreign exchange currencies held by the government, and (3) liabilities to central banks.

The balance of payments account is considered to be in equilibrium if over a 3- to 5-year period its surpluses more or less balance its deficits.

Exchanging Currencies Around the World

In the section about money (currency), we refer to it as a commodity whose value is determined at the marketplace and is affected by governmental actions. Most countries have their own currencies though we experienced in the recent years a trend toward collapsing them, under a central currency, as is the euro for many European countries.

Within a single country, the currency that is considered legal tender for exchange purposes is the local one. However, when we move into international environments, we must pay (except if otherwise agreed) in local currencies. Therefore, we need to exchange our home country currency with that of the host country. But how does the currency exchange work? In its most simple form, and if we assume 1.25 U.S. dollars equals 1 euro, 1 U.S. dollar equals $1/1.25 = 0.8$.

Currencies fluctuate constantly according to market pressures. Accordingly, we need to find the applicable exchange rate. We refer to the *spot rate* for the immediate exchange between two currencies, usually for delivery within 2 days. Otherwise we refer to the *forward rates,* if let's say our contract indicates delivery within 30 days, 60 days, or so on. Traders estimate the currencies' present and future values and determine exact exchange rates. The exchange rate fluctuation represents a risk. Most companies are not in business to take risks in the currency exchange markets. To avoid the risk from exchange rate fluctuation companies *hedge,* for a price.

Toward a New Theory: The Era of Global Business

In a couple of previous instances I stated that this book became a mix between the technocratic needs of the global enterprise, an economic theory, and a philosophical perspective of our era. Also, I believe that major corporations will become the substantive societal players of the near future in terms of research, significance, size, employee happiness, philosophy, and ethics, in a more profound way that state governments previously attempted to be.

In fact, in the section "Managers, Self-actualize!" some working propositions were presented; three of them having some bearing with the present conceptualization:

1. The framework of analysis is a function of the knowledge we possess at a specific time; it constantly evolves.
2. Without data we cannot draw conclusions. *The quality of data is critical.*
3. Have we studied the trends that will shape the decades to come? *Presently corporations are most suited to lead the social change!*

Therefore, it is important to repeat a statement made at the preface and, that is, to be reminded of the relative revenue size of the world's largest corporations as compared to the GNP of countries.[33] Thus, in a table where countries and large global companies are presented together, the largest global company may rank around the 25th position, whereas more than 80 countries have GNP smaller than the revenues of the 500th largest corporation. Do these depictions have some bearing to the previous conceptualization? Yes! Using the same data as before (but with some variation due to definitional issues) consider that the 500 top companies have sales that correspond to more than 40% of the global GNP.

By analyzing similar data, and according to the methodology used, this writer believes that by 2033, in other words in less than 20 years from now, almost two-thirds of the then global GNP potentially will be handled by the 500 largest corporations (and their subsidiaries or their equivalents),[34] and that the role of national governments will be substantially lesser. In addition, consider how much more current, flexible and focused are the corporate governance documents and operation manuals of a modern well-run enterprise than the state-supported constitutions, the laws and the bureaucracies of the great majority of counties. In my own thinking corporate governance documents are the equivalent of country constitutions and operation manuals the equivalent of their laws and bureaucracies. *Thus it is my opinion that the economic theories of the past do not suffice in this new era and that one addressing the preeminent role of the major global business entities should be added. The previous discussion is a first attempt in this direction.*[35]

In this chapter, we studied some of the uncontrollable variables by the corporation environments, namely the political, legal, and economic one. The backbone of all of them is the cultural thinking of the region which we studied in Chapter 2. We also saw the impact of philosophy in the corporate thinking and the enormous social changes that have been happening in the past 100 years.

The next chapter, which also deals with the global business environment, studies some of the major players in the geopolitical arena, such as the United Nations and the European Union.

CHAPTER 5

Global Organizations and Unions of Nations

About This Chapter

Up to now this book addressed the uncontrollable by the corporation environments. It started with topography, explained how it affects the culture of a region, and discussed elements of culture. Then, it studied two very significant elements of culture, philosophy and ethics, their origins, how they were reshaped during the past 100 years, and about the "new" societal player, the business corporation. Three other elements uncontrollable by the corporation variables: the political, the legal, and the economic environment, were then analyzed. These environments do not stand independent from each other. There is a reasonable sequence from the cultural to the legal environment, though there are many overlaps, constant evolution, and feedback.

But where does the "new" societal player, the business corporation stand? As we discussed, for many students of the modern world, geopolitics[1] defined the operating business environment. Different operating environments for business were created in President Theodore Roosevelt's United States, Adolf Hitler's Germany, and Leonid Brezhnev's Soviet Union. We shall revisit the geopolitical arena in the last section of this chapter.

Meanwhile, we address issues about the international organizations which shaped the socioeconomic realities of the 21st century and how they affected the business environment. Such organizations like the United Nations (UN), some of the UN agencies that have indirect or direct bearing on social growth and creation of business opportunities, the European Union (EU), other unions of nations like the North

American Free Trade Association (NAFTA) or Association of Southeast Asian Nations (ASEAN), and other global organizations catering to the worldwide industry-specific needs.

For a moment imagine a world where each nation was following a mercantilistic socioeconomic approach and building tall military and trade borders. Imagine a world without research and development, production advantages, trade exchanges, or global traveling. Or, a world, shredded in tiny independent nations, such as the Republic of Kiribati, population 77,000; the Republic of Vanuatu, population 170,000; or the Kingdom of Tonga, population 105,000.[2] More than 50,000 such nations are needed to represent the earth's population. And, then, imagine today's borderless world with about 200 nations peacefully discussing issues on food, agriculture, human rights, business corruption, or trade development. And to top it all off, one single nation, the United States, commanding an impressive amount of the world's GNP, and 28 European nations working as a single unit, commonly sharing social and business objectives.

United Nations[3]

Immediately after World War II, with its enormously catastrophic repercussions, the UN was established in an atmosphere of hope and idealism with a mission to provide a peaceful social and economic world for everyone. It was not the first time that such an effort was made. Previously, the League of Nations had similar objectives.

The country members of the UN, then and now, can be classified in two major categories: developed countries (DCs) and less-developed countries (LDCs). The great majority of the UN is LDCs, which because of their characteristics, have different needs and objectives than the powerful and dominant DCs. One will immediately sense that the "haves" aim to influence the UN in a different way from the have-nots. This is only the beginning for possible UN conflicts, since the UN includes every cultural segment of the world, prompting again potential "civilization clashes."[4] In spite of differences among the member states and dozens of active military fronts that exist today, in balance, the UN appears to have mastered its initial objectives. The UN has four main purposes: To keep peace throughout the world; to develop friendly relations among nations; to help nations work together to improve the lives of poor people; to conquer hunger, disease, and illiteracy; and to encourage respect for each other's rights and freedoms; to be a center for harmonizing the actions of nations to achieve these goals.

Due to its unique international character, and powers vested in its founding Charter, the organization can take action on a wide range of issues, and provide a forum for its 193 member states to express their views, through the General Assembly, the Security Council, the Economic and Social Council, and other bodies and committees.

The work of the UN reaches every corner of the globe. Although best known for peacekeeping, peacebuilding, conflict prevention, and humanitarian assistance, there are many other ways the UN and its system (specialized agencies, funds, and programs) affect our lives and make the world a better place. The organization works on a broad range of fundamental issues, from sustainable development, environment and refugees protection, disaster relief, counter terrorism, disarmament and nonproliferation, to promoting democracy, human rights, gender equality and the advancement of women, governance, economic, and social development, and international health, clearing landmines, expanding food production, and more, to achieve its goals and coordinate efforts for a safer world for this and future generations.

> The whole history of the world is summed up in the fact that, when nations are strong, they are not always just, and when they wish to be just, they are often no longer strong.
>
> Winston Churchill[5]

Characteristics of LDCs

It is, therefore, necessary to start by describing some the LDCs characteristics. Not all of these characteristics exist in every LDC, but we need to see these characteristics both as social and business challenges. Water pumps exist in the Sahara desert and mobile phones are marketed in the surrounding areas of the Amazon tropical forests, both business ventures being motivated by traditional entrepreneurial objectives, but eventually promoting social well-being. Some of the characteristics that are primarily found in the LDCs are as follows:

- Poor topography
- Low annual per capita income
- High unemployment and disguised unemployment
- Unequal income distribution, usually with a small middle class
- Large population percentage in agriculture
- Low levels of education
- High birth rates
- High mortality and low life expectancy
- Poor health and nutritional conditions
- Dependency on limited exports, usually agricultural or mineral
- Low levels of infrastructure
- Low saving rates and low capital investments
- Not developed banking sector
- Political instability
- Technological dualism
- Regional dualism

Organization of UN

The UN is a very complex organization, which extends much further than its impressive New York building. In its simplest organizational format, it is comprised of the following major divisions:

- The *Secretariat.*
- The *Trusteeship Council.*
- The *International Court of Justice.*
- The *Security Council* (with five permanent members having veto power including China, France, Russia, United Kingdom, and United States and 10 nonpermanent members, each of them being elected for two years)
- The *General Assembly,* where every country, irrespective of size, political might, or wealth has one vote. This has direct impact on the UN orientation, which is primarily led by

the needs of LDCs, such as education, health, infrastructure projects, industrialization, agriculture, and so on. Under the General Assembly there are 17 major programs, including the UN Commission on Trade and Development (UNCTAD) and the UN University (UNU).

- The *Economic and Social Council* which includes all functional and all regional commissions. It also includes well-known organizations, such as the International Labor Organization (ILO), the World Bank—usually referred as the International Bank for Reconstruction and Development (IBRD), the International Development Association (IDA), the International Finance Corporation (IFC), the Multilateral Investment Guarantee Agency (MIGA), the International Monetary Fund (IMF), the UN Industrial Development Organization (UNIDO), the World Trade Organization (WTO), and so forth.

The World Bank[6]

The World Bank is comprised of five organizations, namely: (1) the IBRD, aiming to lend to governments of middle-income and creditworthy low-income countries; (2) the IDA that provides interest-free loans—called credits—and grants to governments of the poorest countries; (3) the IFC, the largest global development institution focusing exclusively on the private sector and aiming to help developing countries achieve sustainable growth by financing investment, mobilizing capital in international financial markets, and providing advisory services to businesses and governments; (4) the MIGA, created in 1988, to promote foreign direct investment into developing countries to support economic growth, reduce poverty, and improve people's lives. MIGA fulfills this mandate by offering political risk insurance (guarantees) to investors and lenders; and (5) the International Centre for Settlement of Investment Disputes (ICSID) that provides international facilities for conciliation and arbitration of investment disputes. The official motto of the World Bank is "working for a world free of poverty." In doing so, since 1947 the World Bank has funded around 12,000 projects in more than 170 countries.

The reader should recognize the efforts of the World Bank, as well as that of all UN agencies, to promote the well-being of the planet's citizens. However, the bank was designed in an era that focused on country-centered programs and public enterprises. Although the bank is evolving, the new financial landscape, including privatization of public entities and the growth of the private and the regional development banks, in the long run, maybe will reduce the traditional banking role of the World Bank.[7]

The International Monetary Fund[8]

The IMF is an international organization of 188 member countries. It was established to foster global growth and economic stability. It provides policy advice and financing to members in economic difficulties and also works with developing nations to help them achieve macroeconomic stability and reduce poverty. Moreover, the IMF promotes international monetary cooperation and exchange rate stability, facilitates the balanced growth of international trade, and provides resources to help members in balance of payments difficulties or to assist with poverty reduction.

The IMF and World Bank have endorsed internationally recognized standards and codes as important for their work and which Reports on the Observance on Standards and Codes (ROSCs) are prepared. The ROSCs refer to sets of provisions relating to the institutional environment—the rules of the game—within which economic and financial policies are devised and implemented. Standards exist in the areas of data and fiscal transparency, and monetary and financial policy transparency have been developed by the fund while others have been developed by other standard setting bodies including the World Bank, the Basel Committee on Banking Supervision, and the Financial Action Task Force.

The ROSCs are prepared and published at the request of the member country, by the IMF, World Bank, or both in each of the standards development areas. In some cases, detailed assessments of a countries' observance of standards are also published. From this the reader can see that the UN has gone far beyond its worldwide peaceful mission. The UN is establishing a global operating environment that, while bridges the gap between the poor and the wealthy, also establishes the rules and standards of state and business interaction.

Let's summarize some of the main areas of standard setting by the IMF, World Bank and, effectively by UN country members:[9] Data and policy transparency, good practices on fiscal transparency, good practices on transparency in monetary and financial policies, financial sector standards, core principles for effective banking supervision, objectives and principles for securities regulation, insurance supervisory principles, core principles for systemically important payment systems, anti-money laundering and combating the financing of terrorism, standards concerned with market integrity, principles of corporate governance, international accounting standards, international standards on auditing, and principles of corporate governance.

However, do note that *all the well-intended UN projects, and those of its agencies, are implemented through business activities, sometimes with debatable principles of corporate governance.*

From GATT to WTO[10]

But where did all the above start? At the Bretton Woods Conference in 1944, the UN in their efforts toward the world's economic recovery post-World War II, proposed the creation of an *International Trade Organization (ITO) to establish rules and regulations for trade between countries.* The ITO would have complemented the other two Bretton Woods Institutions, the IMF and the World Bank. However, business-related and political fears in the United States diminished the ITO dream and only a part of it survived, the *General Agreement on Tariffs and Trade (GATT).*

The GATT aimed to reduce tariffs and other international trade barriers and did very well, through seven worldwide negotiation rounds. It achieved significant progress in many areas ranging from general anti-dumping measures to balance-of-payments restrictions to settlement disputes and, of course, to the reduction of industry-specific tariffs and other barriers of the international trade.[11] During the eighth round of negotiations, the Uruguay Round, GATT's principles and agreements were adopted by the WTO,[12] which replaced GATT and became the body charged with administering and extending them.

The WTO, which formally was established on January 1, 1995, is the only international organization dealing with the global rules of trade between nations. Its main function is to ensure that trade flows as smoothly, predictably, and freely as possible. *Its main functions are in the following areas*:

- Administering WTO trade agreements
- Forum for trade negotiations
- Handling trade disputes
- Monitoring national trade policies
- Technical assistance and training for developing countries and
- Cooperation with other international organizations.

At its heart are the WTO agreements, negotiated and signed by the world's trading nations and ratified by their parliaments. The goal is to help producers of goods and services, exporters, and importers conduct their business. In fact, WTO, directly but also indirectly, creates not only a more peaceful business environment, but also at the same time, handles trade disputes, establishes worldwide rules of engagement, and offers more choice, higher incomes, more jobs, better governments, and improved living conditions.

From the discussion on the UN, and only three of its agencies, it becomes very clear that the UN contributed not only toward a better and more peaceful social environment for all people, but also toward establishing a worldwide business environment acceptable by most rules, regulations, and industry standards. Obviously, the UN, through its various agencies, has a tremendous impact in many other areas, not immediately related to the purpose of this book.

> "WTO economists have carefully scrutinized the use and the impact of government support in a variety of sectors. While some subsidies can benefit society and can offset the negative externalities of economic activity, other types of government support are clearly more controversial and can be damaging. One significant part of our Doha round negotiations involves reducing subsidies which distort trade while encouraging governments to use other forms of support which can facilitate development and environmental protection. Shifting support in this way is politically difficult and requires determination and courage, but the evidence is clear that such reforms can level the playing field and provide real rewards across the board."
>
> Pascal Lamy, Director-General, WTO[13]

The European Union[14]

The idea of a united Europe, a concept that can be traced back to the Roman Empire, was also a dream in the minds of philosophers and visionaries. Victor Hugo, for example, imagined a peaceful "United States of Europe" inspired by humanistic ideals, and statesmen like Konrad Adenauer or Winston Churchill expressed similar visions.[15]

From a Coal and Steel Community to the European Union

In 1950, in a speech inspired by Jean Monnet, the French Foreign Minister Robert Schuman proposed integrating the coal and steel industries of Western Europe. As a result, in 1951, the European Coal and Steel Community (ECSC) was set up, with six members: Belgium, West Germany, Luxembourg, France, Italy, and the Netherlands, who were, just a few years ago, on opposite sides in World War II. The power to take decisions about the coal and steel industry in these countries was placed in the hands of an independent, supranational body called the "high authority." Jean Monnet was its first president. Note that during that time this bold move was a previously unheard of scenario, let alone that the coal and steel industries, to many minds of that era, were symbolic of the means of the most catastrophic war in the human history.

The ECSC was such a success that, within a few years, these same six countries decided to go further and integrate other sectors of their economies. In 1957, they signed the Treaties of Rome, creating the European Atomic Energy Community (EURATOM) and the European Economic Community (EEC). *The member states set about removing trade barriers between them and forming a "common market."* Ten years later, the institutions of ECSC, EURATOM, and EEC were merged. From this point on, there was a supervising Commission, a Council of Ministers, and a European Parliament.

Originally, the members of the European Parliament were chosen by the national parliaments. But, in 1979, with the EU already having nine member countries, the first direct elections were held, allowing the citizens of the member states to vote for the candidates of their choice. Since then, direct elections have been held every 5 years.

The *Treaty of Maastricht* (1992, the EU then had 12 member countries) introduced new forms of cooperation between the member state governments, for example, on defense, and in the area of "justice and home affairs." By adding this intergovernmental cooperation to the existing "community" system, the Maastricht Treaty created the EU.

EU Integration, Common Policies, a Single Market, and the Euro

Economic and political integration between the member states of the EU meant that these countries have to take joint decisions on many matters. Accordingly, *they had developed common policies in a very wide range of fields: From agriculture to culture, from consumer affairs to competition, from the environment and energy to transport and trade.* These *common policy and standard setting objectives were creating a better, smoother, more interactive business environment.* Moreover, these objectives were pronounced by countries, which had similar levels of political maturity (democratic, human rights observance, and so on) and, more or less, they were at parallel levels of economic growth (or had shown promise to achieve expected levels of economic development).

In the early days the focus was on a common commercial policy for coal and steel and agricultural policy. Other, industry-wide, policies were added as time went by, and as the need arose. Often these policies required political willingness as choices had to be made between the expected benefits from state intervention and the promotion of free competition.[16] Since their initial inception, some key policy aims have changed in the light of changing circumstances. For example, the aim of the agricultural policy is no longer to produce as much food as cheaply as possible but to support farming methods that produce healthy, high-quality food and protect the environment. The need for environmental protection is now taken into account across the whole range of EU policies. The EU's relations with the rest of the world have also become important. The EU negotiates major trade and aid agreements with other countries and is developing a Common Foreign and Security Policy.

It took some time for the member states to remove all the barriers to trade between them and to turn their "common market" into a genuine single market in which goods, services, people, and capital could move around freely. The Single Market was formally completed at the end of 1992, though there is still work to be done in some areas. In addition, it became increasingly easy for people to move around in Europe, as passport and customs checks were abolished at most of the EU's internal borders.

In 1992, the EU decided to further its *Economic and Monetary Union* (EMU). The move involved the introduction of a single European currency managed by a European Central Bank. The single currency, the euro, became a reality on January 1, 2002, when euro notes and coins replaced national currencies in 12 of the (then) 15 countries of the EU. The countries that initially used the euro were Austria, Belgium, Finland, France, Germany, Greece, Ireland, Italy, Luxembourg, the Netherlands, Portugal, and Spain. For international business this is a major achievement in favor of the single European market. There were no more exchange risks or surprises. Going with euros from Austria to France was similar to going with U.S. dollars from Arizona to Florida.

A 28-Member Union

The EU has grown in size with successive waves of accessions. Denmark, Ireland, and the United Kingdom joined in 1973 followed by Greece in 1981, Spain and Portugal in 1986, and Austria, Finland, and Sweden in 1995. The EU welcomed 10 new countries in 2004: Cyprus, the Czech Republic, Estonia, Hungary, Latvia, Lithuania, Malta, Poland, Slovakia, and Slovenia, and two more, Bulgaria and Romania, in 2007, and Croatia in 2013.

Nevertheless, the process of joining EU is demanding and often countries have second thoughts after their initial enthusiastic hopes of joining EU. Let's take the example of Turkey,[17] where at a point the polls showed more than 70% of Turks wanted to join the EU. A year later, there were frictions over the divided island of Cyprus where the Turks felt that Brussels was bullying them into making further concessions; leaders of small and medium size firms, responsible for 55% of the country's GNP and 70% of the jobs, were increasingly skeptical of the benefits versus costs of this marriage; "the cost and hassle of implementing the EU's 80,000-page Acquis Communautaire—the vast canon of rules and regulations on everything from air quality to the size and shape of bananas," is for the first time examined by the Turkish government in its complete dimensions. These, and many others, are examples of the tedious process of integration of any new member state. There are *unquestionable benefits of participating in the largest economic union of the world.* But at what cost will a new member state accept to bend its present operational practices?

Furthermore, to ensure that the enlarged EU continues functioning efficiently, it needs a more streamlined system for taking decisions. That is why the *Treaty of Nice* laid down new rules governing the size of the EU institutions and the way they work. The Treaty came into force on February 1, 2003. An effort toward accepting an *EU Constitution* by all member countries, for the time being, has failed, though a newer version will be proposed at a later time.

More than half a century after the "High Authority, through prudent cooperation efforts and carefully planned steps, the EU member states are working together toward peace, safety and security, economic and social solidarity, and the European model of society."[18]

How the European Union Works[19]

The EU is founded on four treaties:

- The *Treaty establishing the* ECSC, which was signed on April 18, 1951 in Paris, came into force on July 23, 1952 and expired on July 23, 2002.
- The *Treaty establishing the* EEC, which was signed on March 25, 1957 in Rome and came into force on January 1, 1958. It is often referred to as "the Treaty of Rome."
- The *Treaty establishing the* EURATOM, which was signed in Rome along with the EEC Treaty.
- The *Treaty on* EU, which was signed in Maastricht on February 7, 1992, and came into force on November 1, 1993.

The EEC, in addition to its economic role, gradually took on a wide range of responsibilities including social, environmental, and regional policies. Since it was no longer a purely economic community, the fourth treaty (Maastricht) renamed it simply "the European Community" (EC). At Maastricht, the member state governments also agreed to work together on foreign and security policy and in the area of "justice and home affairs." By adding this intergovernmental cooperation to the existing community system, the Maastricht Treaty created what is known as the EU and a new administrative structure with three "pillars" which is political as well as economical. These "pillars" refer (1) to most of the common policy areas (community domain), (2) common foreign and security policy, and (3) police and judicial cooperation in criminal matters. Some of the most important institutions of EU are as follows:

- The *European Parliament*: This is the "voice of the people" through their 785 directly elected representatives. Each of the 27 countries has a preset number of seats. Elections are held every five years. Parliament has three main roles. (1) Passing European laws—jointly with the Council in many policy areas. The fact that the EP is directly elected by the citizens helps guarantee the democratic legitimacy of European law. (2) Parliament exercises democratic supervision over the other EU institutions, and in particular, the Commission. It has the power to approve or reject the nomination of commissioners, and it has the right to censure the Commission as a whole. (3) The power of the purse. Parliament shares with the Council authority over the EU budget and can therefore influence EU spending. At the end of the procedure, it adopts or rejects the budget in its entirety.
- The *Council of the European Union* is the EU's main decision-making body. It represents the member states, and its meetings are attended by one minister from each of the EU's national governments, who is empowered to commit his or her government in a variety of issues ranging from consumer affairs and competitiveness to education and environment. The Council has six key responsibilities: (1) To pass European laws—jointly with the European Parliament in many policy areas. (2) To coordinate the broad economic and social policies of the member states. (3) To conclude international agreements between the EU and other countries or

international organizations. (4) To approve the EU's budget, jointly with the European Parliament. (5) To develop the EU's common foreign and security policy. (6) To coordinate cooperation between the national courts and police forces in criminal matters.

- The *European Commission*: The commission is independent of national governments. Its job is to represent and uphold the interests of the EU as a whole. It drafts proposals for new European laws, which it presents to the European Parliament and the Council. It is also the EU's executive arm—in other words, it is responsible for implementing the decisions of Parliament and the Council. It manages the day-to-day business of the EU by implementing its policies, running its programs, and spending its funds.

- The *Court of Justice*: Its job is to make sure that EU legislation is interpreted and applied in the same way in all EU countries, so that the law is equal for everyone. For example, it ensures that national courts do not give different rulings on the same issue. The court also makes sure that EU member states and institutions do what the law requires. The court has the power to settle legal disputes between EU member states, EU institutions, businesses, and individuals.

The EU has created an environment that encompasses practically every social or business aspect. To achieve this complete coverage, many other agencies, committees, or individuals participate in performing specific tasks. Here are some examples: The *European Court of Auditors* checks that EU funds, which come from taxpayers, are properly collected and spent legally, economically, and for the intended purpose. It has the right to audit any person or organization handling EU funds. The *European Economic and Social Committee* is the "voice of the organized civil society." The *European Investment Bank* finances EU projects. The *European Central Bank* manages the euro. The *European Ombudsman* investigates EU citizens' complaints, and if he can, deals with them on a variety of "maladministration" issues as unfairness, discrimination, abuse of power, lack or refusal of information, unnecessary delays, and employment of incorrect procedures.

Other Unions of Nations

From the previous discussions it is evident that the UN and the EU have greatly contributed toward a social and business environment that, to a significant extent, supports the needs of the 21st-century borderless world. Although the EU presents a more functional operational model of a common market than the UN, one has to recognize that the homogeneity of objectives among its member states was always at the core of EU decision making. Similar country efforts, capitalizing on regional similarities exist from the Middle East to South America. In this section, we address two other arrangements between countries: The North America Free Trade Association (NAFTA) and the Association of Southeast Asian Nations (ASEAN).

The North American Free Trade Agreement (NAFTA)

January 1, 1989, was a milestone date. Two DCs, Canada and the United States, by themselves being excellent examples of common markets having absorbed dozens of states through the elimination of trade barriers, regulation standardization, and common currencies, agreed to eliminate the trade tariffs between them. The two countries understood that this was creating an ideal partnership with superb potential for trade.

> Some investors come in order to participate in a vibrant, open economy; others simply view the United States as a safe haven for their savings that is not available in their home country.
>
> Alan Greenspan[20]

The next step was January 1, 1994, when another agreement, this time the NAFTA between Canada, Mexico, and the United States became law containing the following actions:[21]

- Abolishing within 10 years tariffs on 99% of the goods traded between Canada, Mexico, and the United States.
- Removing most barriers on cross-border flow of services.[22]
- Protecting intellectual property rights.
- Removing most restrictions on foreign direct investment between the three member countries.

- Allowing each country to apply its own environmental standards, provided that such standards have a scientific basis,[23] and establishing two commissions with the power to impose fines and remove trade privileges when environmental standards or legislation involving health and safety, minimum wages, or child labor are ignored.

From the above, the reader can see an effort among the three member states to establish a parallel to the EU, without EU's vast administration, paperwork, and bureaucracy. The arguments in favor and against NAFTA as well as those comparing NAFTA with other similar agreements are beyond the scope of this text.

In addition, the reader can see that NAFTA was a major turning point for the economies of the three member states, which aimed to create a borderless economy, a cost-cutting mechanism, and a social growth opportunity carefully balancing potential risks of employment losses[24] and shifts of financial influence. More than 10 years later, and in spite of all sorts of unexpected implementation and administrative problems, NAFTA critics and skeptics have become more positive about its future, whereas others vividly express opinions to expand this model of cooperation to other nations of the Americas.

> "The three Southern Cone nations (Argentina, Chile, Uruguay) prefer a broader free-trade union with the U.S. to the continuation of the Mercosur in its present form."
>
> Gary S. Becker[25]

The Association of Southeast Asian Nations (ASEAN)[26]

The ASEAN was established on August 8, 1967, by the five countries, namely, Indonesia, Malaysia, Philippines, Singapore, and Thailand. Today it has 10 members with a great variation in their economies, social, and income structures. They are as follows:

- Brunei Darussalam
- Cambodia

- Indonesia
- Laos
- Malaysia
- Myanmar
- Philippines
- Singapore
- Thailand
- Vietnam

The ASEAN Declaration states that the aims and purposes of the association are: (1) to accelerate economic growth, social progress, and cultural development in the region and (2) to promote regional peace and stability through abiding respect for justice and the rule of law in the relationship among countries in the region and adherence to the principles of the UN Charter.

This is another "model" of regional national cooperation, probably less demanding than the EU or NAFTA, nevertheless promoting a borderless world for the benefit of any business and individual citizen of this planet. The ASEAN Vision 2020, adopted by the ASEAN leaders on the 30th anniversary of ASEAN, agreed on a shared vision of ASEAN as a concert of Southeast Asian nations, looking outward, living in peace, stability and prosperity, and bonded together in partnership, dynamic development and a community of caring societies.

> "Today, ASEAN is not only a well-functioning, indispensable reality in the region. It is a real force to be reckoned with far beyond the region. It is also a trusted partner of the UN in the field of development."
>
> Kofi Annan[27]

Global Organizations

Many other international organizations have been created with a variety of objectives and various degrees of regional economic and regulatory strength. Examples of them include in the Middle East, the Gulf Cooperation Council (GCC); in Africa, the Economic Community of West African States (ECOWAS) or the Preferential Trade Area for Eastern and Southern Africa (PTA); in South America, the Andean Pact or Mercosur,[28] and so on.

For industry-specific needs, countries have created organizations assisting their export potential, from coffee to petroleum, the most known, influential, and powerful among them being the Organization of Petroleum Exporting Countries (OPEC). In our global economy, which heavily depends on energy recourses, OPEC has managed very well the worldwide oil prices and the resulting financial benefit to its member states. The OPEC's decision making affects even the global currency balance. The present practice of pegging petrodollars to U.S. dollars occasionally appears to be counterproductive for the OPEC countries and, for some economists, oil exporters should link their currencies in some way to oil prices. However, given the trends and volatility of the energy industries, for certain cases monetary discipline is a reasonable approach.

In addition, to globally establish industry-specific operational and regulatory frameworks, other organizations proved to be invaluable. The example of the International Maritime Organization (IMO),[29] operating under the UN umbrella of agencies, is used to present similar organizations' potential impact for the global business environment.

Shipping is perhaps the most international of all the world's great industries and one of the most dangerous. It has always been recognized that the best way of improving safety at sea is by developing international regulations that are followed by all shipping nations and from the mid-19th century onward a number of such treaties were adopted. Several countries proposed that a permanent international body should be established to promote maritime safety more effectively, but it was not until the establishment of the UN itself that these hopes were realized. In 1948 an international conference in Geneva adopted a convention formally establishing IMO (the original name was the Inter-Governmental Maritime Consultative Organization, or IMCO, but the name was changed in 1982 to IMO).

The purposes of the IMO, as summarized in its charter, are "to provide machinery for cooperation among Governments in the field of governmental regulation and practices relating to technical matters of all kinds affecting shipping engaged in international trade; to encourage and facilitate the general adoption of the highest practicable standards in matters concerning maritime safety, efficiency of navigation and pre-vention and control of marine pollution from ships." The organization is also empowered to deal with administrative and legal matters related to these purposes.

The IMO's first task was to adopt a new version of the International Convention for the Safety of Life at Sea (SOLAS), the most important of all treaties dealing with maritime safety. This was achieved in 1960 and IMO then turned its attention to such matters as the facilitation of international maritime traffic, load lines, and the carriage of dangerous goods, while the system of measuring the tonnage of ships was revised.

Although safety was and remains IMO's most important responsibil-ity, a new problem began to emerge: pollution. The most important of all these measures was the International Convention for the Prevention of Pollution from Ships (MARPOL). It covers not only accidental and operational oil pollution, but also pollution by chemicals, goods in pack-aged form, sewage, garbage, and air pollution. But adopting treaties is not enough—they have to be put into effect. This is the responsibility of gov-ernments and there is no doubt that the way in which this is done varies considerably from country to country. The IMO has introduced measures to improve the way legislation is implemented, by assisting flag States (the countries whose flag a ship flies) and by encouraging the establishment of regional port State control systems. When ships go to foreign ports they can be inspected to ensure that they meet IMO standards. By orga-nizing these inspections on a regional rather than a purely national basis resources can be used more efficiently. Moreover, IMO has developed a technical cooperation program, which is designed to assist governments that lack the technical knowledge and resources that are needed to operate a shipping industry successfully.

The Geopolitical Map Revisited

We cannot isolate business from its environment. Large countries, such as the United States, China, Japan, India, and Germany with huge markets and production potential; small countries with energy and other strategic resources; and supranational organizations as those we examined in this chapter, all of them greatly contribute toward a global borderless business arena, by reducing tariffs, establishing industry standards and regulations, and facilitating trade.

Although from many aspects the world appears to be converging toward a borderless state, we need to learn from political reasoning and notions that shaped the thinking of the past rulers and "wise men."[30] We need to understand the "cultural embeddedness of geopolitics" and recognize that *changes will be slow, requiring accurate balancing of past predispositions and of modern-era implementation of visions toward a better, more fair and equitable world for all human and nonhuman life.* We need to revisit belief platforms, to mention just a few, from Theodore Roosevelt's assertion about the Monroe doctrine to Hitler's statement that "Germany today is no world power" to Samuel Huntington's "clash of civilizations" to Edward Said's "clash of ignorance" to Robert Kaplan's "coming anarchy" to Philippe LeBillon "resource wars" to Osama Bin Laden's "Letter to America," to Jeremy Rifkin's "European Dream" and how it is quietly eclipsing the "American Dream."[31] Many influential people, and their followers, subscribe to these ideas and have their own agendas to support their own thinking. We need to identify the deeper motives of people behind their actions.[32]

To better visualize future geopolitical dynamics, some interesting findings taken from an *Economist's* survey are worth mentioning.[33]

> China, India, and other developing countries are set to give the world economy its biggest boost in the whole history.
>
> Pam Woodall[34]

"America is less important as locomotive of the global growth than it used to be, thanks to the greater vigor of the developing economies" and soon we may experience a rise in cost of capital in the DCs with a potential of sluggish growth, financial shocks, and recession.[35]

What are the forecasts for GDP (in market exchange rates) for 2040? China will be at least as big as the United States with India third, Japan, fourth, Mexico fifth, Russia sixth, Brazil seventh, followed by Germany, Britain, and France. Consider that in 2000 China was number seven, Brazil number eight, India number eleven, Mexico number fifteenth, and Russia number sixteenth.[36] Isn't that a dramatic shift of economic power indicative of where the new markets will be, and where the production and technological capabilities will lie? Consider that more university students in sciences and engineering already graduate in India than either in the EU or the United States. Consider the resource potential of some countries and, therefore, the ability to reposition themselves as global economic superpowers. For example, in the case of Russia, with its vast land mass of 11 time zones, cannot be underestimated. Consider the unions of nations, such as the EU or NAFTA, which may greatly affect the geopolitical dynamics of that future era.

Meanwhile, expect that quality of life will be improved for the developing nations. For example, in 2040, the forecast of car ownership will be more than 400 million in China, more than 300 million in India, and a little more than 200 million in the United States.[37] In addition, and given technology and demographic projections, the service sector will predominate and, in some industries, such as medical and health care, will take a leading role in the marketing and human resource areas.[38]

Old and New World Order: The Ruling Class

However, from another perspective, one should see the evolution of the world's ruling class. The pharaohs and the kings of the past became the czars and the emperors of other eras and eventually the presidents and the prime ministers of today. These people had the power and the means to shape their environments and, at the same time, many of them, their own well-being. For our era, a new world order is present,[39] and business is its primary engine.

But who are the equivalent of the rulers of the past during the epoch of business? Businessmen and entrepreneurs command the creation of value, the economic welfare, the research potential, the quality of life and, in the process, accumulate their own material wealth, assume a higher social status, and increase their influence and power.

We think that before we start discussing elements of the structure of the enterprise we should refer to Albert Jacquard's[40] need to understand our limitations as a prerequisite to sustain human existence and civilization growth in our planet.

If we do not study ourselves and understand our own limitations how can we establish worldwide industry standards or reduce the civilization barriers (not to mention tariffs) between nations? In our opinion this responsibility will rest in the future on the shoulders of businessmen who must be able to see their ethical roles and elevate themselves to higher levels of the Maslow's hierarchy of needs, perceiving their own purpose within the realm of self-actualization, not only amassing material wealth and power. Business and other organizational leaders should be the role models of the generations to come. Their in-depth education and potential of self-actualization[41] will determine the quality of human and nonhuman life on planet earth.

CHAPTER 6

Accounting and Finance Perspectives

About This Chapter

Under the broad assumption that in our era practically all business is global, the previous chapters of this book dealt with the environment of the global corporation. How and why culture, philosophy, ethics, the social changes of the last century, the politics, the legal perspectives, and the various global organizations shaped the business environment and transformed the business enterprise so that it became the defining player of the social fabric of our era.

This part of the book deals with the functions of the global business. International accounting and finance perspectives are presented in this chapter, international marketing perspectives are presented in Chapter 7, and international management perspectives in Chapter 8. Chapter 9 is a "Capstone" chapter, presenting the main elements of a successful global corporation as well as its governance principles.

In the following sections of this chapter, a variety of issues are presented, which are viewed as essential to the topic, although, given the general objectives of this book, the analysis of these issues bypass the depth that specialized books in international accounting and international finance have. The topics covered in this chapter are: evolution of international accounting, comparative accounting around the world, accounting standards, inflationary accounting, transfer pricing, international taxation, accounting in the era of enterprise resource planning, international accounting and business ethics, financial developments and corporate governance, foreign exchange markets and risks, finance and banking issues at a global level, and the financial management of global corporations.

Evolution of International Accounting

From the very beginning of human history people have tried to keep accurate records of their business dealings. In Mesopotamia, for example, thousands of years ago historians discovered detailed records of business activity,[1] but it was only thousands of years later, during the 15th century, in Venice, where business people found that "double entries" can result in recording more accurate accounts.

Moreover, before the emergence of telecommunications and computers, the business world was moving at a very different—comparatively very slow pace. For example, a couple of centuries ago, colonial enterprises, which were operating in a similar way with modern era's corporate subsidiaries, also had needs of accurate recording of information, management, and control. However, information was not travelling through the telephone, fax, or Internet. From India critical information was coming to the home treasury in Great Britain, 6 months later, onboard sailing ships that circumvented Africa. The managers of these colonial enterprises had time to think, revise plans, study options, and generate business and political support.

> Understanding the international dimensions of accounting is vital for anyone who wants to do business or invest across national borders.
>
> F. D. S. Choi, et al.[2]

Today, accounting is not anymore a record-keeping profession or a business control mechanism. Accounting requires creative thinking and ability to deal with a variety of operational environments. Accounting provides all sorts of managerial information for decision making and statistical analyses. It operates within certain standards and rules that depend on the local regulations. The correctness of accounting statements concerns every single one of its stakeholders, sometimes millions of them. Since World War II, computer technologies further boosted the accounting profession. All record-keeping information automatically enters into the corporate accounting system and, through enterprise resource planning (ERP) modeling; even the finest ripple effects in business are sensed by the decision makers, who react with knowledge after weighing options.

International accounting is a direct result of modern-era business demands. Companies need reliable mechanisms to record information and to provide decision-making tooling for subsidiaries that are all around the world and operated under different economic, legal, and accounting parameters. Information is coming to the home headquarters treasuries and, through complex algorithms, is translated in the home accounting language. For example, different currencies, exchange rates, tax levels, marketing processes, commissions, license fees, and so on, have to be accounted and presented in a unified sum that is legally correct and meaningful for the decision makers and the stakeholders of the corporation.

Given the highly specialized knowledge that state-of-the-art accounting demands today, how is the training in accounting as a field of study? Even one European educational institutions 100 years ago did not recognize accounting, or, for that matter, the other functional fields of business administration, as worthy of university-level study. For example, accounting was not even at par with economics. Accounting, finance, or marketing required only technical training. Since then, dramatic changes have happened propelled by industry demands and educational pioneers,[3] especially in the United States.

Information diversity is of essence. It brings new insights and promotes evolution. Today, hundreds of doctoral degrees in accounting are produced annually, very challenging corporate internship and training programs exist, and highly specialized modules cater to the most focused company needs. The accounting educational landscape has changed from that of the past century, and, therefore, the quality of those choosing to serve this profession has dipped. In fact, the same applies for finance, management, and marketing professionals.

When all think alike, then no one is thinking.

Walter Lippman[4]

Comparative Accounting Around the World and Accounting Standards

Almost in every country of the world the accounting practices evolved according to local economic reasoning and peculiarities, or were imported from other counties and modified to fit the local realities. Culture, level of economic development, education, the political and legal environment played a major role in shaping these realities. For example, in countries that in the past had significant hyperinflation, like in South America, tend to use anti-inflationary processes in their evaluation of accounting statements. Similarly, in countries with a tradition in the financial markets, like Great Britain, methods that allowed broad measures of accounting disclosure were adopted.

The theoreticians of international accounting recognize four schools of thought in the accounting practices used.[5] In summary, these schools of thought, though they are not absolute as they often include elements from others, are as follows:

- *Macroeconomic:* In this approach, the observer sees the whole economy functioning with the individual business entities staying outside of this framework. The countries define formal and informal priorities, policies, and administrative processes, within which business functions. For example, within this national framework, one can see the tax laws or the disclosure policies. An example of a country following this approach is Sweden.
- *Microeconomic:* Here the central player is the business entity and of central concern to the country's policies is how this entity will survive and grow. For example, accounting tenants like the replacement cost have been designed to maximize the corporate worth. The Netherlands is an example that follows this approach.
- *Independent discipline approach:* This approach is preferred in countries like the United States or Great Britain. Accounting practice, processes, and standards have been designed to serve business organizations. They do not refer to the needs of the overall economy.
- *Uniform accounting approach:* This school of thought dictates that the government dictates all accounting laws and forces all business organizations to follow them in a uniform way. France is an example of a country that follows this approach.

We must also observe that depending on the region[6] there are different *accounting value dimensions,* to a great extent depicting the cultural thinking of the population. These dimensions are as follows:

- *Professionalism* versus *statutory control,* where usually the dimension of professionalism is preferred as people have a sense of equal rights and citizens are not afraid of each other being at a different economic or societal level.
- *Uniformity* versus *flexibility,* which exists usually in nations where people are having a sense or order and demand an exact pronouncement of the legal tenants.
- *Conservatism* versus *optimism,* given the operating risk in a particular region.
- *Secrecy* versus *transparency,* where usually more transparency exists in societies where the individual is more respected *(accounting disclosure).*

Accounting standards are accepted procedures that dictate the manner in which accounting reports, statements. or any related concept should be processed and presented. Accounting standards are changing over time and depend on the accepted local practices. For example, the British accounting thinking greatly influenced that of the United States, Canada, and of the ex-colonies of Great Britain. At the same time we witness a tendency to establish worldwide common accounting standards. The *International Accounting Standards Committee* (IASC),[7] *since 1973, aims to establish common accounting standards, to continuously improve them and to standardize them worldwide.*

At this point, it is necessary to restate that *subsidiaries should follow the accounting practices of the host countries,* something that complicates the work of the treasury at the home headquarters. Accounting and tax practices change very rapidly. The following analysis may further clarify the complexities at the different host accounting environments, but provides only a historical basic platform of reference.

France

The French accounting practice is a classic example of the uniform accounting thinking and has its origins in the directives of the French

Department of Economics, back in 1947. Since then, there were many amendments, and in 1986, it was extended to also include EU directives. The French accounting system extends to every accounting manifestation, from tax issues to statistics, and effectively depicts the evolution of the French commercial code *(Code de Commerce),* which exists since Napoleon (1807). If needed, corporate accounting data are considered as court evidence and, therefore, a lot of formalities are required, their truthfulness is expected, and a minimum of corporate accounting statements is published annually, including balance sheets, profit and loss accounts, and reports and notes from directors and auditors.

United States

In the United States more than 4,000,000 companies get their legal status at the state level and they are subject to the state laws—not the Federal ones. Each state has its own unique corporate legal system, which often do not demand detailed accounting statements.[8] This is in contrast to the corporations that are traded at the stock exchanges and which are under the jurisdiction of the *Securities and Exchange Commission* (SEC), a Federal body of supervision.

Beyond the SEC, the accounting and financial reporting of these companies is regulated by the *Financial Accounting Standards Board* (FASB), a private domain organization, which in the past 30 years has issued *Statements of Financial Accounting Standards* (SFAS) aiming to provide useful information to investors, creditors, or stakeholders, who are interested in having a truthful representation of the companies.

It is expected, therefore, that occasionally FASB and SEC are seeing the corporate world under their differing objectives with the potential of implementation conflicts. In spite of their different approaches, FASB's and SEC's efforts resulted in a very conducive business operating climate.

Partly because of this regulatory environment, American business grew and matured. And for many students of world business affairs, this sensible environment helped American business to become the model for others to imitate. Finally, in 1990, FASB went beyond the U.S. business realities, recognized the borderless world and its globalized dynamics, and turned to the lessons learned in the international accounting arena. Since then, it has included in its mission statement to "promote the international compatibility of accounting standards concurrent with improving the quality of financial reporting."[9]

The Netherlands

Institutionally, the Dutch can be considered as more liberal than the average European, and this also characterizes their accounting practices. At the same time they are highly professional and academically very competent, initiating sensible accounting reporting practices. Due to the small size of the land, the internationalization of their people and the very large corporations that are headquartered there, like Uniliver, Philips, and Shell, the Dutch accounting practices were always flexible and accepting of foreign influences.

More meaningful accounting regulations appeared in the Dutch business environment only after 1970, when the law required annual accounting statements. Through the same legal processes, the standardization of accounting reporting, transparency issues, and corporate auditing practices were introduced. This law became part of the country's civil legal system and was amended per the directives of the EU. It must be noted that during the past 20 years private Dutch organizations, such as the *Netherlands Institute of Registered Accountants,*[10] defined accounting processes which, although they are not legally binding, are observed by major corporations and are in line with the accounting statements of major international organizations, such as the *International Accounting Standards Committee (IASC, now Board).*[11]

China

In spite of the fact that Chinese history indicates that even 2,000 years ago the Chinese had effective recording of business activities, the present main body of Chinese accounting procedures was developed in 1949, following the Soviet prototypes, the Marxist principles, and the central administration of economic and state systems. However, in the past 25 years there was a dramatic shift of Chinese accounting thinking. The central government directs the overall macroeconomic thinking and, to a great extent, leaves the microeconomic roles to the market dynamics. Privatization of state enterprises and China's position as a global superpower define new priorities, methods, rules, and regulations.

The responsibility of the design and implementation of accounting principles lies with the Department of Economics, which oversees the 1993 accounting law and its subsequent amendments. This law applies to all corporations and organizations that are not at the public domain and effectively unified more than 40 different accounting systems that existed in China until then. With this standardization China entered in a new much more efficient era and there is little doubt that more changes will occur in the future. Each private corporation is obliged by law to annually provide a balance sheet, profit and loss accounts, liquidity statements, statements of financial transactions, notes, and all necessary timeline obligations.[12]

The EU

Since 1957, the EU has issued many directives aiming to harmonize the manner with which accounting practices are followed throughout the EU countries. Milestone EU decisions are relevant to the purpose of this book.

The EU's fourth directive issued in 1978, required that corporate accounting should present a true and fair view. Moreover, it provided specific instructions about the format of balance sheets and profit and loss accounts, the valuation of the enterprise (primarily based on historical costing), and the publication of accounting records which, to some extent, was based on the average thinking of member states.[13]

Through its eighth directive (1984), the EU established the minima of training and qualifications of those dealing with accounting reporting and the ways that EU member states should treat the auditing differences and practices among them.[14] By 1995, EU, closely observing IASC's and FASB's statements, started following a strategy toward compatibility, comparability, and convergence of accounting practices among member states in order to facilitate corporate trading in global markets.[15]

Inflationary Accounting

In many parts of the world accounting, following simple routines, plays the very basic role of recording business activities. However, in other parts of the world, given the advanced demands of the business community, accounting plays a greater role, being creative or identifying solutions to specific problems, like dealing with inflation. In a previous section of this chapter, *Comparative Accounting Around the World and Accounting Standards*, it was mentioned that there are countries with significant levels of inflation, even with hyperinflation.

For illustrative purposes, let's assume that vehicles that are produced in country (a) where annual inflation is 0%, will be sold by the company's own subsidiary in country (b) where the annual inflation is 40%, and where the present exchange rate is 1A$ = 10B$. 100 vehicles at an average price of 10,000 A$, that is, 1,000,000 A$ (or 10,000,000 B$) have been produced today at the A country, and are shipped to be sold at the country B, in average, three months later. In this example, the reader readily understands that three months later the average car price in B$ should be a least 10% higher than its price tag when it arrived, in order to accommodate the inflationary effect, the expected new exchange rate, and the hedging costs that are necessary to reduce the transaction risks.

To calculate the fair inflationary effect of the previous example, exact methodologies are employed by those dealing with inflationary accounting based on complex algorithms. These *calculations are based on current and replacement costs using historical data and expected inflationary levels.*

Worthy theoretical approaches of the inflationary accounting exists in countries like UK and the United States as both countries had extensive business activities with countries with high inflation. At the same time one can find useful similar approaches in countries that dealt with inflation, such as Brazil or Israel.[16]

Transfer Pricing and International Taxation

In our global business village another topic of great interest is transfer pricing, especially as the topic relates to the levels of international taxation.

> Some of the biggest tax heavens are in fact OECD economies, including America and Britain, that many would see as firmly onshore.
> *The Economist,* Special Report on Offshore Financing[17]

Transfer price is the charged price to a corporate member, for example, the price charged from parent company to its subsidiary, for a product or a service for a transaction that crosses national borders. Transfer pricing may apply to finished goods, semifinished goods, or even raw materials. This price, given taxation, legal, political, and business-related concerns, often do not follow the within-the-home country mode of price determination, its price escalation, or its profit margin. The reason is simple. In the international business arena conditions exist for higher profit margins, by capitalizing on tax-haven countries, flags of convenience, tax treaties, tax rates, and so on.

The transfer pricing decision which effectively circumvents or lessens national tax rates and controls, requires knowledge of many issues that are country-specific, changing over time, and differing according to the transaction. For example, the United States has different tax rates for portfolio investments, direct investments, interest, or royalties for Australia and different for Austria. Efforts toward *tax harmonization* among countries might reduce the transfer pricing effect, but should not be seen as a realistic business tool for the foreseeable future,[18] though there are indications of tax rate convergence.[19]

Nevertheless, many tax treaties among countries have produced significant results in the areas of exchange of tax information and of *double taxation* (an issue of great concern to the business executives that are subject to taxes in more than one country).

Accounting in the Era of Enterprise Resource Planning

Traditionally, the accounting reporting was organized around functional fields, such as finance, management, or marketing. Hand-written records on huge ledgers, meticulously recorded all necessary transactions or bits of managerial interest. Needless to say that it was extremely tedious to retrieve a single record, to change a policy, or to answer specific management queries, such as regional sales or average prices. Moreover, retrieval of data meant to manually work the existing information that was not automatic and required additional cost and time. For example, it was possible to compare regional sales, but this required extensive manual labor of skilled and trusted employees. As a general rule, companies before

World War II used accounting systems to just record information and rarely as an aid of meaningful managerial decision making.

The introduction of the computer changed all that. For the first 20 or so years after the war, the use of computers facilitated accounting recording and speed up processes. For example, punching invoices gave the corporation the ability to immediately summarize relevant data and to provide meaningful information. Managers were quickly able to react to ask even what-if questions. Accounting entered into an era of real service to the corporate management. Hence, Managerial accountancy was born.

Meanwhile, consulting corporations, such as SAP or PeopleSoft, saw that *a systemic approach, combining the accounting experiences and the computer technologies, was necessary to provide a truthful virtual picture of the corporate decision making.* The Enterprise Resource Planning (ERP) era was a reality and ERP the *modus operandi* for any corporation that wanted to be globally competitive. Information technologies (IT) brought into the ERP system usable data from other, usually secondary, sources. Through ERPs, managers were able to see even the slightest ripple effects at the corporation's bottom line—before a decision was to be made. Every bit of information, from tax rates to exchange rates and from commissions to profit margins, was now entering into "intelligent" IT systems. A new *techno-bureaucracy,* based on similar systems, was possible, requiring sensitive, sensible, knowledgeable, and prudent executives to supervise it.

Immediacy is key in the decision making and, modern international accounting, does provide well-developed methodologies and accurate ERP systems. However, there are several caveats. *ERPs can create a corporate technocracy* that, if not properly audited, might result in systematic and systemic errors. Accounting can become so sophisticated that only well-trained professionals can fully understand corporate reports. *Accounting can hide issues and become the vehicle for frivolous decision making or for unethical managerial behaviors,* as we saw in the cases of Enron or Parmalat.

International Accounting and Business Ethics

From the previous discussion it is obvious that a corporate accounting system provides a managerial picture, a snapshot of the company, using legally acceptable processes, appropriate technologies, and academically valid methodologies. Given the regional realities and observing when this picture was taken, it must be truthful. As we saw in Chapter 3, truth is at the core of philosophy and ethics and, therefore, of business culture, business philosophy and business ethics. An international company can operate in a variety of environments and use a variety of business practices. Manipulation at an accounting level resulting in unethical behaviors is very possible.

The most known example of corporate unethical practices was that of Enron, once a global energy leader, which was followed to its demise by its corporate auditors, once one of the best accounting firms in the world, Arthur Andersen. Accountants are responsible for the meaningful picture of the corporations they advise and ethical conduct by both. Because of examples like Enron, the American Sarbannes–Oxley Act was initiated.

Enron's case was not the only management unethical behavior linked to accounting practices. This is happening all around the world in companies irrespective of size. The most-known European example is that of Parmalat, a major Italian dairy producer where the amoralistic behaviors of its leaders resulted in substantial sums of money being lost.[20]

The fact of the matter is that today's accountant has not only "bean counting" responsibilities. He must also be a highly educated, adaptable, creative, mature, and an ethical person capable of dealing in accordance with the specificities of a variety of legal and business environments. The previous sections of this chapter dealt with international accounting issues. Accounting, as we saw, helps us to get a snapshot of the enterprise. Now we shall focus on a few selected international finance issues that are deemed necessary for the person who needs to get a broad perspective of international business, namely about financial developments and corporate governance, foreign exchange markets and risks, finance and banking issues at a global level, and the financial management of global corporations.

Financial Developments and Corporate Governance[21]

Corporations operate within financial realities which develop according to the countries in which they or their subsidiaries are present. They need to understand these realities, how they are changing and, given the competition, how they can benefit from them.

Over the past two decades, the financial systems[22] underwent profound changes all over the world, driven by both institutional and market-driven developments. Prominent among the former are the rules and regulations,[23] which decreased the degree of financial repression, increased competition in domestic financial markets, and led to a largely liberalized financial system. Other changes included pension reforms that diminished expectations of pension benefits, the enactment of laws for minority-shareholder protection, and the privatization wave in both developed and developing economies.

As for the market-driven developments, they included the worldwide trend toward market economies and the resulting momentum for integration of national financial markets. In addition there were also technological innovation which lowered transaction costs and facilitated competition, information dissemination (thus reducing the problem of asymmetric information), and capital-market participation and trading. As a result, the role of traditional bank intermediation decreased, that of capital markets increased, while other forms of intermediaries, such as, pension funds and mutual funds, grew significantly, responding to a shift toward institutionalized management of savings.

Corporate governance, which from a finance perspective are the rules that *"deal with the ways in which suppliers of finance to corporations assure themselves of getting a return on their investment,"* as Andrei Shleifer and Robert Vishny have defined it,[24] affects firm's performance, efficiency, growth, financial structure and treatment of shareholders and creditors, and ultimately economic growth. In bank-based systems, banks monitor firm performance and exercise external control. In capital-market-based systems, corporate control is exercised via the market mechanisms, usually hostile takeovers. As for the institutional infrastructure, capital-market-based systems require better investor protection than bank-based systems. This, in turn, requires both rules and enforcement; that is, laws and regulations against expropriation by insiders, both managers and controlling shareholders, and an efficient legal system that enforces them.

Under the pressures of the evolutionary changes on financial systems, corporate governance became an important policy issue in many countries. Rules and regulations that refer to information disclosure, corporate transparency, oversight, and control have been put in place almost worldwide, as a response to the increasing role of capital markets. Additionally, cross-border issues of corporate governance became more pressing, due to the expanding investment and trade flows plus the higher cost of settling cross-border disputes. Financial development and trend of convergence of the financial systems toward the market-based norm have resulted to pressures on corporate governance to converge to the Anglo-American model,[25] setting the goal of maximizing shareholder value as their primary objective.

Foreign Exchange Markets and Risks

Foreign exchange markets are the mechanism through which individuals or corporations transfer financial power from one country to another or minimize their international *foreign currency exchange risks*. These markets transfer more than one trillion dollars[26] daily and they utilize "players," like:

> Experience shows that neither a state nor a bank ever has had the unrestricted power of issuing paper money without abusing that power.
>
> David Ricardo (1817)[27]

- *Major international banks:* These banks are often very large[28] and act as market makers although they do not participate in every market. In tandem with them are the *nonbank foreign exchange dealers,* which, due to the nature of their trade, they are in a position to buy and sell very large sums of money.
- *Central banks:* Countries have their own central banks, which are in a position to buy and sell currencies, increasing or reducing the available supply of their currency and, therefore, affecting its price.
- *Organizations and companies:* These "players" are entering into the market usually in order to *hedge* for their international transactions, in other words to protect their foreign currency holdings against adverse movement of the exchange rates

(hedging). As a general rule, organizations and companies do not enter in this market in order to profit from it.

- *Other "players"*: Many other types of players are in this market, including the *arbitragers,* who buy and sell foreign currency for a profit arising from price differences among or between markets,[29] and *foreign exchange brokers,* who facilitate international currency transfers for a commission often utilizing hundreds of dealers and automated trading systems.

Foreign exchange markets, because of currency fluctuations, constantly present international foreign exchange risks, which need to be countered, called earlier as *hedging.* Let's see the currency exchange risk through a very simple example.

Our company headquarters are in country A. Our subsidiary in country B persuades us that there is a great business opportunity in that country, which should yield 40% of the invested capital in three months. Therefore, we transfer the requested A$1,000,000 to the country B which there equals to B$10,000,000 (the then exchange rate is 1A$ = 10B$). True to its word, three months later our subsidiary has on its balance sheet B$14,000,000. However, now 1A$ = 20B$. When this money is translated back to A$s, we realize that it equals only to A$700,000 (14,000,000/20). Our company actually lost 30% of the invested capital without either the headquarters or the subsidiary making a managerial error. Simply no one observed the currency risk involved and the need for hedging. No one observed how the company is affected by the fluctuation of exchange rates—what is generally known as *exposure.*

We have different types of exposure. *Accounting exposure* involves the currency conversion of financial statements of foreign operations to the home country ones. The company needs to consolidate all its accounts and report them in a single currency. The *translation* of the accounts may result in losses, as in the previous example, but also in gains. The translation exposure can be managed through a variety of methods which are addressed in more specialized books.[30] Another type of exposure is the *transaction exposure,* which involves a corporate obligation to a foreign currency transaction. The home company, for example, makes a foreign sale but gives six months' credit to get its money back. This involves, of course, a pricing decision and pricing decisions offer a combination of benefits to the receiving party for a cost to the home corporation.[31] We also have *operating exposure*, which involves the home country currency appreciation and calculates changes of the corporate present value due to future cash flows.[32]

Finance and Banking Issues at a Global Level

In the previous section we saw that foreign exchange markets are the mechanism through which individuals or corporations transfer financial power from one country to another or minimize their international foreign currency exchange risks. The currency exchange markets and risks are affecting the international finance issues. Corporate financing within a specific country is not much more different than financing anywhere within the global business arena. The principles are the same.[33] However, on the one hand, the legalities, processes, and culture of the global financial institutions are different, fact that requires knowledge, information, and speed of reaction, from the other, the ability to be in a global domain, gives the corporation many more options for better rates and other related benefits. For example, though within a country there may exist specific strict banking regulations, the eurocurrency markets have less red tape, making them very competitive.

There exists thousands of financial institutions worldwide, which offer many different products and utilize separate transaction processes. These institutions develop according to local cultures, needs, and practices and, therefore, they serve their own mission statements. Case in point is the banking institutions in two EU countries, Austria and Belgium, which are economically and population-wise about the same: However, there are significantly more bank branches in Austria than in Belgium and, therefore, the ratio of loans to deposits are higher in Austria.

To operate a business one needs funds. In principle, this funding comes from banks, corporate headquarters, corporate subsidiaries, or other stakeholders, including suppliers. Financing approaches are born according to the peculiarities of each local system. Nevertheless, for the finance needs of international trade, some specialized instruments, like *banker's acceptance drafts, discounting* or *factoring* can be used. These are extensively discussed in specialized international finance books.

Another way of financing international trade is *counter trade*. Through that the seller receives as part or the total sum of the obligation, nonmonetary instruments, such as goods, raw materials, and so on. Therefore, this is a form of financing the repayment obligation, though some people will classify it as a marketing tool to achieve sales when this may not be possible when cash repayment is required. Counter trade is used very often in international business.

There are many forms and overlapping definitions of counter trade. The classic form of counter trade is *barter* where goods are exchanged for other goods. *Counter purchase* exists when two contracts are negotiated at the same time, for example, one company offers its technology patents and the other the rights to sell a product in another country. *Switch trading* involves a third party, which facilitates the exchange between the others, for example, when a barter agreement is channeled through a facilitator, who pays part of the deal in monetary instruments in exchange for distribution rights of goods in another country. A *compensation deal* often requires part of the agreement to be paid (to the A company) by the production generated at the facilities built by the A company for the B company. In an *offset trading* situation, the exporter agrees to create additional employment, export opportunities, and so on, to the host country.

The Financial Management of Global Corporations

> Potential investors do not want flexibility, they want fixed rules of the game.
>
> John Gavin, U.S. Ambassador to Mexico[34]

As we saw in the section on transfer pricing, the global enterprise enjoys a unique benefit: To be able to transfer cash, funds and profits between its headquarters and subsidiaries. At the same time, the company needs to coordinate a very complex system of financing—options, rates, promises, and confirmed obligations—for the benefit of its stakeholders, to provide the following:

- A clear picture of the enterprise at every moment.
- The required capital at the lowest cost possible.
- Maximization of the firm's consolidated profit, taking into account the different taxes from various countries.
- The required liquidity—a critical element is the management of the cash flows. Often companies are in danger because of lack of liquidity.

Therefore, we need to examine the main tasks that the international financial manager has to complete. They include the following:

- Minimizing liquid capital
- Investment of surplus liquid capital at high-yield opportunities, but not in high-inflation economies
- Reduction of stocks and receivables
- Use of hedging when needed
- Accelerating payments from subsidiaries to the home headquarters
- Handling of financial obligations
- Getting loans for the subsidiaries at the host countries
- Minimization payments in advance

The above list is only partial of the many obligations the international financial manager should have to undertake. From the previous discussion, it becomes clear that this person should be knowledgeable, experienced, culturally adaptive, and ethical.

In this chapter, we discussed accounting and financial perspectives of the global business. For the interested reader we should mention that the previously stated concepts are only a brief summary of the field, and we advise you to study any standard text on international accounting and international finance for further details. The next chapter deals with another topic central to international business issue, international marketing.

CHAPTER 7

Marketing Perspectives

About Marketing and About This Chapter

Marketing is the process where an organization meets its own objectives, and, at the same time, satisfies the target consumer's needs in terms of product design, promotional activities, pricing, and place where this product is offered (the 4Ps of the marketing mix). In essence, the consumer becomes the center of the organization's attention. The organization studies the consumer product (or service) needs and delivers them through actions that provides each desired product these 4Ps, the variables controllable by the organization. These 4Ps must be delivered in a way that they are *internally consistent*—the consumers expect consistency in the desired marketing mix, for example, they might think that a luxury item cannot be sold at a bargain price or through a convenience store.

Around these controllable variables, there are those uncontrollable by the organization, for example, a country's culture, political environment, legal system, economy, technology, and so on, variables that we discussed in the first part of this book. We can visualize this concept as three concentric circles, where in the middle is the target consumer, next is the 4Ps, and outer the variables uncontrollable by the organization.

Then, what about international marketing? Is there a difference? The answer is negative. We employ the same variables, we meet consumer and organizational objectives, but, usually, in international marketing, one faces a lot more complexities, different legalities, new distribution channel strategies, foreign languages, unexpected custom practices, and so on. Consider, therefore, that the organization must develop a different marketing mix for each market it operates and coordinate efficiently all of these markets, wisely utilizing its limited resources.

It is necessary to stress that the corporation first identifies markets and then produces the product that will satisfy them. In fact, this was not always the case. We first had the *production era,* where producers were producing whatever they perceived was needed and the consumers were "beating a path" in their efforts to get the product. Next, we had the *selling era* where salesmen were selling the products produced, and, finally, we had the *marketing era*—what we now experience in many of the developed parts of our world. It must be mentioned that, depending on the region the company markets its products or services, a different era than the marketing one might be present.

In this chapter, and following the previously explained marketing mix, we address marketing issues with particular attention to those that the corporation faces at its international markets. We address consumer, business-to-business (B2B), and service marketing for product design, pricing, promotions, and place issues of international marketing. Then, we discuss about international business research, primarily focusing on the international marketing research concepts, and, finally, we discuss entry methods that a company has at its disposal when entering into foreign markets.

> You can no longer rely on your home market, because your home market is an export market—for everybody else.
> Niels Christien Nielsen, Danish Technology Institute[1]

Product Design in International Marketing

The consumer purchases a product because she wants the *benefit* that this product promises. Benefits are both tangible and intangible in character. She wants, for example, a warm coat to face the winter or a brand name shirt to show to her friends that she buys from that fashionable source. The combination of benefits, tangibles and intangibles, offers us the concept of the *total product.*

Every product has *primary characteristics,* often called *salient product characteristics,* which define the essence of the main benefits that the consumer derives from this product, the *core of the product.* Every product has also *auxiliary dimensions.* For example, one prefers a luxury hotel because it offers a great suite to sleep and amenities that go with his or her lifestyle (core of the product). The hotel also offers some auxiliary dimensions that he or she occasionally likes—a spa, meeting rooms, a rooftop revolving restaurant where he or she can entertain his or her distinguished friends. The core and the auxiliary dimensions of this hotel represent for the particular target consumer the *augmented (or total) product* that he or she needs, the benefit he or she seeks.

From the other side, the corporation that owns this hotel calculates that there are enough target consumers who, if satisfied with the benefits the hotel provides, will pay for these services, meeting thereof the corporate organizational objectives.

In international marketing we follow the same rule. We research the target consumer's needs, and if the business plan shows that we also meet our organizational objectives, we proceed to offer the needed product. We must clarify that this is a long-term study of options with different scenarios and changing environmental conditions. We must also understand that penetrating a foreign market is a highly complex task that requires our understanding of how the target consumer thinks. Let's see some factors that will facilitate *market penetration.* As you study the factors subsequently, consider the differences in thinking of the assumed consumer segments in different international markets, for example, in Anchorage (a suburban elitist), Alaska versus in Zambezi (a villager residing on a river), Zambia:

- *Trialability* gives the target consumer the opportunity to try the new product, often through small sizes, taste trials in a super market, and so on. The consumer now feels more confident that this product meets his or her needs.
- *Observability* gives the target consumer the chance to observe how the product functions, especially when the producer cannot give his customer the opportunity to touch it or to feel it. For example, we cannot bring into a store the action of a windsurf, whereas we can show it on a DVD.
- A product may face difficulties in penetrating foreign markets, if its *compatibility* with the existing support systems does not allow it. For example, if a product needs an additional electric converter to function in a foreign market, it will be less desirable from one that does not need one.

- The existence of *relative advantages* may also determine the product's success in a foreign market. Customers are willing to invest in a product that offers relative advantages over the existing ones.
- Product *simplicity* versus product *complexity.* The more complex the product is, the more difficult its market penetration is. Also, it needs a lot more support in terms of personal selling, warranties, reverse distribution channels, and service.

We must stress that organizations are not the only for-profit ones. We also use the same marketing concepts for the not-for-profit ones, like churches or political parties. Products can be classified as consumer and as industrial ones (business-to-business, or B2B). We should also see the service dimension, in international marketing, as a separate subsection of the present section. Pertinent thoughts in these three areas follow.

Consumer Products

> Foreknowledge must be obtained from men who know the enemy situation.
>
> Sun-Tzu[2]

In international marketing we may face some issues that we do not see in the same light as in our domestic market. Some of them are discussed as follows.

The *self-reference criterion* (that we examined in Chapter 2): SRC usually is a serious issue when there is a distance between the home and host markets' cultural understanding about the need or use of a product. For example, in our home market "make up" may be a very acceptable and expected characteristic of a modern, sociable, well prepared for her daily routine woman. However, in another cultural environment a woman's face should not carry make up. Thus, our assumption that all our cosmetic product lines will be successful may be in error. Some of them may be very successful indeed, like plain aromas, or moisturizing lotions, and others will have very limited use, indeed!

The *innovation element*:[3] Marketing books indicate that, over the course of the product's life cycle (during the diffusion process), innovators, though opinion leaders, command only 2.5% of the market. So, why is innovation in international marketing so very important? There are degrees of *newness of a product* depending on the innovation level. From the one side of the spectrum we have products belonging in the category of *breakthrough* innovations, which often are termed *discontinuous innovations,* for example, horse-driven carriages to engine-propelled cars. These products perform a function that was not performed by any previous product and, therefore, there is a need for behavioral change at the market place.

From the other side of the spectrum we have ongoing product adaptations, which are usually termed *continuous innovations*, as in the case of a new car model over the previous year's model. These products present only a variation of existing products, and therefore, there is no change in the existing consumption or use patterns. In the middle of the spectrum is what is termed as a *dynamically continuous innovation,* for example, a landline phone versus a satellite cell-phone, effectively offering performance improvement (or other benefits the consumer desires) but not requiring significantly different consumption or use patterns.[4]

In global markets, especially while marketing in the underdeveloped or in the developing world, we often face a unique element: Products in our domestic market can be characterized as *continuous* or *dynamically continuous innovations*, but in those markets it may be considered as *discontinuous innovations,* requiring an in-depth understanding of how to approach the local innovators, who are going to be the opinion leaders eventually affecting the diffusion of a relatively new idea. For example, for a decade now the developed world observes the future of computers providing enhanced reality, digital walls, pen-size computers, "placeshifting," and smell technology.[5] For researchers and knowledgeable users these cutting-edge technologies might be continuous innovations. However, if an international marketer plans to introduce them to Sudan, he or she will soon realize that even the early Sudanese adopters will see them as discontinuous innovations.

Innovation, of course, should be related to technology challenges. Recent research shows that technology and marketing alliances are the most popular types of strategic alliance among the larger firms. For long term marketing alliance success, the size of the enterprises, undertaking joint ventures, can be a determining factor. The larger the company: the better, though outstanding joint ventures among smaller companies exist, and will continue to exist.[6]

Product adaptation based on the needs of a foreign market. Compatibility with obvious market characteristics, like offering a left-hand driven car in Australia or Japan, is a must. An equally important element, however, is compatibility with culture-related or personal growth and knowledge-based elements of the target consumer. An Albanian old lady will enjoy a simple radio set more than an MP3 player. Remember that entering into most new markets and introducing simple products will be more successful than complex ones.

Similarities of markets segments. As one advances in the social strata, more similarities exist among segments. Elitist and well-off customers from Madrid (Spain), Managua (Nicaragua), or Manila (Philippines) are mature buyers of the very same expensive watch, top Parisian fashion, or a world-class sports car. The same customers will send their kids to an expensive Swiss school or join others for a rare cruise. On the other side of the spectrum, we expect some markets will be satisfied with products that were successful in developed countries years ago. The German VW "beetle" that sold so successfully around the world and since the 1980s, can be seen today in production in South America.

Business-to-Business Products

Experience guides us to make a few suggestions in producing industrial or B2B products for foreign markets.

Product adaptation to local legal, energy, and industry standards is a must. Initial market entry requires product simplicity, especially in the auxiliary product dimensions and for developing or less-developed industrial markets. Note that in some markets *obsolete technologies* of others are most welcome and should be used everywhere possible. They are proven to work and cheaper to maintain and buy. Do not offer anything except appropriate technologies.[7]

Instructions-user education will be needed. Industrial products can be dangerous if not used properly. Expect that in many emerging markets a significant learning curve of the workers will be required. Quite often these workers do not have any previous experience with these types of products (or services). Well-translated instructions in the local language, repetitive and intense learning, on-the-job training, teaching of safety and ecology rules, and gradual introduction into performing the desired tasks are required.

Service and product maintenance. The following apply especially in emerging markets. When a small part of an industrial process is malfunctioning, this may affect the total production line. Expect expensive repercussions on everything and everybody. Service and necessary parts must be immediately available. Moreover, routine tasks, like lubrication of a pump or a lift truck, maybe easily forgotten. Attention to well-defined duties, timetables, and control of these actions is necessary. Similar concerns are not important in developed markets where process experiences on similar matters are abundant.

Warranties are also vital to the market penetration of industrial products. Experience from other applications are indicative of past successes, but primarily, the provider's ability to offer the necessary service and product maintenance promise will be a determining factor for market success.

The Service Dimension

Totally different category in international marketing is services, such as, banking, insurance, education, consulting, and so on. In addition, the service element is part of most tangible products marketing mix, and, in fact, at the continuum tangible to intangible products, the services end increasingly weighs more. Reviewing some of the characteristics of services is necessary for any aspect of service marketing.

Services are *intangible.* People cannot "hold" an insurance coverage or a lecture. As services are intangibles in character worldwide, it is a good idea to promote them through tangible evidence. This gives to the customer a more concrete *feeling* of the service. An example is the insurance company Prudential which includes a "rock" in its logo. Moreover, as we are an unknown variable, when we enter into many foreign markets customers doubt the quality, consistency, usefulness, and the competitive advantage of our product. We need to build customer trust and loyalty.

The more expensive the target market considers the services to be, the more difficult it is going to be to build this trust.

Services are *perishable.* When a cruise ship leaves with only three-fourths occupancy, all these empty cabins (and the resulting revenue) are forever lost. In-depth cost study of break-even points is necessary. A minimum global pricing of services should generate enough revenue to cover fixed costs and use marginal pricing wherever possible.

Services are *inseparable* from their provider. A lecture is uniquely tied to the lecturer. No other can deliver it in his or her exact manner. This has implications with respect to the need to standardize the provided service. Customers expect at least a specific promised minimum. Otherwise their long-term loyalty is in jeopardy. Additionally, wherever possible, auto-mated processes should be used, as in the case of banking services and ATM machines.

Service *consistency* is another issue. Even the same actor, performing the same act for her one-hundredth time might deliver it differently from the previous ones. Minimum expectations from the product–service mix is necessary.

In summary, we should design for our international markets specific product mixes that satisfy target markets at least at the minima promised and provide a reliable and consistent customer service level.

Pricing Elements in International Marketing

In this section, we examine pricing elements in international marketing at two levels: Strategy pricing concerns and practical issues in global pricing.

Strategy Pricing Concerns

The corporate pricing strategy is dictated by the company's overall orientation in a foreign market. Usually we refer to three different types of objectives orientation:

- Income (e.g., profit maximizing)
- Sales (e.g., maximizing sales)
- Competition (e.g., establish price levels)

When entering into a market, pricing-wise companies use the following approaches: *Penetration pricing,* aiming to acquire a large market share through low prices. This policy requires corporate liquidity, produces low short-term profits, and also protects the market from intense competition. *Skimming pricing,* where companies price their products at high levels usually on the assumption of exclusivity, limited production or high quality, resulting in high profit margins and potential of other competitors to enter into the same market.

If the product is already in the market, traditional product life cycle (PLC) considerations should predominate our strategic thinking. For example, at a maturity level, "me-too" products are expected and pricing should be very competitive. The corporate benefit of international marketing is the capacity to avoid being at this stage, constantly "rolling" its products to an earlier PLC stage allowing for higher profitability. Constant innovation and creativity will ensure the company's ability to pursue strategies that will allow remaining at the growth stage and to recycle products that are at maturity.

Practical Issues in Global Pricing

For most of the companies around the world, pricing is based on a *cost-plus approach,* after calculating price escalation for the foreign market. The product has an ex-factory price, to which the accountants add freight and insurance to a port, after that they add related transportation (and again insurance) costs, duties at the port of entry, delivery costs to the foreign agents, and so on. It is obvious that, through this process, the total per unit cost will become higher.

Another approach is based on *what the market can bear.* International markets, exactly because they are at the introduction or growth stage of the PLC, may allow for pricing above that of the domestic market.

Usual practical concerns of our pricing relate to how the company is paid in foreign currencies and how to face inflation in the host country. Both issues are discussed in Chapter 6. Hedging, for example, counters foreign exchange risks but at a cost, which needs to be factored in the pricing of our products. Another practical concern relates to the pricing in itself in the foreign markets. *In the foreign market, pricing follows the legal frameworks of the host country and of the international conventions.* If a host law imposes a *price ceiling* we must follow it. Also, *dumping*, in other words selling abroad at prices lower than those charged at home or other markets, is another unacceptable practice.

Promotions in Global Markets

> Doing business without advertising is like winking at a girl in the dark. You know what you are doing, but nobody else does.
>
> Stuart H. Britt[8]

Promotions aim to inform, remind of messages, and persuade. Under promotions, another controllable by the corporation variable, marketers classify advertising, personal selling, other forms of sales promotions, and public relations. The following discussion centers in these four areas and it is followed by an analysis of promotion ways in international marketing.

The Basics of International Promotions

A classic definition from the American Marketing Association is that *advertising is any paid form of nonpersonal presentation of ideas, goods, or services by an identified sponsor.* Within the home environment, communication, linguistic, and cultural understanding may give a comfortable advertising platform. However, various host-country dimensions give the topic a far more complex identity. Coordination of advertising campaigns worldwide deals with business priorities, timelines, introduction of new products, complex budgets, different advertising themes, different media usage, and so on. For many years the "programmed management approach,"[9] or any equivalent tactic, modified to meet specific needs, has been used as the backbone of international advertising efforts for major corporations. During this process the subsidiary develops from marketing strategy to options to specific implementation tactics to budgets and, at every level, the subsidiary checks with the mother company to alter plans if they are outside the mother company's specifications or objectives.

During the above process, the choice of the company that will implement the different advertising concepts is of paramount importance. On the one hand, major host country advertising companies are more often effective in the creative part and identifying suitable mass media to transmit the desired messages. On the other hand, major international advertising companies are more suited to undertake global accounts because they are in a better position to coordinate their own advertising subsidiaries.

Advertising is an efficient way of promotion, but *for certain product classes personal selling is more effective.* A large percentage of the promotion budget should be allocated for personal selling efforts especially if the company sells

- industrial products;
- tailor-made goods;
- expensive products or services;
- luxury products;
- high technology products;
- products that need parallel services;
- in rural areas;
- in underdeveloped or developing markets.

Public relations (PR) are nonpaid (though this can be debated) activities in promoting the corporate image, the company's good deeds, ethical behaviors, best practices, and so on. Public relations are highly important in international markets where a foreign company is often scrutinized much more than the domestic counterparts and it has less clout with the local politicians, people of influence, or media. A good PR department is also vital if something goes wrong. The largest ever industrial accident, in Bhopal, India, at a Union Carbide plant, is a classic case requiring immediate and top-level attention of the issues involved.

Finally, *sales promotions, meaning any other promotion not included in the three above categories, namely, advertising, personal selling, and public relations,* heavily depend on each foreign market and its overall development. In a developed market, for example, existing supermarkets can easily entice future buyers through sample tasting efforts, whereas in an underdeveloped market even the simplest such promotions may be in vain since the target consumers are not accustomed to similar experiences. Creativity and sensitivity to the local cultural behaviors is key to marketing success.

Promotion Ways in International Marketing

From the previous discussion it has become evident that the marketer has a four-account promotion budget for advertising, personal selling, PR, and sales promotions. She has to allocate the budget to get the best results, given the corporate overall strategy (skimming, penetration, and so forth, within a framework of information, persuasion, and reminding of messages). In effect, in the international markets, she faces combinations of promotion-products, altering or keeping them the same, according to the perception and use of the product by the target consumer. Let's examine the following options through examples:

- *Change neither the product nor its promotion.* Goods that are in this class are perceived and used by the target consumers in a similar way the consumers did in the original or in another market. A soda drink with global appeal (e.g., Coca-Cola), an expensive Swiss watch, scuba gear of particular specifications, are within this classification. Obviously, small changes are to be expected, like translation and listing on the bottle the locally expected nutritional information.
- *Change the usual auxiliary dimensions of the product but keep its promotion.* Target consumers have the same perception about the product, but they want some changes in the product itself. Some Europeans, for example, have a more limited space and different purchasing practices than Americans. Therefore, they want their refrigerators to be smaller and quieter.
- *Keep the product as is but change its promotion.* Target consumers use the same product but in a different way. Americans use their bicycles for exercise and sports. On the other hand, in China the bicycle is usually used for transportation of goods and people.
- *Change both the product (usually at its auxiliary dimensions) and its promotion.* This is an often used practice in

international marketing as[10] the degree of *newness of a product* changes from market to market. A new product commands its own appropriate promotion. Obviously, if the company enters into its foreign market with a discontinuous innovation, the product will necessitate a totally new promotion.

With the exception of poor developing countries at the lower rungs of the economic development ladder, marketing infrastructures and management practices are becoming more sophisticated and similar across the world. At the same time consumers all over the world are becoming more demanding. The net effect of all these developments is that global markets are getting intensely more competitive. Long-established global brands are challenged by new brands both in domestic and global markets. Because of such intensive competition, consumers in all countries are demanding value in product quality and accompanying services at lower prices.

These issues, which are well recognized by both opponents and proponents of globalization, pose several marketing challenges to all markets of the world. For example, the need for green marketing from the perspective of sustainable development is gaining momentum in all countries. The rich-poor globally and within countries infuse social responsibility in global marketing with great intensity. These and other emerging globalization related challenges should be the future concern of marketing academicians and practitioners."[11]

Distribution Policy and Logistics

The main barrier to exporting for small business enterprises isn't resources, it is knowledge of how to identify and secure export opportunities.

Göran Sljöberg, Swedish Trade Council[12]

After many years of practical experience in international marketing, it appears that the most vital controllable variable of the marketing mix when first entering into a new market is the existence of a solid distribution network. Choosing a good distributor and having efficient sales channels is more important than having better product, price or promotion, and a weak distributor. The choice of the distributor also relates to the chosen entry method, something we will revisit in the following section.

What does the exporting company aim to succeed through its foreign distributor? To achieve its overall marketing objectives for this market, to have all necessary warehousing, trucks, distribution outlets and logistical support, to reach its final consumers in a timely and efficient way, to provide a reverse distribution mode for rejects or product returns, to have the necessary support in dealing with customs, insurance brokers, advertising agencies and state bureaucracies, and to be paid according to the contractual stipulations.

How the Logistics Function Came About?

Logistics, which in today's business terminology has evolved as supply-chain management, started from the military. Without suitable logistics no war can be won. The same applies to the business arena. It needs the coordination of trucks, trains, airplanes, and ships. It is a tremendous task to operate a global maritime company reaching practically every major port with its vessels or to synchronize UPS's hundreds of aircraft and tens of thousands of vehicles. People tend to underestimate the size of logistical support needed to satisfy the global demand. Early in the morning in Louisville, Kentucky, UPS Worldport handles every hour hundreds of thousands of packages. To do so, Worldport must process more data every 30 minutes than that which is processed at the New York Stock Exchange in an entire day. In Memphis, Tennessee, FedEx's global hub processes one aircraft every 90 seconds and, similar images are constantly processed from Cologne to Dubai and Manila to Mumbai.

Today's global logistics support has given unique marketing advantages to companies which capitalize on the responsive potential of companies like FedEx or UPS. *Effectively, a new era of one-to-one marketing has been created both at the consumer and B2B level.* Dell, for example, sells from its own website and call centers, gets paid in advance, then builds to order, and individually ships the product to the final consumer within days. Zara, a fashion company, gets new designs into its shops in around 5 weeks, avoiding mass production, buying unfinished products in Asia, and reprocessing them close to its major manufacturing facilities, in Spain. Such a process, only a few years ago could have taken 6 to 9 months.[13]

Approaching the Final Consumer

Whatever the product and its market is, an expensive Swiss-made watch or a German-made water pump in Sahara, marketing in a borderless world must seek and identify consumer or B2B needs. As the producer may be far away from the final consumer it is a middleman or a strategically positioned company subsidiary who senses these needs. According to the type of product or service marketed, there are two different types of channels.

> Go the extra mile for your customer.
>
> Richard Templar[14]

The role of the retailer is to be a middleman, an intermediary in the marketing chain, and reach the final consumer through particular functions like providing an assortment of products and services, breaking bulk, holding inventory, and providing services. The retailer buys directly or indirectly from the manufacturer or the producer. The retailer has to be highly sensitive to the market trends, the products needed, and the processes employed. Beyond business objectives, the retailer plays key roles, for example, becoming a socialization and information-exchange opportunity as it is in small rural communities, or responsible for major undertakings, as it is with the ecology-green consciousness that Wal-Mart,[15] the world's largest retailer, promotes for its own operation but also, indirectly, to its suppliers. In both instances, the retailer listens to what the consumer wants and adjusts his product–service mix accordingly.

> Huge video screens bombard people with ads while shopping,[16] a worldwide phenomenon for retailers, from Wal-Mart to Carrefour.

In a parallel sense industrial buyers will seek their own intermediaries, usually promoted through industry association, specialized magazines, and trade shows. Business-to-business exchanges command larger payments, fewer accounts, more in-depth analysis of requirements and standards, capability to tailor-made production to the individual buyer needs, involvement of more specialized persons from each side of transaction, lower price volatility, higher service demands, and long-term partnerships.

Distributor Qualifications

For an exporter it is critical to identify a suitable distributor. Embassy trade experts, industry associations, publications, advertisements, consultants, trade shows, web analyses, or specialized databases[17] can provide profiles of distributors in foreign markets. Then, it is up to the company to choose the one who fits best its purpose. But what are the traits a distributor should have?[18]

- Necessary personnel, facilities, and equipment.
- Financial strength, reliability, capability to face market fluctuations.
- Market recognition.
- Years of experience in the foreign market similar to our lines of products, and the ability to deal with the product's character (e.g., tailor-made, specialized service, etc.).
- Proven and extensive sales network, and ability to deal with the exporter's unique market character (e.g., original equipment, government, industrial, consumers, etc.), and ways (e.g., offer exclusive distribution arrangements).
- A corporate image in the foreign market that complements our company's promotional aims in that part of the world.
- Knowledge of related resources (e.g., ad agencies), bureaucratic facilitators, competitors, and good PR with all of them.
- Corporate culture of the same wavelength, so that potential problems can be avoided (e.g., ethical conflicts).
- Good chemistry between the distributor and exporter executives.
- Business processes that meet the exporters standards (e.g., efficient ERPs), and so on.

From another perspective the distributor chosen must be able to offer "sufficient space" to accommodate the exporter's strategic effort in entering this market. Quality of personnel, ability to offer the required service support, product complementarities, or existing lines of distribution must be closely examined by the exporter before he decides to commit to a particular channel. The choice of a distribution channel results usually in long-term relations and has to be studied very carefully before the final commitment. In some cases, for the exporter, it will be difficult to withdraw from its contractual (or from the assumed) obligations. A long-term plan for market expansion might be necessary to outline future intentions for joint ventures, wholly owned subsidiaries, and so on, between the exporter and foreign partner.

In the previous discussion we addressed main points of the controllable variables of the international marketing mix. Specialized books on this topic can address these issues in depth. Attention should be focused to identify *market segments* and *market niches*. Profitability is rarely built on products at the maturity stage of the PLC. Inventiveness should lead the marketers toward unexplored market segments with products that fit target consumers, not necessarily the wealthier customers. Actually, research offers some "features" of successful business models on marketing to the poor.[19] They tend to propose ideas as the following:

1. Focus on low-margin but high-volume products without compromising quality.
2. Develop single-use, small quantity, and other innovations in packaging.
3. Products should be high quality, durable, functional, simple, and inexpensive.
4. Leverage the use of local people, nongovernmental organizations, and other low-cost resources.
5. Where appropriate, use technology to minimize investment and to keep costs low.
6. Build trust with your customers—resist short-term financial goals that compromise such trust.
7. The poor are different—develop inexpensive sources of continuing customer feedback.

The previous arguments project also one of the major societal functions of the global corporation: To bring goods and services to the masses of the underdeveloped and developing markets, previously being far away from the corporate growth business plans.

International Business Research

> In business, competition will bite you if you keep running; if you stand still, they swallow you.
>
> Semon Knudsen[20]

International business research assists a corporation in better understanding its foreign operating environments through factual knowledge. It offers information on a variety of matters including legalities, personnel matters, consumer preferences, competition, and so on. Most of international business research refers, however, to international marketing research and, therefore, usually it can be found in this chapter. Actually, some people tend to start first with international marketing research as its aid to better understand the consumer. But what is marketing research? Marketing research is the objective and systematic gathering, analysis, presentation, and use of data aiming to improve the decision making in the area of marketing. The internationalization of marketing research adds several issues of concern.

Researching International Markets: Issues of Concern

Complexity of the primary research design is an issue as we have to face many countries and different languages and cultures. The complexity of research can be faced, and appropriate methodology can be identified if the problem definition is clear. Researchers should be very careful as underlying characteristics of behavior might not be evident to them. For example, a young up-and-coming professional in Northern Europe might have more material motivation than another from South India who perceives the self-actualization elements of behavior as very important.

Lack of secondary data will make research very difficult. Expect that developing and underdeveloped nations often do not have them, but if they do, they might not be reliable, comparable, or recent. Private organizations can provide some industry-specific secondary data, at a cost.

Data sampling is very critical. Samples have to be representative and properly stratified to extrapolate data for the whole population. We cannot compare Indians, Bangladeshis, and Pakistanis. Although their countries share common borders, Indians alone are more than 1 billion people. Biased sampling frames and generalizations will produce ambiguous and unusable results, or both. Then, the *quality of instruments used* will determine the real value of the answers received. Focus groups are necessary to develop appropriate instruments which must be pretested before their actual use in the field.

International business research costs are high. Due to difficulties in mining secondary data, primary research design complexities, research administration, and so on, expect that research in developing, underdeveloped markets, or both, though the cost of researchers will be low, might be more expensive than that of developed markets.

Secondary data taken for granted as quality data. Often we use existing data believing that the source (national census, major pharmaceutical company, and established company with many years of experience) are methodologically correct for our purpose. This can lead to conclusions that are correct for those who drafted the survey but can only partially justify our intended thinking.[21]

Main Steps in International Research

Success in international business is related to the experience curve the company (or its associates) has. The same applies to the international business research. The following steps delineate the process:

1. Defining the research objectives and determining an initial cost (budget).
2. Using the corporate data bank, and examining what has been previously found with respect to the research problem.
3. Collecting secondary data.
4. Evaluating steps 2 and 3, and restating research objective, if necessary.

5. Preparing research design, paying particular attention to methodological and sampling issues.

6. Determining, from an administrative perspective, how the research will be conducted, steps, personnel, timelines, and final cost estimation.

7. Implementing research, and gathering primary data.

8. Analyzing data and group findings.

9. Presenting research findings, and proposing further research needs.

10. Integrating findings to the overall marketing plan and the corporate data bank.

Entry Methods in Foreign Markets[22]

Worldwide, hundreds of companies exist that are capable to export, but they do not. Also, for the past 30 years there are very worthy export assistance programs in dozens of countries. So, why do not more companies export? The answer is lack of knowledge of the foreign realities, complacency of the individuals involved, as well as fear of risk, and its potential business repercussions. Enterprising leaders of these firms are happy with the yield from their domestic markets and are unwilling to venture further. They do not feel that their home market is an export market for business all around the world, and they do not understand that if they do not expand their own frontiers they are bound to be taken over by the competition. Obviously, this unwillingness to export phenomenon is much more prevalent with small- and medium-sized companies that with large ones.

Let's examine different scenarios in a company's effort to internationalize its business.

Indirect Exporting

A well-established company with modern facilities, profitably operating in its home market for half a century and employing in its two plants more than 200 employees, is content to collect premium local produce, package it, and market to the major domestic super-market chains and to several local wholesalers.

Then, while in specialty stores in London and New York, the daughter of the owner sees their fine-looking jars of olive oils and marmalades proudly being exhibited to be sold at a premium price, at least three times over the price at their local market. They also carry a small adhesive label stating in English all necessary nutritional information. What is happening? One of the wholesalers buys their products at the local market and sells it overseas. He sees an opportunity and, since there is no contractual obligation against it, he explores it and gains from it. In fact, the wholesaler had told the marketing manager about his export ideas, but the company never took them seriously. The company continued to market its products only domestically, but, indirectly, and without the company's involvement whatsoever, they were exported.

There is profit to be made in the export markets, and proof of that is the company's product is indirectly exported to them. Somebody else benefits from this opportunity—not the company. In fact, the wholesaler now knows the export markets well and is in a position, if he so desires, to switch suppliers (reducing the sales of the original company), which has no knowledge of venturing into export markets. Is there any financial benefit to the company by using the particular wholesaler? Is there any risk by not seeking alternative export possibilities? How should the company proceed? The expected profit margin at no additional risk.

Direct Exporting[23]

The same company now gets serious and thinks about starting its own export sales. The first step, which has some risk but also promises more profits, is through direct exporting. But how to do it? A suitable strategy, options, and the appropriate business plans are needed. The local industry association and a visit to a major trade show have provided some names of potential distributors in foreign markets. Identification of a good foreign distributor appears to be a good initial solution. His existing network of retailers seems to be a far better approach than the sporadic foreign sales of the wholesaler. To identify this distributor, make all the necessary arrangement and plans, print new product labels, prepare for exports, actually export the products, pay dues, expect payment in arrear, hedge for possible foreign exchange fluctuation, build a new warehousing facility, and so on, the company incurs some costs. Direct exporting means more company involvement, higher risk because of the additional capital outlay, and potential more profit and market knowledge.

Joint Ventures

A few years down the road the New York distributor appears to be ready for greater things. In fact, he wants to go beyond the City of New York, cover the whole state, and prepare himself for a multistate expansion. He relates his business vision to the company which concurs and proposes to start a joint venture, to be owned by the now exporting company by a certain percentage and, the rest, by the distributor. They each have areas of specialization in production and in marketing, and they do have a good "chemistry" between them. The joint venture which is a further step into foreign market expansion, will necessitate more investments, we call them *foreign direct investment* (FDI[24]). Enlarged warehousing and distribution center and own production facility in the United States using locally available produce will carry more risk, counter competition, promise more profits, and have significant better market penetration.

Wholly Owned Subsidiaries

Finally, the company decides that it is time to take over the whole operation. It now knows well the U.S. market, it invests more in FDI, it further expands its production and distribution facilities, and administratively it needs to integrate all its global efforts which now cover Europe, Japan, and Australia. It proposes to buy out its ex-distributor (after a point partner in a joint venture) who accepts the offer.

A wholly owned subsidiary means, of course, higher levels of investment (and therefore business risks), but it also promises more profits, better market coverage, and expansion potential. In fact, *exporting is not always a plausible option*. Production in the host market has advantages: Transportation, insurance, and currency exchange costs and duties are avoided; utilization of foreign facilities is a plus which is appreciated at the host environment; exports from the host country facility to neighboring areas is easier; production in itself maybe cheaper and the technology used more appropriate for the local realities; overutilizing the home country facility maybe counterproductive and, after a point, more expensive; possible trade restrictions are avoided; products produced at the host market follow the standards of the host market, and so on.

In a summary form, we see *that going from indirect exporting to direct exporting to joint ventures to wholly owned subsidiaries, the involved company progressively has more foreign direct investment, undertakes more risks, and also enjoys more profits, potential market growth, and operational control.*

Licensing and Other Arrangements

Another company produces faucets and other bathroom accessories. It holds very worthy patents and its corporate logo is recognized for its reliability and quality. Production expansion from their own factories is not a very desirable option as the owners are well-off and they do not care in having more business headaches. The company (*licensor*) decides to proceed via a licensing agreement, where the *licensee* is granted an exclusive license[25] to use for a specific period and specific geographic area its patents, proprietary rights, inventions, trademarks, and knowhow in return for a certain percentage on sales.

The licensor has now the opportunity to gain without investing anything or handle other administrative or market issues. The arrangement is often very reasonable and desirable but, as with every case, potential problems may exist. For example, what if the licensee produces at a lesser quality than required and this affects the long-standing good name of the licensor? What if products sold at the specified geographic region find their way into the licensor's area through "gray" channels? Obviously, a carefully drafted contract is essential covering all these details—and many more.

A third company (*franchisor*) produces its famous Italian pizzas and decides to enter into several new markets through *franchising*. Franchising is a form of licensing where the franchisor undertakes the responsibility to assist its franchisees with training, promotions, knowhow applications, accounting systems, and so on. To some extent, we can think that the franchisees operate as quasi-own corporate subsidiaries, but they are independently owned and, therefore, they do not require a capital outlay from the franchisor's point of view. In fact, the franchisees pay a fee to enter into the system and a prespecified sales percentage as a fee to the franchisor. Certain modifications of the product offering(s) according to market peculiarities are necessary.

Finally, many other different arrangements should be considered when a company decides to enter into foreign markets, ranging from selling whole "turnkey operations" to managing specific contracts.

In this chapter, marketing issues were addressed. It is reminded that any corporation must first identify its markets and then produce the products needed. In the global business village it is of paramount importance to act very quickly. There are very few barriers to counter competition. The next chapter addresses issues on international management, especially about human resources, corporate structures, and information technologies.

CHAPTER 8

Management Perspectives

About This Chapter

Here are some ideas about what management is:[1]
- Lot of folks confuse bad management with destiny.

  Elbert Hubbard

- Good management consists in showing average people how to do the work of superior people.

  John D. Rockefeller

Management is any set of activities aiming to achieve organizational goals. In other words management refers to any business function, from accounting to marketing, and includes specific processes, such as administration, directing, planning, decision making, organizing, teaching, controlling, and so forth. Focusing on global business activities, this chapter examines management processes, especially as they relate to international human resources (HR), to corporate structures, and to information technologies (IT).

Management existed always. Management is responsible for the material and intellectual capital left throughout the human history, from building temples in India to fighting wars in Troy. Judging from specific achievements, people in some areas developed better administrative and managerial tools. For example, the British, given the times and the then accepted rules, advanced their colonies more than the Portuguese, as a comparison of economic growth between Hong Kong and Macau indicates.[2]

Furthermore, the *essence of management is strategy*, a term that was coined in the military. Alexander the Great, a military strategist, was probably the first major international manager. With 30,000

Macedonians, at the age of 33 years, he had conquered the then known world, and when he returned back, he was so influenced by cross-cultural adaptation that he had merged practices and ways of life from many of the lands his forces had taken over. Another very well-known example is of Sun Tzu, the Chinese author of the *Art of War,* which even today is used in management classes to teach approaches in management strategy. Today, most of the management textbooks heavily capitalize on "strategic" notions.

It also appears that management principles have universal followers. A few opinions from distinguished Japanese managers are as follows:[3]

- There is no end to restructuring. Rather than fear change, we must welcome it and understand that it brings new opportunities and business (Tadashi Okamura, President and CEO, Toshiba Corporation).
- I believe the most important concern for business is the kind of value it creates (Yasuo Nishiguchi, President, KYOCERA Corporation).
- Two things are essential in today's management—the ability to look ahead into the future and to establish a distinct identity for all your products (Ichiro Taniguchi, Mitsubishi Electric Corporation).
- We can achieve global success only if we genuinely listen to our customers (Akira Gemma, President and CEO Shiseido Co.).
- We will transform to respond to our global customers and to stay at the apex of technological and product development (Akira Chihaya, Representative Director and President Nippon Steel Corporation).

On the other hand of this global thinking, there are the local managerial realities deeply rooted in their native cultural upbringing and predispositions. Many long-established small family operations can easily convince the visitor that business thinking is based on local practices and tradition with many references to the local environment and little concern about modern-era universal concepts. For example, business ethics, although revered in large corporations, for many, especially smaller, businesspeople, is an oxymoron phrase. In international management we need to merge the ways local business is conducted with the globally successful managerial principles, practices, and technologies. Adaptation and creativity offer a more realistic and flexible operational platform.

Creativity showed to people better organizational approaches, more efficient utilization of resources, and ways to avoid unnecessary risks—today, we call this process entrepreneurialism. One of the main resources utilized were humans. For most part of our history humans were the propelling power of economic growth, usually as slaves of the rulers. During the past 300 years, and due to the industrial revolution, we have been approaching an era where every citizen of the planet will have the possibility to equally enjoy the rewards of his efforts. We are in front of an era where fair and ethical standards are transforming the work environments, everywhere.

> When John Kenneth Galbraith was asked about his greatest hope for America, he answered: "My greatest hope would be for more equitable rewarded people … From the bottom up."[4]

HR Challenges: Culture, Technology, and Generation Gaps of the 21st Century

Throughout history, cultures and subcultures, developing within topographic confinements and socioeconomic realities, shaped the roles, the thought processes, and the work habits of individual populations. Today, with emergence of a borderless business arena, corporations operate in diverse environments and employ workers with very different attitudes and work behaviors.

Let's hypothesize that we need to identify a suitable workforce for a worldwide operator of a luxury hotel chain—from managers to chefs. As we will see in this chapter, of paramount importance are the workforce selection process, the purpose-specific, intense and periodically revised training, and the evaluation of this workforce. After all, this hotel chain must standardize its service in Paris (France), Quebec (Canada), Rio de Janeiro (Brazil), Shanghai (China), or Tangier (Morocco), and, at the same time keep the local "flavor" of every of its facilities. How are we going to proceed?

In Chapter 1, we saw that cultures, as they veer from generation to generation, are changing and, to some extent, they are converging. The workforce of the 21st century follows this pattern. To make this point more obvious, let's use the American paradigm of generational changes.

The generation that was born before War World II (1925–1945)—known as the *silent generation* and affected by family patriotic sentiments—can be characterized by traditional behaviors and devotion to the principles of the nation, laws, and faith. The next generation, known as the *baby boomers,* effectively many of the people born in the next 20 years, are defining new trends, take more personal risks, do not feel that they must sacrifice themselves, or reduce their own pleasures, for the common good. They challenge hierarchy, religious, and ethical conduct often with a "mix" of beliefs, avoiding dogmatic positions of specific philosophical theories.

In the next 20 years, the *baby busters* or *generation X*, appears. Probably due to the high loans of the previous generation, the nonsecure working environment, and the understanding that baby busters witness a socially mutating era, this generation feels it must secure itself with ties of family and friends. Alas! As we saw in Chapter 2, the societal structure is rapidly moving from the society of the unit to the society of the individual.

We are now in the 21st century and today's generation is often called *generation Y.* It is expensive and demanding. It develops in the "society of the individual," the mass media, the computers, the mobile phones, and the Internet.[5] The family patriarch is not there to bring in perspective issues and questions. To a great extent IT influences the thinking of this individual and reprioritize culture-related learning objectives. In Chapter 2, we called this person as *homo technologicus* and indicated that, occasionally and probably, due to his lessened social involvement during his upbringing, this person might prefer technology to social interaction, might be a weak learner of complex, abstract concepts, and might be an unsuitable member of the global workforce.[6]

For a moment, we should observe the era of global corporations, which effectively started only after World War II, *vis-à-vis* the employee's attitudinal changes and principles within the same period—going from the silent generation status to generation Y. For example, at a worldwide level, the principle of self-sacrificing for the betterment of the social sum and the respective personal beliefs appears to be culturally embedded from antiquity, as the well-known example of Socrates indicates, to about the end of World War II. Since then a deterioration of patriotic principles and social ideals is evident at a global level, in favor of self-propelled motivation. Therefore, today's corporation needs to thoroughly reexamine the value system of its future workers as it needs corporate cultural stability, in the same way the empires of the past saw their own cultural and philosophical tenants.

In our borderless world,[7] talented, suitable home-country, host-country, or expatriate workforce exist in ample supply, or it can move to where the demand for their services is needed. Therefore, in its global quest, the corporation, as in the previously mentioned case of a luxury hotel operator, seeks to identify, develop, and use suitable talent and workforce from a variety of environments. During the selection process, *attention is needed toward bridging socioeconomic, cultural, generational, and technological gaps.* This is possible in theory, but how? Learning what is available worldwide is almost an impossible task. Comparing what is available with the HR needs of the corporation is even more challenging, especially at a time when these gaps mutate constantly.

People and their leaders, workforce and their executives, and students and their teachers must learn from each other of the available job placement opportunities through interactive, culture-specific, and meaningful information exchange. This is an era of business–education partnerships. *In-depth understanding of each individual's separate attributes, motivation, and needs; sound selection of the workforce; state-of-the-art education; and direct, one-to-one communications are keys for the sensible development of all stakeholders: The individual, the corporation, and the social fabric, as a whole.* Teamwork is highly in demand in international business situations.

Executive pay in the United States: The three top executives of major corporations received during 2000 through 2005 more than 100 times the average salary of a single employee of the same corporation.[8] Let's move forward, allow a reasonable time in administering the affairs of corporations (for 7–10 years), and examine the potential executive severance pay. For the top 12 executives severance pay exceeds 2 billion U.S. dollars![9]

HR Management in a Global Context

To survive, any organization must continuously adapt to the demands and changes of its environment. Global business organizations should not only change their production methods according to the technological developments, adapt to the financial methods, modify old products, or introduce new ones, but also change themselves. They must change their corporate culture in a timely way, must organize their subsidiaries both per headquarters' culture and per the environment they operate, must recruit HR capable to adapt to the changes of the global business or technological environment, and must understand the cultural diversity and capitalize on cultural complexities, such as cultural heterogeneity or linguistic differences. In addition, global business organizations must have corporate cultures that quickly adapt to environmental changes and personnel that are sensitive, calm, flexible, well-trained, ethical, understanding, and tolerant of new people, new experiences, new processes, and new situations.

In a parallel manner the business environment must be quick to adapt to the needs that organizations have for skilled employees. In a borderless reality, potential needs of organizations must be faced before its competitors lure the better work "talents." "The bottom line: After tech industry lobbying, the (U.S.) Senate bill raised the number of visas for skilled foreign workers from 65,000 to 115,000."[10]

Typology of Corporate Cultures

Initially corporate cultures depict the thinking of their owners. As time passes, corporate cultures are influenced by the belief systems of their managers and stakeholders of the enterprise. Additionally, the components of corporate cultures should parallel the thinking of individuals of an organization. These individuals work for extensive periods with their companies and, therefore, they should be content with the corporate philosophy and culture. Capitalizing on the assumption that the global corporation, to some extent, must have a corporate culture based on cultural diversity, Fatehi classifies companies as follows:[11]

- *Monolithic organizations:* These are highly homogeneous organizations where one dominant cultural group dictates corporate culture and thinking. Prejudice and discrimination against the members of the cultural minority are prevalent. The homogeneity of workforce leaves little room for inter-group conflict. Monolithic thinking is found at the early stages of a firm's international business involvement; however, eventually the heterogeneity of plural organizations takes over.
- *Plural organizations:* The home organization recruits host-country citizens for its subsidiaries for a variety of reasons, including acquiring indigenous knowledge about its host markets, having culturally sensitive personnel supervising local workforce, dealing with bureaucracies, and so on. This makes the plural organization culturally heterogeneous, though its home executives continue to have ethnocentric attitudes.
- *Multicultural organizations:* These organizations recognize the value of cultural heterogeneity and capitalize on potential contributions and synergies because of cultural diversity. They are characterized by structural and informal integration, absence of prejudice, discrimination, and intergroup conflict.

Speaking of cultural diversity... PepsiCo, the U.S beverage icon, has as CEO the Indian-born Indra Nooyi. She leads the 2006 *Fortune* American list of the most powerful women in international business.[12]

Motivation of the Individual

An individual's motivation to achieve an objective or to perform a task is a complex psychological construct that recognizes needs and ways to satisfy them. There are different levels of need, starting from simple physiological ones to security to belongingness to esteem, and ending to self-actualization. Abraham Maslow first proposed this classification in the 1940s.[13] In practice, material-financial rewards may satisfy physiological needs, even security needs—let's say through a pension plan. For some, belongingness needs can be satisfied through the socialization environment at work or at home; esteem needs and self-actualization needs are more advanced processes[14] that may be satisfied through a job title or through challenges induced by the work itself. In general, we accept that a satisfied need is not a motivator anymore, therefore, that it cannot be used by the business world to advance organizational objectives any longer.

The above had merit, especially in the post-World War II business environment, which was predominated by Western-type corporations, operating in a world with well-defined borders. *To a great extent, Maslow's thinking has merit even today,* in spite of world's rapid changes and unexpected demands: Far away cultures affect others; cultural imperialism creates new perspectives; mass communication media simplify and transform people's understanding toward materialistic happiness; social mutation is ever present; IT pushes the frontiers of knowledge; technology and computers isolate the individuals; the borderless world is a reality; and great masses of people are able to obtain the necessary means to feed themselves, be warm, be safe, be educated, and cater for their future. These people are the operators and the managers of the new societal player, the corporation, which, alas, tries to satisfy their needs primarily through the traditional motivator: Material and financial rewards.

Is this realistic in our era? Or is it necessary to invent new motivational platforms? Nowadays *the global corporation has an ethical responsibility to advance the social fabric and sustain the environment, wherever it operates.* The old modus operandi is not sufficient in a world where the average individual employee of the 500 *Fortune* companies commands more than $1,850,000 of assets and more than $450,000 sales.[15] This is an enormous social capital that has to be respected. *The employee should be motivated at higher levels, enjoy more than financial rewards, and, through his employer, be able to advance her own social, philosophical, and* raison *d'être perspectives.*

At the same time today's borderless world magnifies the differences of cultural confinements. Let's say we need to operate a team that, among others, includes an American and a Japanese. The American culture promoted the American's individualism and his win-lose behavior. The Japanese, on the other hand, has been taught that he is an equal member of the team and for him a promotion or an award may make him feel bad—certainly it is not much of a work motivator. Additionally, in the work environment unsatisfied needs may result in a series of problems, such as, accidents, low performance, absenteeism, and so on. In turn, the same unsatisfied needs create home problems, social unrest, and even affects the health of the workforce.

Work motivation also relates to the individual employee's happiness. We have stressed that *companies have social roles. One of them is to cater to their workers overall happiness levels.* We are in the 21st century not in 1849, when Thomas Carlyle wrote that economics is "not a gay science," or when Jeremy Bentham discussed his "utilitarian" philosophy and his peers looked forward to an invention that was to promote hedonism, a kind of a psychological machine.[16] Since then we have learned a lot about human happiness. When someone feels warm, fed, and safe, additional material adds very little to her happiness level. Some people "forget" themselves in a work-related function, doing what is expected of them better than their peers, effectively "losing" themselves in their work.

> Know your enemy and know yourself, and you can fight a hundred battles with no danger of defeat.
>
> Sun Tzu[17]

In the international work environment the basic understanding of the motivation theory and human happiness remains the same as within the domestic environment. Sensitivity and cultural understanding are needed to successfully accommodate the thinking of the plural or the multicultural organizations we saw previously, where the impact from differences in *ethnic cultures* may be lessened by the worldwide standardization of *professional cultures* and the specificities of their own *corporate cultures*. In fact, the existence of professional cultures allows the individuals to focus on issues and avoid cross-cultural references. For example, the Australian accountants of that subsidiary will examine an audit discrepancy (almost) under the same light as the controllers at the Swiss headquarters.

HR Activities at a Global Level[18]

As one can surmise from the previous discussion, historically, HR management has focused on activities related to recruiting, hiring, training, evaluating, compensating, and terminating employees. Doing these activities well contributes significantly to company performance and profitability.[19] This is hard enough to manage in a single country; however, when an organization works with employees in multiple countries it must understand the cultural attitudes toward work, and one additional important aspect: The law.

Over long periods of time the difference in cultures between countries produce differences in laws. All of the HR activities must be performed with the knowledge of different cultural attitudes toward employment and in compliance with the local laws. For example, in different countries organized labor unions might be required, tolerated, or forbidden. Another example is job security. In the North America, the prevailing laws support employment-at-will, meaning that just as an employee can quit any job at any time for any reason, so can an employer fire any employee at any time for any reason (or for no reason at all). In most of the EU, there are significant protections that prohibit employers from terminating employees after they have been on the job for a while. With the global growth of businesses, imagine the complexities that arise when dealing with workforces that have different sociocultural expectations for each of these, HR, activities and different legal protections for employees.

In addition, technology[20] is increasingly having an impact on HR management. For example, recruiting can now be done on a global basis through the Internet. Researchers[21] have shown that they can influence attraction to a company simply by altering the type of feedback they provide to potential employees that answer questions on a website. This means that due to the interactive capabilities of the Web, not only can employers reach out to the best possible employees anywhere in the world, but that they can also get the candidates that would be the best fit with their company culture, *want* to work for the company.

Practical Issues

The organizational, and this includes the *business, environment is the place where the HR factor creates value. The quality of the employee and her working environment directly correlates to her performance and thus, to the achieved results, creativity and societal growth—both economic and noneconomic.* Corollary to these thoughts is that the selection, evaluation, education, and overall growth of the employee are the defining variables for value creation. An organization to be successful must have well-selected managers and continuously offer its HR department meritorious opportunities for education and promotions.

> Behind a capable man there are other capable men.
>
> Chinese proverb.

With respect to international management, here are some practical advices:

- Businesses should try to recruit people for the host subsidiaries from the host countries. These people have more cultural congruency, behavioral understanding, knowledge of, and acceptance from their environments than the foreigners.
- The ideal individual for a foreign assignment, beyond sound knowledge of his functional field, must have a positive personality, flexibility, ability to adapt, team spirit, proven capacity to work under stress for many hours without immediate guidance, limited resources, and dealing with frustrating local bureaucracies. He must also acquire in-depth country-specific knowledge and cultural empathy for the specific foreign environment he is being sent to. Additionally, it is desirable that he has previous similar experiences and linguistic abilities.
- For an international business career, the stability of the individual, both at a personal and professional level, must be carefully scrutinized. Behavioral ups and downs of the individual who has responsibility over an international post can be very damaging to the operation.

- Selection criteria for international assignments may vary according to the place the individual is going. Locally accepted values and ethical norms must be compared and contrasted with those of the individual who has to deal with them.
- The individual undertaking a foreign assignment must want to be there. If his management wants him to go, but he does not, expect that he will be unhappy, may make errors, and underperform.
- If the individual selected is moving from his own familiar environment to another, particular attention must be paid to the spouse and the rest of the family members traveling with him (kids and parents). Studies show that negation to a foreign environment often comes from the spouse, not from the individual selected for the assignment.
- The company must continuously upgrade the potential, both at a personal and at a professional level, of its foreign personnel through education. The fluidity of the global environment and the resulting IT repercussions, demand in-depth understanding, and catering of the educational needs.
- Professions and professional cultures develop in different ways across nations. The global company can get the best ideas and practices from a host of environments and, thus, improve its overall operations.
- Home management must deal with its global ventures in warm, ethical, sincere, and supportive ways. It should use exact, well-tested, and efficient processes, and should avoid any personal interaction. Processes are not sentimental. They should apply equally to all.

International Labor Relations

Traditionally, labor resources have worked very hard. They built pyramids and vast tracks of rails. They worked under very cold or humid conditions. They rarely enjoyed their work time. They experienced little of the carrot and much more of the stick approach. The laws were not in their favor; there was no concern about the work hours, work conditions, safety of the workers, sickness, or retirement. In an Aldous Huxley's sense citizens belonged in different classes.[22] Only after the industrial revolution working conditions started changing, not only because of profound statements of the left-wing leaders, but mainly because of *the realization by the industry leaders that higher productivity was a function of a better work environment*. Meanwhile, all around the world, labor organizations mushroomed trying to protect the rights of the workers and, at the same time, labor laws were written depicting the understanding of each society about the rights of the workforce. A momentum had started reprioritizing human values, dictating respect for the individual and his environment, and pushing toward philosophical repositioning in favor of an ethical and balanced world, where both the human and nonhuman life had clear rights toward their betterment.

Obviously, the working realities and the conditions in Malaysia were different than those in Mexico, and those in the United States different than those in the USSR. The respective legal systems and labor unions evolved according to local pressures, dynamics, and politics. Corporations, in need of workforce, had to deal with the local unions and labor laws, which were vastly different and according to each country's norms and values. It was not always for the "good" of the workers necessarily, but often local labor unions, which sometimes were quite powerful and very political, were able to shut down whole industries for elongated periods of time. In those cases corporations were frustrated, unable to do anything, except to accept losses. Fifty years ago, it was not feasible to move a whole production facility.

Then, the borderless world, almost unexpectedly, appeared. Many localized labor organizations, entrapped in their internal political games were slow to react to the globalized realities. At the same time, as we saw, a new player came—the international corporation, which by now was much more sophisticated, flexible, and adaptive. This new player had a much better grasp of marketing, accounting, and financing possibilities. The managers of these businesses had a better understanding of human motivation and the reasons behind their productivity. Their firm's *plan-*

ning process was starting with an exact definition of the organizational mission, and the corporate values, principles, and objectives. The objectives and the respective plans were strategic, tactical, and functional. And, naturally, the human factor was an integral element of all of the above and for all the diverse environments in which the corporation was operating. The international corporation was in a position to place, educate, motivate, and reward its workers in a much more realistic and creative fashion than what the local unions had in mind. After all, local labor unions were strictly local, whereas international corporations had experienced and validated productivity factors in many global working environments. They were in a better shape to study the real motivation of their workers and to offer the appropriate working conditions for each different country's environment.

Moreover, the global corporation was now in a position to move where suitable conditions were abundantly available. This corporation was not locked anymore to a particular place because of the existence of a warehouse or production facility. The bottom line was a financial equation, not subject to local political pressures, bureaucracies, or demands. At the same time, and to a greater degree, fears of moving to the lower-cost-producing areas proved to be unfounded when the appropriate working force education was timely taking place and the respective HR were again able to undertake higher level and, therefore, better-paid jobs. In fact, competitive conditions at the global village were creating a better and richer societal environment for all.

Are we, therefore, approaching the end of the useful life of labor unions? Of course not, if they adapt according to the needs of the times by offering real value to their memberships and, by the same token, if they continue to respect the core cultural predispositions of their regions. For example, in Germany the essence of *codetermination* is vital, whereas in Japan the concept of *keibatsu* (from *kei* meaning family and *batsu* meaning group or faction or clique[23]) is instrumental for any business function. Going a step further from the localized labor unions, attention should be also directed to international efforts. Since 1919, the now United Nations International Labor Organization[24] has contributed significantly toward the betterment of workforce conditions, as well as many other international unions, all of them with millions of members, for example, the International Confederation of Free Trade Unions (ICFTU), the European Trade Union Confederation (ETUC), the World Confederation of Labor (WCL), and so forth.

Summarizing this section, we may say that "most admired"[25] companies realize that higher productivity is a function of a better work environment, which they do offer. And that for them and their betterment, local and international labor unions will continue to play a significant role even though on a worldwide basis substandard working conditions still exists. It is the opinion of this author that governments, supranational organizations, corporate entities of all sizes, and labor unions have not sufficiently aimed to create a better working environment for all.

Managing the Global Corporation

From the discussion up to now it is evident that the international manager faces a complex work place where management of thousands of people in diverse environments requires not only workplace standardization but also differentiation, flexibility, and adaptability. Behind this thinking there are classic principles of management, such as the following:

- Existence of organizational competency allowing constant evolution in the ever-changing global business arena and a competitive corporate culture aiming toward upgrading HR through education.
- An appropriate organizational structure (see below).
- Existence of a meritorious process for selection, recruiting, and evaluation of personnel.
- Existence of global reward systems, taking into consideration the varying motivational elements when one crosses country borders.
- Efficient worldwide communication and information systems, and thorough use of suitable IT technologies (see the end section of this chapter).

We accept, of course, that all business is global. However, some companies are better fitted to expand internationally. Experience in foreign environments, ability to capitalize on lower cost conditions without affecting quality required, and risk reduction through joint ventures are some of the reasons that companies quickly move to the international business arena. However, common denominators for global success are being entrepreneurial and culturally aware of the conditions to be faced.

Corporate Structures

Thirty years ago Peter Drucker said that corporate structures must have clarity, not simplicity. This is very true for the case of international corporations. Basic types of corporate structures are as follows:

- *International division structure* is the organizational form that has as a separate division all its international functions, including marketing, production, joint ventures, and so on. Effectively, the corporation remains domestic, but under a separate entity it deals with everything outside the home country.
- In a *functional organizational structure* the organization is divided according to functions, let's say production, marketing, finance, and so forth, and under each function the corporation has home and international divisions.
- In a *product division structure* the organization is divided according to product categories, let's say computers, copy machines, services, and so forth, and under each product category the corporation has home and international divisions.
- In a *regional division structure* the organization is divided according to the geographical regions it operates in and has divisions under each region, for example, Europe, Americas, or Asia.
- Finally, in a *matrix organizational structure* the organization combines at every possible occasion functional, product category, and regional inputs.

The above is a typical classification found in management books, it offers a generalized understanding of the corporate structures, but it does not give the daily detailed operative format of the organizations.

The Born-Globals[26]

From the beginning of the book we have used interchangeably the combination of the words *international–global* and *firm–company–enterprise–organization*. Now, it is time to introduce something that is more appropriate to the realities of the 21st century. *The growing globalization of the past couple of decades resulted in a new form of business enterprising, the born-global firm. These born-global companies take a global perspective from their inception and play the "borderless world" to its fullest ramifications.* Born-global corporations may have first been recognized in Europe and Australia, but born-globals now exist everywhere in the world.

Traditionally, companies start domestic.[27] Then, slowly, they move to some export activities, often through independent sales representatives; establishing a formal department dealing with export activities (usually within the marketing function), which is the next step; following that, these companies establish a foreign division or subsidiary; and, finally, they proceed to have their own foreign manufacturing, production, or operations. When Henry Ford, Colonel Harland Sanders, Sakichi Toyota, Walt Disney, and Sam Walton started their companies, they were thinking purely domestic. But as time progressed, they followed the approaches similarly to the ones described above toward their corporate internationalization.

> Think globally, invest locally (an investor strategist's advice; think GLOCAL[28])
>
> Jack Rivkin, CIO Neuberger Berman, Lehman Brothers

Born-global enterprises don't have a standard way of developing. These organizations do not follow an established growth pattern. However, all born-globals start off with a global mindset. They view the world with many ever-changing submarkets, sometimes requiring even one-to-one marketing. Their organizational styles, structures and configuration, operations and strategy, and decision making and management styles, usually jump, skip, or leapfrog the traditional growth models we discussed in the previous section. When the need be, they employ anti-organizational or centerless organization formats. They use patents and employ appropriate productions worldwide. Many born-global firms apply cutting-edge technologies and ERP systems, have an entrepreneurial spirit, and mutate to other types of enterprising when conditions change. *We can see the born-global corporation as the equivalent of a quasi-living organism, continuously adapting to every single environment it operates.*

Therefore, as students of international business, we need to be aware of this organizational type, which is a step beyond the previously described formats. Born-global firms are expected to become more prominent in the near future requiring their employees to have higher levels of technical expertise, knowledge of the functional international business fields, and in-depth understanding of self. Moreover, these organizations will be looking for associates that have the appropriate attitudes, multiproject management skills, ethical standards, ability to adapt, team spirit, flexibility, adaptiveness, and stable behavioral characteristics.

Trends

Military-type, command-and-control organizational structures were very appropriate for the corporate needs 50 years ago. Then business thinkers started introducing newer iconoclastic concepts. The *virtual corporation* was one of them, capitalizing on other people's knowhow, marketing expertise, production facilities, and so on. "What a virtual corporation looks like? To the outside observer, it will appear edgeless, with permeable and continuously changing interfaces between company, supplier, and customers. From inside the firm the view will be no less amorphous, with traditional offices, departments, and operating divisions constantly reforming according to need."[29] The concept of a *centerless corporation*[30] was an evolution of the previous concept allowing constant corporate reinvention and transformation according to need, effectively acquiring better organizational control and sense of direction. Steps toward the corporate transformation were proposed by others,[31] but practically all insisted on commitment,[32] building on creativity,[33] and being entrepreneurial.

Academics, consultants, and practicing managers saw the emergence of the global organizations and the need for prompt adaptation to their needs. Subsequently, they started building on strong corporate culture beliefs, corporate merging and corporate raiding specificities, capitalizing on market potentialities and HR talent, and investing in information technology. Case-by-case, firm-by-firm constant transformation resulted in more flexible formats of management. The results appear to be rewarding to all stakeholders of the corporation. More people enjoy the products made and services produced than ever before; IT is expanding at phenomenal rates; creativity, new process, and new products are everywhere; more corporate profits now than any time in the past; society and environment benefits; and HR enjoys a more fulfilling work environment than in the past. Everyone appears to be a winner.

Management in an Information Era[34]

Information projects knowledge. Knowledge projects creativity. A major asset of any corporation is the ability to identify, mine, and exploit appropriate information as well as to efficiently manage it to achieve its objectives in a rapidly changing global business landscape. Let's see some examples:

- A major law firm begins a legal document retrieving appropriate information from known sources and electronically distributes it to all involved personnel who add, either by voice or by text, pertinent material. In this way the firm saves steps, speeds up the deal-making process, and prepares its legal battles.
- In a commercial aircraft electronics plant, the entire set of systems has been designed to support high-performance work teams using floor data to build proactive processes, to identify defects, and prevent them. The work teams can reorganize product-line flows, change the manner in which a product is build, retool a product, or change how a machine is used.

- A fund manager using S&P 500 stock index, 11 variables, and the appropriate neural network program says, "The computer will detect patterns in stock prices that are too subtle or too diffuse for a human to detect ... (and finds) those 'undervalued' stocks where those patterns remain unrewarded."

If someone feels that the previous examples exaggerate reality, it must be noted that all of them were practiced at least 20 years[35] before the publication of this book. Today's management, to survive, must integrate IT, related processes, and appropriate enterprise resource systems. This section has two parts. The first refers to international management in an IT environment and the second to the globalization of the high-tech industry.

International Management in an IT Environment

In the modern corporate environment the integration of computer information systems into business strategy, managerial processes, and executive decisions has simply become not a weapon against competitors but a necessity for the contemporary enterprise.

Studies indicate that corporate management should integrate through technology all levels of operation, from functional routines to strategy concepts.[36] Currently, the penetration of computing and IT is far above the mean in all industries. Even industries which did not initially require computers and IT, only a few decades ago, currently have not only adopted IT but have even mastered the art of computing. One such notable example is the Gallo Wine Corporation in California which in the past few years has consistently been rated at the top in the list of best IT companies in the United States. One of the reasons Gallo gained such a prestigious rating is that people at Gallo have enthusiastically embraced IT and have ingeniously and successfully applied new technologies in their business operations. For instance, Gallo engineers have devised a method to monitor the quality of their grape vines from satellite images which are maintained in a database for easier archiving, access, and retrieval purposes. Naturally, computing and IT are an integral part of the daily operations at Gallo.

Another area where IT has proven an invaluable ally is the area of distributed operations. A good example of a corporation with highly distributed operations and decentralized organization is Nike Corporation. Nike makes athletic products such as shoes which are manufactured often in Asia and then distributed and sold around the world. Nike follows a relatively flat organizational structure. The U.S. headquarters coordinates everything through its streamlined top management. All other operations are distributed around the world. Top executives communicate with all other organizational units and manage their operations through the use of IT. Naturally, computing and IT are an integral part of the daily operations at Nike.

The management of international corporations has become much more effective, energetic, and dynamic through the adoption and creative use of IT. Contemporary managers using IT have tighter control over their organizations, can easily and quickly obtain valuable information for the short-term navigation of their company, and chart an optimal long-term course which can ultimately benefit the corporation and their shareholders.

Globalization of the High-Tech Industry

During the recent past the computing and IT industry has been truly transformed into a global industry. A confluence of factors led to this development. In the late 1990s two unfortunate events had a significant impact on the economy of the United States, and decisively distorted the appearance as well as the esoteric nature of the high-tech industry as a whole.

The first unfortunate event was the collapse of the stock prices of all the new high-tech Internet startup companies also known as dotcoms. These high-tech companies were typically founded strictly on the basis of an idea by young, inexperienced, and newcomers to the stock market arena, IT entrepreneurs. It did not take long before these young and promising persons were baptized as prodigies by well-known stock market analysts although they acted prematurely giving the stock market a euphoric climate and a presumption of value for their companies.

Although their companies had very few, if any, hard assets in their possession, they were allowed to enter the stock market on the alluring promise of endless future earnings via international, unlimited, and frictionless electronic commerce over the Internet. Often and prior to the initial public offer in the stock market, their companies were funded on the basis of a single idea—typically from venture capital firms only for a limited time period which, is not uncommon, did not exceed a full calendar year.

Not only were these newly formed high-tech companies unwisely allowed to enter the well-established U.S. stock markets, but also, despite continuous losses, they showed constantly rising share prices, often supported by expert accounts of well-known and respected analysts who presented glowing reviews and cases of potential future earnings. This highly inflammable mixture of conditions created an environment of euphoria and an ensuing feeding frenzy for investors, who could not stop pouring massive amounts of capital on the shares of these promising but short-lived companies.

Consequently, the share prices of these high-tech companies exploded, reached their zenith, which could be characterized more than excessive even by not so conservative thinkers. The majority of these companies had massive stock value compared to their hard assets and as a result when their share prices collapsed a chain reaction occurred and the severe ripple-shock waves affected, to an extreme degree, the whole U.S. stock market. The U.S. stock market suffered tremendous losses and was extremely depressed due to catastrophic damages of trillions of dollars. This series of events is also known as the dotcom crash.

The second unfortunate event was the telecommunications sector stock market crash. In 1996 Congress enacted the Telecommunications Act, which was signed by President William Clinton into public law 104 and motivated telecommunications companies to invest $500 billion to install fiber optic lines while increasing significantly the available capacity for broadband Internet, data, and voice telecommunications.

One of the unforeseen results of this enormous capacity increase was the inability of global corporations to absorb the newly available colossal telecommunications capacity. The result was a diminished demand by corporate service providers, quite a few of which were the already vulnerable and ill-fated dotcoms. Subsequently, the ensuing reduction of individual consumer prices and the eventual loss of half a million jobs in the telecommunications industry further damaged the US-based IT prospects.

As a result of this series of unfortunate events corporations and new enterprises as well as their silent funding sources, venture capital firms, immediately changed their course of action. Methods of conserving capital were immediately introduced, excessive expenses were eliminated, and audits of expenses allowed for a tighter control of costs, outsourcing, and offshoring prevailed where feasible.[37]

Offshoring and outsourcing are simple manifestations of the globalization of the IT industry including research and development. Globalization offers some merits as eventually it will lead to worldwide competition, elimination of localized monopolies, higher wages in low-wage countries, access to previously unreachable medicine, and improved quality of goods and services as well as equality of wages and *justice for all in a global free trade market*. IT globalization has both short-term positive results such as cost minimization as well as long-term positive results such as economic justice for all as well as the increase of quality of software or hardware products, the progression of computing and scientific research, and all other scientific fields where computers are used. Hence, what naturally ensues is the advancement of science, medicine, and the quality of life worldwide.

On the other hand, globalization does incur some short-term adverse effects as well, such as the loss of a plethora of jobs in a local national market where previously workers enjoyed a monopoly of employment at usually high wage rates. For instance, millions of jobs have been lost in the North American markets. However, as mentioned earlier, optimistic point of view is that from an economic perspective according to the comparative advantage theory, globalization of the IT industry along with offshoring are necessary conditions for the greater well-being; they benefit worldwide employment, commerce, and profitability. They act as catalysts increasing international trade; making possible long-term economic viability, stability, and prosperity while steadily building the wealth of nations and people involved in the global IT industry around the world.

The countries with the most work offered and accomplished offshore are first and foremost the United States closely followed by the United Kingdom and the well-developed countries in Western Europe, such as Germany, France, and the economically prosperous countries in Asia, such as Japan, South Korea, and even Australia.

The recipient countries of the work offshored have low-cost wages and due to special geographic or demographic characteristics they are the best candidates for undertaking the work. For example, countries such as India and China, which have a very deep pool of talented workers highly educated in universities of the United States and Western Europe, are prime candidates for offshoring.

Another example pertains to countries with language specialization, such as India, which can easily serve the English-speaking world, and the Philippines, where bilingual workers in English and Spanish can offer customer care to the North and Latin American markets.

A further example pertains to countries with a close proximity to the country of origin of the work contracted. This close proximity makes possible for the recipients of the work a better understanding of the work, language, customs, and culture of their customers. In this category, examples include countries such as Canada which can undertake work from the U.S. market and the Czech Republic which can undertake work from the German market.

Furthermore, another example pertains to countries with a unique expertise in a specialized high-end sector such as Israel which enjoys a local deep pool of highly skilled HR and the ensuing contribution of very talented scientists in computer security, antispam, and antivirus software.[38]

Apple is a good example of an international corporation with truly global operations. One of their flourishing product lines includes the iPod music players, which bear an inscription saying designed by Apple in California, made in China. Another very successful product line includes the power book laptop computers, which bear an inscription saying designed by Apple in California, made in Taiwan.

In synopsis, the globalization of the computing field and IT industry has become a reality and in this new market of global competition, the corporations and individuals, who will emerge successful are the ones that embrace and enthusiastically pursue the leading edge of technology, are gifted with innovative thinking, and can offer new ideas in the field of computing and in the IT industry.

In this chapter, we examined issues related to international management, from international HR and labor issues to practical matters to the evolution of corporate organizational formats and applications of IT in international management. We also tried to point out the fact that corporate structures and usage of HR have moved during the past 50 years from a model that resembles a military-type organization to a model, which is much more fluid, flexible, and adaptive to all the diverse environments the corporation operates. This was possible only after the world achieved a borderless IT state.

The following chapter, given that today "all business is global" operating within a corporate governance environment, is a "capstone" one and summarizes essential characteristics of a corporation. The characteristics described in the next chapter refer to (1) the creative, (2) the consumer-based, (3) the HR-centered, (4) the IT, and (5) the ethical corporation.

CHAPTER 9

Capstone: Global Business Challenges

In General

This chapter discusses the elements of today's global corporation that are central to the enterprise of the 21st century: What are these elements, why are they important, why do they constantly change, how do they function within the corporate framework, and what are the challenges they present? In this chapter, which assumes an understanding of the previous parts of this book, we attempt to answer these questions and connect them with notions, such as corporate culture, philosophy, ethics, governance, technology, and so on. At the end, guidelines on preparation of any corporate governance document and concerns about the employee of the global corporation are addressed.

After many years at the corporate helm, business leaders express their life experiences and advice in a less technocratic, more ordinary, and prudent way. Following are some examples of "the best advice (they) ever got":[1]

- You are right not because others agree with you, but because your facts are right (Warren Buffett, CEO of Berkshire Hathaway).
- Make a fool of yourself. Otherwise you won't survive (Richard Branson, Founder of the Virgin Group).
- Recognize the skills and traits you don't possess, and hire the people who have them (Howard Schultz, Chairman of Starbucks)
- Have the courage to stick with a tough job (A. G. Lafley, Chairman and CEO of Procter & Gamble).

- Follow your own instincts, not those of people who see the world differently (Sumner Redstone, Chairman and CEO of Viacom).
- Be yourself (Jack Welch, Former Chairman and CEO of General Electric).
- Don't listen to naysayers (Sallie Krawcheck, CFO of Citigroup).
- Don't limit yourself by past expectations (Vivek Paul, President and CEO of Wipro Technologies)
- All you really own are ideas and the confidence to write them down (Brian Brazer, Academy Award and TV producer)
- Get good—or get out (Peter Drucker, Business consultant)
- Balance you work with your family (David Neelman, CEO of JetBlue)
- Keenly visualize the future (Klaus Kleinfeld, CEO of Siemens)
- Respect people for what they are, not for what their titles are (Herb Kelleher, Founder and Chairman of Southwest Airlines).
- You can learn from anyone (Clayton Christensen, Professor, Harvard Business School).
- Do what you love (Ted Koppel, ABC Nightline Anchor).

Let's get back to any enterprise. This author believes that *in the future the world will focus more on the business activities and will be less ethnocentric. In the global village the "tribe" or the "nation" may continue to give an individual cultural identity, but we already witnessed an additional cultural identity that relates him or her to the activity(ies) he or she preferred to associate his or her business enterprising.*[2]

For most part of the human history, it was philosophical tenants that outlined our beliefs in terms of purpose, ego satisfaction, or social fabric. Only in the past 100 years, the enterprise, as we know it today, presented its vitality, structure, and challenges. Therefore, in the future, a great deal of *attention should be focused toward balancing the individual's mental, emotional, and philosophical development against the classic business motiva-tor, which is materially based.*

> "The ability to demand high performance without being heartless has been part of GE for a long time."
>
> Jeff Immelt, GE[3]

The overall "happiness," self-actualization, and development of the employee should be a central managerial concern. It is worth mentioning that the previous advices of distinguished business leaders focus on the human development itself. This is particularly pertinent for global operations where self-actualization and cultural knowledge will enhance the understanding, promote business efficiencies, and avoid potential cultural clashes.

In the future it is business that will bear the main responsibility for economic development, progress, human happiness, research, education, health, and employment, not national or supranational efforts. Since all business nowadays is already global, annual sales of some corporations are often significantly larger than the gross domestic products of nations and their per employee output is many times higher than the gross national product (GNP) per capita even of the most advanced nations.

In the sections that follow we analyze essential dimensions of any operation beyond those discussed in the second part of this book. They are central to the corporate success in the ever-changing global environment. Such dimensions deal with the following:

- The continuous R&D, leading to a creative enterprise.
- A consumer-based corporate philosophy.
- A corporate structure that is centered on the individual.
- Capitalizing on information technology (IT) and the society of knowledge.
- The adaptive and ethical corporate governance.

It is obvious that, to some degree, the above dimensions overlap and interrelate.

The Creative Enterprise

During the past 100 years the existence of patents or registered corporate logos were giving unique market advantages to the holder of these patents or logos. Indeed, there exist many agreements, starting from the Madrid Convention to the Paris Agreements, protecting these business rights. However, in the 21st century the business landscape changes. Consumers demand ultralight multifunctional cellular phones or Google services. Were they in existence 25 years ago? No! How and why these products are now in prominence? Why the three major automotive U.S. companies, rulers of the U.S. market, allowed newcomers to set and profit in their own backyard? Innovation, creativity, and research from less complacent companies is the answer.

> "An innovative product can last three to four years at most. You need to do continuous research."
>
> Fabrizio Lori, CEO Nuova Pansac
> 16th European "Hot Growth" Company 2005[4]

In the 21st century continuous renewal has become the element of progress and the innate feature of the corporate culture. However, and at a global level, we listen that "companies in the U.S., Europe, and Japan are struggling with innovation. Despite spending huge sums on R&D, most corporations have dismally low levels of innovation productivity. The brutal truth is that up to 96% of all new projects fail to meet or beat targets for return on investment."[5]

Known companies like Procter & Gamble or General Electric already understand that the "Knowledge Economy" is being eclipsed by the "Creativity Economy," effectively raising creativity to the core of business competence.[6] The consumer, investor, employee, or any other corporate stakeholder should see any business undertaking with admiration and beyond expectations. He should see that creativity is deeply rooted in the corporate DNA and that the company faces the global challenges foreseeing the changes and implementing solutions before they emerge.

"Creativity and imagination applied in business context is innovation. We are measuring GE's top leaders on how imaginative they are. Imaginative leaders are the ones who have the courage to fund new ideas, lead teams to discover better ideas, and lead people to take more educated risks."

Jack Welch,[7] Former GE President

To some extent, innovation becomes the core of creativity. There are innovations, we call them macro-innovations, which affect whole industries and can be used from any business in the industry to improve performance, use new technologies, and market better products. At the same time, micro-innovations at the individual corporate level create unique competitive advantages to companies that embrace this thinking in their corporate culture. Companies, such as DaimlerChrysler, Pfizer, Ford Motor, Toyota, Siemens, and so forth, invest billions of dollars annually in R&D. The existence of a corporate culture allowing creativity and continuous innovation demands corporate agility to adjust and structure itself as a "centerless corporation."[8] The following steps outline the creation of a creative company:

- Think out-of the-box. Research institutions, universities, conferences, competitors, trade shows, consultants and, sometimes, sound internal thinking may provoke creativity. However, in general, we have to avoid in-group thinking, if we believe that new knowledge is essential.

- Existence of a corporate board and a leader that believes in creativity. Here is a caveat: Creativity necessitates change. People do not like change. Expect a "revolution" and get ready to face it. The established status quo will try to avoid the new thinking, ideas, processes, influences. Get ready to change positions of directors, structures, or rewards.

- Implementation goes from the consumer toward the research lab. Not the opposite. As with any reverse engineering effort, a well-prepared and time-bound plan and specialized educational efforts are imperative.

We must mention that for creativity we do not need to expect the "large" corporation to spearhead the effort. As MIT professor David Birch showed in the 1980s, the small- and medium-sized companies offer more to economic growth than the large ones. A proof of that are the 500 top "hot growth" European companies that created 130,000 new employment opportunities from 2001 through 2005.[9]

The Consumer-Based Company

In the previous section as well as in Chapter 6, we implied that the creative enterprise should focus on the consumer. The company develops unique marketing mixes to satisfy his or her needs. These marketing mixes are products of in-depth global research. In a multicultural, ever-changing global business arena we need to be creative and adaptive to gain and retain the global consumer. We are not in a production or a sales era anymore, neither are we in the safety of our well-protected home market.

Why are new business icons appearing and old ones seizing to exist? How a small supermarket in Bentonville, Arkansas (Wal-Mart), within 50 years, become the largest business entity in the world? How a food chain can enter in a market thousands of miles away from its home and displace traditional local restaurants with a simple pizza?

To a great extent the old marketing principles apply: Understand the consumer and offer value. Another reason is name recognition and continuous efforts to keep this recognition growing. Coca-Cola is still considered the most valuable brand in the world, and Apple computers has the largest annual change in the value of its brand for 4 years running.[10] Moreover, we need to see that the world is changing rapidly, the trade barriers are gone, and the global consumer can be approached through a variety of media. We must have foresight of these changes, the willingness to undertake risks, readiness for speedy actions, and ability to categorize our marketing options.

Let's discuss one aspect of the marketing mix, product. Annual Designs Awards[11] assist us to visualize this challenge. Some of the successful products have personality like a simple pair of inexpensive, Indian-made sandals or an elegant coffeemaker. Others have tactical advantages like merging in a single palm-size apparatus, a camcorder, camera, MP3 player, webcam and voice recorder, or offering a showerhead that adapts to different uses. More categories can be designed according to the consumers' psychography, targeting the product design to elegance, "ripple effects," image enhancement, and so on. Attention: *We must examine the consumer in every market. The emerging markets may have more potential than the saturated ones.*

Another aspect of the marketing mix is price. Unquestionably, some markets will buy the $200,000 Bentleys and Ferraris. However, local manufacturers in Brazil and India will sell their $3,000 automobiles and the French Renault will invest in the Romanian Dacia $600 million to be able to produce a $5,000 vehicle for the emerging markets.[12]

Let's observe distribution channels. At least in the beginning close cooperation between the host and home partners is necessary. For example, when Metro, the German supermarket giant, entered into the Vietnam market, customers were unwilling to approach the stores in fear of the security personnel. Replacing them with ladies wearing the traditional ao dai dress sufficed to overcome this obstacle. In the same market they changed their practice of offering wrapped-in-plastic products as the customers wanted to touch, feel, and smell their food.[13]

The HR-Centered Corporation

In Chapter 8, we discussed the human resource (HR) needs of the global corporation and we studied different company structures. One of these structures is based on what we called centerless organization, or what others may discuss as an antiorganizational design. This is an efficient and adaptive corporate structure that caters to the needs of today's fast-changing business world, products offered, technology needed, or markets served. Enterprising is very important in a multicultural environment requiring sensitivities and understanding of all stakeholders, owners, employees, customers, suppliers, and so on. To do so *the HR available are of paramount importance. Organizations must be able to mutate according to presented realities, immediately sense and adjust to any organizational "ripple effects," and take advantage of opportunities as soon as possible.*

Andrew Gould, CEO of Schlumberger Ltd, an oil-field services giant in 80 countries, says that "the capacity to develop talent from anywhere in the world is one of our key strengths" and capitalizes on a corporate data-base that marries HR information concerning people's past performance and salary with each of the workers curriculum vitae.[14]

Byrnes says that "the secret of every high-performing company is great people—and that there aren't enough stars to go around."[15] Talent development is crucial to business success and tens of billions of dollars are spent annually to develop the managerial skills needed. At the same time HR incompetence is a major reason that results in losing the corporate competitive advantage. John Kenneth Galbraith writes that " ...as regards the modern great and often bureaucratic corporation there [is] more to be feared from incompetence than from market power."[16]

> "Talent should be a weapon and should be used as a weapon.… But it is amazing how little attention companies put into this"
> Marc Effron, VP for talent management at Avon Products[17]

Here are some following thoughts on personnel development:

- *Track the performance of the people a manager promotes. If they don't do well, the manager is failing.*
- Focus more time on natural strengths of the company's HR. Research shows that the best managers spend 80% of their time trying to amplify their people's strengths. Copy them.
- Drive hard toward solving recruiting and training needs. Good talent can be imported at a significant price and often helps to think out-of-the-box. However, the best companies grow their talent in-house.[18]
- *Understand the quality, experience, and potential cost savings from part-timers.* Treat them well.[19]
- Capitalize on host HR talent and expatriates. They know well the foreign realities, they are enterprising, and they are well-priced.
- Great people are balanced people. *Consider spending money not only for their professional development, but also for their personal enhancement. The materially based motivation does not satisfy the self-actualization criteria that mature people seek.*[20]
- Motivate HR according to own dispositions. Most people are motivated by material-based incentives. Some others are

seeking higher level satisfaction from their work environment, for example, self-actualization or "forgetting" themselves in a work-related function.

- Consider a variety of "perks" according to the workforce preferences. Individual "happiness" and "good life" factors play a key role. According to *Fortune,* Google ranks number one for 2007 among the 100 top companies. Part of its philosophy is that "home is where the perks are. Googlers can climb, play beach volley, lift weights, and go for a dip—without ever leaving work."[21]

- Carefully screen the leaders and the persons in command. They are responsible for market opportunities, business growth, talent development, and corporate social responsibility. They must be knowledgeable, experienced, and prudent. They must be able to see the whole picture of the enterprise and keep things in perspective—it has been reported that "once a second somewhere in the universe a star explodes with the brilliance of an entire galaxy."[22]

- Seek talented people and retain them. They can create opportunities and motivate the whole organization. In those cases a forced distribution appraisal method of the employees, with predetermined percentages of success (like grading on a curve), might be an appropriate solution. Often major organizations employ such approaches though similar systems are unforgiving and many HR managers are skeptical about them.

> Start young.
>   Ted Turner, Founder of CNN[23]

Global companies should carefully examine HR cost issues in relationship to expected benefits and implications from their multicultural realities. The Irish software developer, for example, maybe significantly more expensive than his Indian counterpart, however by accepting a cost increase he maybe in a better position to serve his customer needs. This is a challenge for the HR departments, which, in addition, need to study, as we discussed in the chapter on management perspectives, educational, IT, and cultural compatibility of future employees. There are also generational gaps, for example, a belief shift from altruistic self-sacrificing to ego-centered motivation. Similar shifts are expected to affect corporate culture stability, especially at the subsidiary level, often on the grounds of local unemployment, politics, and education, for employing people who are not coming from the host countries (guest workers and expatriates).[24]

At the core of sending appropriate personnel to specific positions all around the world is the corporate ability to offer sensible and agreeable accommodations and logistics support. HR departments must be able to foresee and handle (having all necessary cultural sensitivities) all aspects of practical issues, from schooling of an expatriate's children to funeral arrangements. Specialized companies can be used for outsourcing some of these details, using companies like Extended Stay America in the United States or the Ascott Group in Singapore.[25]

The bottom line of the global corporation is its employees and, therefore, the HR department has the most critical role, especially, in the areas of recruiting, evaluation, and training. However, the world's practices with respect to the employment and laws are changing over time. The global corporation has to adapt accordingly.[26]

The IT Company

> Technology makes the weak strong.
>
> Michael Wolff[27]

In a previous section on "The Creative Enterprise," we said that advanced companies already understand that the "Knowledge Economy" is being eclipsed by the "Creativity Economy." We have already addressed issues with respect to corporate creativity. But what happened with the knowledge factor on which the creativity is based?

The "Knowledge Economy" relates to IT. From the moment a baby is born to the age he will be able to vote, the amount of available usable information will have at least quadrupled. As a society we need an appropriate method to constructively utilize all these data and knowledge.

Business, facing similar challenges, has an increasingly important role in the societal improvement and welfare.

A strategic advantage of today's global business relates to the way it administers all data, from accounting to personnel to R&D to marketing, through the use of enterprise resource planning systems (ERP). Not only IT in its classical sense, but industry-specific developments, from bio- to nanotechnologies, offer to business unique competitive advantages.[28] Professor Alfred Chandler says the "The most important difference—and this has been happening since 1880s—is the continuing transformation of big business by high-technology firms."[29]

> "Paper isn't a big part of my day… We're finally getting close to what I call the digital workstyle."
>
> Bill Gates[30]

The company needs to remain competitive by being aware of the global developments in its industry. It is not sufficient anymore to participate in global trade shows, learning cutting-edge lessons from competitors, or to manually seek industry developments from embassies or trade journals. *It is necessary to have the appropriate search engines and transcribe information to knowledge.[31] The IT world goes beyond national borders. There are very few knowledge barriers in the Internet era. The company is unable to monitor global industry changes if it does not have active systems to handle data and knowledge.*

There is a caveat though … as with any kind of technology, IT has to be weighed against the "liability of foreigners," where global corporations are facing functional issues with respect to local business concerns.[32] This usually happens when global corporations aim to capitalize on the host countries IT human capital and knowledge, and starting subsidiary facilities based on cost-cutting concerns. Normally, appropriate licensing agreements suffice, as in the case of India.

> "To organize the world's information and to make it universally accessible and useful"
>
> Google's stated mission[33]

From a practical perspective, *IT can be used in all functional areas of business enterprising*. For example, in the HR area IT greatly assists in delivering the HR "Scoreboard," a measurement system that uses quantitative standards or "metrics" to measure HR activities, therefore highlighting the causal relationship between HR activities, the emergent employee behaviors, and the resulting firm-wide strategic outcomes and performance. In fact, IT can improve HR productivity, self-service, and outsourcing, significantly lowering staff-to-employee ratios, training and career growth options, dissemination of corporate values and HR policies, and so on.[34]

Beyond cost-cutting and legalistic issues, at a global level, we are bracing for an era of IT usage. Information overload can be confusing. Information quality is essential and a vital building block of any enterprise. Poor quality of information will ruin the competitive chances of our corporation. All controllable and uncontrollable business areas are affected by information, information quality, and the technology that mines this information. This applies to accounting, finance, management, marketing, and the environment, in general. We need to walk in an efficient way through millions of pieces of information and examine only those that are pertinent. We need to be very focused on the issue at hand and see as it changes, over time, the business landscape. Take, for example, the radio frequency identification (RFID). A few years ago retailers were happy with barcodes. Now, they are able to retrieve and use, through RFID, a lot more critical information. The development potentially affects billions of users. The example with RFID is typical: Identifying the implementation venues of the new technology and its potential future use in all its societal applications is a challenge in itself that requires understanding of philosophy, civic designs, human psychography, and so many other concerns that necessitate executive motivation at the self-actualization level.

Today's borderless world expedites technology diffusion, every kind of technology, and vice versa. As Professor Aggarwal says, the technology revolution facilitates the globalization of business, and the globalization of business makes technology more profitable and innovations faster.[35] Innovations appear and innovation awards are proposed everywhere covering from the development of *automated DNA synthesis* to Internet file-sharing and telephony using *peer-to-peer technology* to the *commercialization of the wind energy* and *hydrogen-based fossil fuel alternatives* to *multipurpose cell phones*, kind of "remote controls for life," able not only to communicate, take pictures or bring the latest news, but also to monitor health or to be passports, act as burglar alarms, or as weapons.[36] Globalization and technology are reinforcing each other toward a new social status quo where business will have the paramount role in life quality.

We must also recognize that IT brings an era that, from a marketing perspective, leads to a reversal in traditional roles. Many of the seller's functions are already performed by the buyer who takes full initiative on what to buy, what features to have, when to buy, how to pay for it, and so on. The Internet has advanced purchasing self-dependency and has brought one-to-one marketing, both being very desirable societal objectives. In addition, one-to-one marketing becomes the very essence of identifying the consumer needs, satisfying them, avoiding wasteful production or advertising, and, at the same time, using the least possible human effort, as most activities are realized through automated processes.

The Ethical Business

Alan Greenspan, the ex-Chairman of the Federal Reserve, while accepting the Enron Award for Distinguished Public Service on November 13, 2001, answered a young student's question as follows: *"The best chance of making a big success in this world is to decide from square one that you're going to do it ethically."* That was only a few days after Enron had fallen to disgrace following its glory days and being epitomized as the example of an unethical company. Unhappily for Greenspan, he had agreed to accept the award (but not the honorarium) more than a year in advance.[37] Enron's failed business ethics and corporate collapse were financially disastrous for thousands of investors and employees.

We are facing sweeping changes in the global arena of business. The era of the corporations is *ante portas* while, at the same time, we are witnessing diminishing power and effectiveness of national governments. The new player, the multinational global corporation, is taking on a significantly responsible role for quality of life, education, societal growth, and research and development. This new player, which often has more annual revenue than the GDP of whole nations, evolves within certain cultural environments but develops its own culture, as has happened in the past with nations. As a result, *corporations face unprecedented ethical challenges, which in essence determine the limits of their corporate social responsibility*[38] *and value-based responsiveness behaviors.* These behaviors should aim to reverse present narrow-sighted business decision making and be responsive to long-term life sustainability demands. Human "happiness," industrial emissions control, eco-friendly practices, fuel-efficiency, and "green" thinking are typical applications of these business behaviors.

Visionaries of the past, including science fiction writers, could not have foreseen the impact that modern business is having on national cultures. Perhaps these effects resulted from advancements in IT, which are leveling the competitive playing field of global business. Today's business operates in an almost seamless manner, being able to detect even the slightest "ripple effects" on its operating environments. However, society faces the risk of a new techno-bureaucracy.[39] In today's world, all business is global, and it has defined behavioral norms, educational standards, research rules, and economic growth methodologies. We would hope that global business will soon enable every human to enjoy reasonable living standards.

Unhappily *business evolved so quickly that it was not possible to set up control processes to assure that business will operate ethically.* The example of Enron typifies this failure.

Parmalat, a European firm, is another example of corporate unethical behavior, which seems to exist everywhere—to the point that many perceive using the word ethics in the same phrase with business (e.g., business ethics), as an oxymoron. For others, defining business ethics is of major challenge. There is always the danger that *business may become a quasi-dictator of human and nonhuman development, which is at risk when potential conflicts arise between social welfare and corporate mission.* Resolving such issues is a great challenge for global corporations in the future. Business operating domains must accommodate all stakeholders: employees, customers, owners, and the environment in general. Business must strive to enhance the emotional and intellectual development of all people in a way that is mindful of the nonhuman environment.

Business sets its organizational mission within cultural constraints. These limitations, different for each operation, are based on unique philosophical tenets that delineate acceptable parameters for corporate codes of ethics.

It should be said that organizational mission statements are teleological in nature. For instance, consider the ethical question of whether to drop an atomic bomb on Japan to end the war; if so, at what cost? Similarly, business objectives might have peripheral costs to stakeholders. Business objectives must be reached using ethically acceptable means. A major Las Vegas gambling casino would establish its code of ethics differently than would a nonprofit religious organization in Oklahoma. Both organizations will achieve greater success in reaching objectives by having specified understandable philosophical and cultural frameworks for corporate governance.

To build an ethical company, clear philosophical tenets should dominate every aspect of its corporate cultural and operating behaviors. Corporate vision goes through a "tunnel" with at least four sides or dimensions: customers, employees, owners, and responsibilities to the societal environment. Each side of the tunnel is positioned according to the ethical tolerance of corporate philosophy. Consequently, it is of paramount importance to express corporate governance philosophy, operating rules, the limits of ethical behavior, and the implementation processes of the corporation in a clearly written and widely distributed policy and procedure manuals. Implementing societal-friendly "best practices" alone will not demonstrate the cultural predisposition of a corporation. A carefully considered corporate philosophy will contribute to more effective business ethics practices, manageable corporate cultures, and practical governance implementation processes.

Moreover, it is important to understand that *business philosophy and ethics are affected by the area of application.* For example, assume that the overall intent of the corporation is to prohibit the employment of underage children by any company supplier. However, an ethical dilemma arises in a society where the only bread-earners are children. Many other such examples can be cited. Such challenges should be addressed with prudence, maturity, knowledge, plus elements of self-actualization. The utilization of these features of wisdom will determine the characteristics of successful global corporate management that will, in part, define the future of human quality of life.

A few final and summarizing thoughts are in order. First, *even within a culture there is no uniform set of "ethics."* One might see something as ethical but another might not. To that extent we might face ethical "clashes" in global business because of differences in the cultural environments. What is ethical in one culture may not be ethical in others. Then, *corporate "cultures" may conflict with ethical conduct at the local operating level*.[40] Finally, at the macroeconomic levels, one can see that *different political systems might handle the issue of ethics according to their overall position*.[41]

Developing a Governance Document for Any Corporation

The creative, ethical, HR-based, marketing-based, IT enterprise will all be parts of the central core of the future business. As in the past, business organizations must be managed. Businesses are systems. To be functional, they must follow general contentions which work as frameworks of reference in developing the specific rules of corporate ethics, governance, and the respective operations manual.

Companies operate within these rules. These rules are developed by the senior managers, the "elders" of the corporation. There exists a revision process for the rules, but, until the next revision, manuals and processes should be treated as the "constitution" of the enterprise. No one is allowed to bend the rules. People must follow them; they cannot change course midway. The general contentions that apply to these rules can be classified in certain categories:

- *Practical utility:* Real, practical, specific objectives must be met at the end. Overtheorizing is not an objective. The corporate mission is the final objective.
- *Operational validity:* To validate results, the company must consistently measure the results of process implementation against desired yardsticks and through a valid methodology. It should be done in a transparent way. During the implementation process legal and ethics codes must be respected. Continuing feedback is expected.
- *Control and penalties:* The rules should aim to identify and point to all wrongdoings and cases that do not meet the

expected standards and to impose "penalties," if necessary. Feedback should be recorded to allow, in due time, further refinement of the rules. To be successful a well-developed accounting system is necessary.

- *Long-term application:* Corporate governance rules are devised to exist for a long time. They are not developed to handle a specific crisis. They must be flexible and capable to conform to situational changes.

- *In-depth understanding of environmental demands:* Companies operate in a variety of environments with different ethical and legal prescriptions. Corporate governance documents should develop appropriate guidelines for all situations. That's why it is necessary to be drafted by highly experienced and senior executives. These rules have to be broad in nature and adaptable to environmental and industry-wide changes. They should not define specific actions, for example, volunteer assistance to handicapped persons.

- *Appropriate preparation:* These rules must come out of in-depth study of corporate past experiences. All types and levels of stakeholders should offer their insights and normative suggestions. To achieve in-depth understanding of their needs, operation, and performance, appropriate preparation is in order. Focus-group interviews and a comprehensive plan with exact timelines are necessary. Corporate experience in implementing related matters, such as ERP applications, sensitivity training, and so forth, will enhance the chances of success in devising a corporate governance document. Full support from the top management is a prerequisite.

- *Consciousness of actions decided:* This category primarily applies to the individuals who will be in charge of developing the governance documents. They should be proponents of the values that this document implies. They should firmly believe in them. Their life should mirror the actions pointed by the final documents and all their personal influencers, including wives, families, mass media, and friends should see that these individuals adhere to these value systems.

Concerns: Thinking of the Future
of the Corporate Employee

We extensively discussed in this book about the environment, structure, and challenges of the global corporation. But what about its most important element, its employee? Has he or she adjusted to the life style, demands, and social structures of the future? Is he or she going to be happy? Are there any deficiencies in the psychic nature of the modern man that might restrict his societal future role? What are the implications due to the existence of social (like the "death of the family," we saw earlier), cultural, generational, and IT gaps among employees of a global corporation? What are the implications when this man (or woman), after faithfully and forcefully serving his company for years, is forced to leave, faces a psychological breach of contract, sees his or her company merging or downsizing and his or her job devalued? Will he or she survive?[42]

It seems that within the "developed" world, often today's "business executive" "flows" within the predetermined molds of social acceptance. The "new media society" and the technology imposed on him, to a great extent, predetermines his or her social behavior, how many hours he or she will spend at work, in front of the TV, in front of his or her computer, his or her intangible activities, recreation, enjoyment, studies, choices, self-development, social interactions, cooperation, and social offering. This man rarely moves outside the accepted norms (the mold), or, reacts, demands change, participates to a revolution. He or she is a faceless "happy" representative of a "material" world that teaches him or her about reason of existence, objectives, and what fun and future is. Intangible sensors direct him toward group thinking. He or she does not use his or her own senses in an era of virtual realities. He or she believes in them. There is very little room for self-actualization.

> Each person is unique in talent, history, and temperament, and is called to develop these gifts for the benefit of self and others.
>
> Father Timothy J. Cusick[43]

He or she lives in an era where critical thinking is a must but difficult to be integrated in the techno-bureaucracies that surround him or her. Consider how this book started: Philosophy, culture, corporate culture, knowledge, and truth. People do not spend much time around those notions anymore. They should. Otherwise, the modern man will approach an era of culture/IT-based middle ages that will reduce the human potential of free thinking, of hope outside predetermined molds. The global corporation and the social system will offer to this man the material means of happy survival, but is this enough? What about the individual's self-actualization potential?

Epilogue

Teaching and practicing global business, primarily in the United States and Europe, I witnessed an intriguing phenomenon: The evolution of the traditional role of business enterprising from a purely profit-centered one to one that added a dimension of societal responsibility and responsiveness. To some extent, today's business consciously undertakes governmental roles of economic growth, life quality, research, health, and education. Business entities become quasi-nations of the past, sometime larger than them, with their own corporate cultures and philosophies, ethic codes, governance processes, and bureaucracies.

Our world is a global business puzzle with conflicting priorities and potential civilization clashes. The majority of businesses still cater to regional markets with managerial aim toward homogeneity and avoidance of intergroup conflicts. Large companies continue to exist while others merge,[1] catering to the needs of global stakeholders and to varying host-country objectives. In the borderless world of the 21st century, shareholders, employees, customers, and technologies can be mined from everywhere, producing great enterprising incentives for thousands of companies and impressive benefits to their employees. Still some nations, with relatively homogeneous ethnic backgrounds and after becoming entrepreneurial, succeed to provide a fine life quality to their people, achieving global prominence in their particular fields.[2]

Nevertheless we believe that the future societal fabric, research, education, and life quality belongs to the large corporate entities that will also be responsible for a majority percent of the global GNP. The present national entities and their governing bodies will play a lesser role. We believe that meritocracy, not democracy, will be a better proposition for our planetary future. Therefore, well-developed, fair, and human-oriented corporate governance will be the necessary conditions in the era of global business and corporate governance.

Recall the following statement, as mentioned in the Preface: "Prudent people, like Mahatma Gandhi, taught us that one must become as humble as dust before he can discover truth." We indicated that humans should have simple desires and self-actualization objectives.

After addressing issues about geography, culture, philosophy, truth, 21st century realities, the externalities to the corporate environment, perspectives of accounting, finance, management and marketing, we discussed specific elements of the global corporation and its governance, social objectives, and concerns about today's employee.

Unquestionably, today's employees can enjoy far more economic means than their counterparts 20 years ago. However, this "happiness" is usually material based since the traditional business motivator—the reward for success—is also material based. Sometimes it is even an illusion of a "good life" that includes bigger homes and faster cars, yachts and cosmetic surgery. Humility is not always consistent with the material-based desires. Neither is freedom, happiness, or sense of fulfillment. To some extent the employee, and therefore most human beings, are trapped in a business mold that allows little room for self-actualization or for achieving personal objectives without compromising their principles. I worry that because of our enterprising during the last 30 years we witnessed a rapid change of social values, learning habits, and mental fixations. This happens through totally illusionary animation cultures affecting the behaviors of even the very young. Also, it happens through questionable media practices and blogging-(encyclo)peadia fora. Trusting our own senses, having simple life desires, or using local cultural teachings for host-country development is often iconoclastic and against the accepted norms. Traditional formal learning institutions, like universities, are in a transitional state in their effort to meet the global educational challenges in an era of reduced human and financial resources.

I worry because our business-propelled, IT/media world might lead us to a new era of culture/IT-based middle ages.[3]

Wise, prudent, knowledgeable, ethical, enlightened corporate leaders are needed.

If they are successful, they will be the equivalent of the good kings and governors of the past.

We need to preselect, breed, and train this new quad of individuals or identify ways to bring them forward and put them in command of the business structures of the future.

About the Author

John Thanopoulos studied in Greece, France, and
England before receiving his doctoral degree in Marketing from the University of Arkansas, in the United
States. He started his career as a business practitioner
having achieved more than $25,000,000 in sales by the
age of 26. Eventually, however, he joined the academe
and, in 1983, the University of Akron in Ohio as a
Director of the International Business Programs where he also taught
Marketing and International Business. During his academic life he
received various awards and recognitions, such as:

- World Education Congress, Best Professor in International
  Business (2012).
- The editors of the *Internationalizing the Business School: Global
  Survey of Institutions of Higher Learning,* acknowledged him as
  one of the six "early pioneers" of these studies (2000).
- University of Akron, College of Business, Teaching
  Innovation Award (1997).
- University of Akron, College of Business, Publication Award
  (1997).
- Distinguished Sales and Marketing Executives Award,
  Presented by Sales and Marketing Executives of Akron, Inc.,
  February 15, 1994.
- The University of South Carolina awarded him with the
  Academic Achievement Award for Faculty Development for
  his International Business Program (1989).
- University of Akron, College of Business, Teaching Excellence
  Award (1988).
- The Ohio governor honoured The University of Akron with
  the (E) Excellence in Exporting Award in Exporting (1987)
  for his International Business Program.

He also served to various other positions, including Associate Dean for the American College of Greece and co-chair of the Executive Committee of the Greater Akron Export Association.

He has over a 100 academic contributions that have been published in a variety of media, including *Journal of Teaching in International Business, Journal of Economic Integration, Journal of International Business Studies, The International Trade Journal, Issues in International Business, Kyukyo Economic Review, Arkansas Business and Economic Review, Journal of the Academy of Marketing Science, Health Marketing Quarterly, Review of Business, Current Research in Global Business,* editorial volumes, teaching manuals, and so forth.

In 2000 he returned to his homeland, Greece, joining the University of Piraeus, as a Professor of International Business but he continued to teach for the University of Akron and the University of Arkansas until 2007. He has contributed to more than 100 international events, papers, speeches, and related services. Presently, he is the Vice Chair of the Department of Business Administration.

His books in Greek (published by Interbooks, Athens) are in international business (2002, 2006, 2012; 2007, in English), ship management (coauthored, 2005), business ethics (2003 and 2009), and self-actualization perspectives of the international manager (coauthored with 185 of his fall 2009 students, electronic format, 2010). In 2013 Fedimos published the third editions of his books *Global Business* and *Business Ethics*.

Notes

Preface

1. The academic field of international (often called global) business emerged only after WWII. The Academy of International Business (AIB) started monitoring international business curricula since the late 1960s, through a series of studies, usually every four years. Vern Terpstra, John Daniels, Lee Radebaugh, Robert Gross, John Thanopoulos, Reijo Luostarinen, and their colleagues were the pioneer editors of these studies. *See* Arpan and Kwok (2001), p. 4.
2. Ranging from research and development to employee happiness.
3. Goodman (1999), p. 421.

Chapter 1

1. *Scientific American*, August (2011), (edition on "Questions about the Multiverse: What lies beyond the cosmic horizon of 42 billion light-years").
2. Naturally, a comparison between corporate revenues and country GNP presents major conceptual shortcomings. Data were retrieved from *Fortune* (European editions, number 10, July 25, 2011 and July 23, 2012) and from the International Monetary Fund, "Report for selected countries and subjects." *International Monetary Fund*, retrieved June 2, 2012. It is understood that data may significantly vary given definitional and source discrepancies and comparability issues. For example, other GNP sources, like United Nations, the World Bank or the CIA Factbook, may vary between them more than 12% (for the same period 2010–2011).
3. Since the reader may not be familiar with the terms, the following depictions are given by the Encyclopaedic edition of the *Lexicon Webster Dictionary*, English-Language Institute of America, Inc., 1977 printing, p. 268 and p. 1009: Deontology, that which is binding or needful; the study of duty or moral obligation. Teleology, the doctrine of final causes; the study of evidence in nature indicating that final causes exist (etc.).
4. "For thy merchants were the great men on earth: for by thy sorceries were all nations deceived" (in King James translation, 18–23).
5. *See* McGregor (1960); Hammer and Champy (1993); Rodriguez, Siegel, Hillman, and Eden (2006).

6. McLuhan (1967); Cooper (1971); Anglemyer et al. (1980); Goleman (1995); Skelly (1995); Donaldson (1996); Dunkelberg and Robin (1998); Pasternack and Viscio (1998); Cappelli (1999); Drucker (2001); Desjardins (2007).

7. Brock (1978); Tuathail, Dalby, and Routledge (2006); Klein (2007).

8. Reich (2007).

9. For the most recent statistics *see* The global 500: The world's largest corporations (2013, July 22), pp. 1–22, *Fortune*.

10. *The Urantia Book* (1955), p. 780. The Urantia Foundation, Chicago, IL.

11. Rand (1964); Drucker (1974); Blackstone (1979); Goodpaster and Sayre (1979); Jacoby (1985); Davidow and Malone (1993); Beauchamp and Bowie (1997); *The Challenges of Corporate Social Responsibility* (2000); Hartman (2002); Anand (2008); Derensky (2014).

12. Accessed on September 1, 2013: www.Canon.Global.

13. Wise (1966, July 1), p. 89. The very private world of Peat, Marwick, Mitchell, *Fortune*.

14. Lyons (2002, April 1), p. 19. Full disclosure, *Forbes Global*.

15. Coggan (2002, June 8–9), p. 18. The tyranny of the benchmarks, *Financial Times*.

16. Bargh (2014), pp. 20–27

Chapter 2

1. Huang, J. H. (1993), p. 103. *Sun-Tzu: The Art of War* (The New Translation), Quill-William Morrow, New York.

2. Webster, Donovan (2002, January), p. 56. China's unknown Gobi Alashan, *National Geographic*.

3. *See* the very impressive development in Dubai at Afshin Molavi's, Dubai: Sudden city, *National Geographic* (2007, January), pp. 94–113. This does not mean that when valuable resources were found people always had the chance for a better living. For the opposite, *see* Tom O' Neil (2007, February), pp. 88–117. Curse of the black gold: Hope and betrayal in the Niger delta, *National Geographic*.

4. Richard Stone (2006, April), p. 38 and 43. The long shadow of Chernobyl, *National Geographic*.

5. Geopolitics: The study of the influence or application of economic and geographic factors upon the politics of a state; *Lexicon Webster Dictionary* (1977), p. 408.

6. Therefore, it is imperative for the new generation of global managers to have a deeper understanding of philosophy, ethics, and self-actualization

perspectives. In university teaching this has been a major concern. For an example, *The Global Manager: Self Actualization Perspectives*, coauthored with 185 of his Fall 2009 students, 1st electronic edition (in Greek), Interbooks, Athens 2010.

7. Stefan Theil (2005, August 8), pp. 42–48. The next petroleum, *Newsweek*.

8. EU is asking, for example, that by 2020, 20% of energy transportation needs to be supplied by alternative resources. *See* James Boxell (2006, November), p. 3. Peers call for tax incentives to boost use of biofuels, *Financial Times*.

9. *See* Chapter 9, Capstone.

10. The ghostly flickers of a new dawn (2006, November), p. 65, *The Economist*.

11. Ed Crooks (2006, November), p. 1. Only 34% support building new nuclear plants, says poll, *Financial Times*.

12. A white-hot elephant (2006, November), p. 67, *The Economist*.

13. Scott Wallace, Last of the Amazon, *National Geographic* (2007, January), pp. 40–71. Also, The greening of America, *The Economist* (2007, January), p. 9. Also, Pete Engardio (2007, January), p. 53. Beyond the green corporation, *Business Week*

14. "The human footprint" is presented at David Quammen (2005, September), pp. 2–35. Views of the continent, *National Geographic*, Volume 208.

15. Stephen Hawking (2001), p. 159. *The Universe in a Nutshell*, Bantam Press, New York.

16. This was stated in one of his books in Greek, *The Industrial Revolution that Did Not Happen* (Sakkoula Publishing, Athens 2004). For his insights about money in antiquity, *see* Vassilis Doukakis (2013). *Money and Banking in Greek Antiquity*, Champaign, Illinois Common Ground Publishing LLC.

17. *Lexicon Webster Dictionary* (1977), p. 246.

18. There are more than 160 definitions of culture...*see* Alfred Kroeber and Clyde Kluckhorn (1985), p. 11. *A Critical Review of Concepts and Definitions*, New York, Random House, found at Michael R. Czinkota, Ilkka A. Ronkainen, and Michael H. Moffet (1996), p. 298. *International Business*, 4th edition, Fort Worth, Texas, The Dryden Press. Conceptually, many people recognize culture as an iceberg presenting what is obvious and what most people cannot see. For an example *see* S. Tamer Cavusgil, Gary Knight, and John S. Riesenberger (2014), p. 121. *International Business: The New Realities*, 3rd edition, Pearson, Boston 2014.

19. "...and demonstrates the value of multilevel techniques in analyzing the effect of cultural entrepreneurship." Erkko Autio, Saurav Pathak, and

Karl Wennberg (2013), p. 334. Consequences of cultural practices for entrepreneurial behaviors, *Journal of International Business Studies,* Volume 4, Number 4.

20. The acceptance of change argument will be further analyzed in the subsection of material culture.
21. Goodman (1999), p. 710.
22. Don Belt (2002, January), p. 82. The world of Islam, *National Geographic.*
23. Goodman (1999), p. 88.
24. Jon Meacham (2013, February 25), p. 42. A papal benediction, *Time.*
25. Goodman (1999), p. 235.
26. *See* its website, www.aacsb.edu or that of the European Foundation of Management Development, www.efmd.edu
27. Morrison (1994), p. 3.
28. Goodman (1999), p. 485.
29. Let's say that culture A people feel ok when others stand next to them within 5 to 10 inches, where culture B people, accustomed to more space, feel uncomfortable if an individual stands in less than 17 inches from them.
30. *See* subsection of this chapter under the title "Cultural imperialism."
31. Fareed Zakaria (2006, March 6), p. 31. India rising, *Newsweek.*
32. Grondova in his typology has defined 20 such areas. *See* A Cultural Typology of Economic Development, pp. 44–55, at Harrison, Lawrence E., and Samuel P. Huntington (2000), *Culture Matters: How Values Shape Human Progress,* Basic Books, New York.
33. Harrison and Huntington (2000), pp. 296–307.
34. Leung Kwok. Rabi S. Bhagat, Nancy R. Buchan, Miriam Erez, and Christina B. Gibson (2005), p. 359. Culture and international business: Recent advances and their implications for future research, *Journal of International Business Studies,* Volume 36, Issue 4.
35. Samuel Huntington (2001). *The Clash of Civilizations and the Remaking of the World Order,* 4th edition, Terzo Books, Athens, Greece.
36. Kroeber and Kluckhorn (1985); Morrison, Conaway, and Borden (1994).
37. Garreau, Joel (1981). *The Nine Nations of North America,* Avon, New York.
38. Goodman (1999), p. 183.
39. London under attack (2005, July 9), pp. 9, 26, 62, *The Economist.* Evan Thomas and Stryker McGuire (2005, July 18), pp. 14–22. Terror at rush hour, *Newsweek.*
40. Samuel Huntington (2001), pp. 23–24, 53–54. *The Clash of Civilizations and the Remaking of the World Order,* 4th edition, Terzo Books, Athens, Greece.
41. Melinda Liu (2006, April 24), p. 20. War of wills, *Newsweek.*
42. Owen Matthews (2006, December 11), pp. 34–36. Who lost Turkey?, *Newsweek.*

Chapter 3

1. *See* Chapter 9, section on the "Ethical Business."
2. These definitions have been taken from *Lexicon Webster Dictionary* (1977), p. 712.
3. Jacques Thiroux (1998), p. 2. *Ethics: Theory and Practice*, 6th edition, Prentice-Hall, Upper Saddle River, NJ.
4. *Lexicon Webster Dictionary* (1977), p. 1061.
5. Special issue, supplement of *Forbes ASAP* (2000, October 2). What is true.
6. Freiburghouse (2000), pp. 37, 46, 49, 56, 66, 236, 273.
7. *See* Chapter 8, Management Perspectives.
8. Nabil A. Imbrahim and Faramarz Parsa (2005, Winter), p. 28. Corporate responsiveness orientation: Are there differences between U.S. and French managers?, *Review of Business*, Volume 26, Issue 1.
9. Marshalll McLuhan (1967), pp. 320–321. *La Galaxie Gutenberg Face a l'Ere Electronique*, 2nd French edition, Mame, Paris, France.
10. *See* Mike McNamee, Amy Borus, and Christopher Palmeri (2002, April 8), pp. 78–79. Out of control at Andersen, *BusinessWeek*. Wendy Zellner and Stephanie Forest Anderson (2002, January 28), p. 42. A hero—and a smoking-gun letter, *BusinessWeek*. Also, in the same issue, Bruce Nussbaum, Can you trust anybody anymore, pp. 39–40 and Joseph Weber, et al., Can Andersen survive, pp. 46–47 and Byrnes, Nanette, et al., Accounting in crisis, pp. 50–54.
11. *Lexicon Webster Dictionary* (1977), p. 337.
12. Jacques Thiroux (1998), p. 28. *Ethics: Theory and Practice*, 6th edition, Prentice- Hall, Upper Saddle River, NJ.
13. *See* following section "The Legal Versus the Ethical Framework of Business."
14. This maybe legal in one country and ignored in another where pirating this technology maybe acceptable. To that extent, we might have implications and challenges within the legal domain, but those will be addressed in Chapter 4.
15. Carol J. Loomis (2006, July 10), p. 37. The global force called the Gates Foundation, *Fortune*.
16. The short arm of the law (2002, March 2). p. 67. *The Economist*.
17. *The World Almanac and Book of Facts 2000* (1999), p. 889. Primedia Reference Inc., World Almanac Books, Mahwah, NJ.
18. Some useful titles follow: William H. Davidow and Michael S. Malone (1993). *The Virtual Corporation: Restructuring and Revitalizing the Corporation for the 21st Century*, Harper Business, New York. Michael Hammer and James Champy (1993). *Reengineering the Corporation: A Manifesto for Business Revolution*, Harper Business, New York. Bruce A. Pasternack and Albert J. Viscio (1998). *The Centerless Corporation: A New Model for*

Transforming Your Organization for Growth and Prosperity, Simon and Schuster, New York.

19. *See* also Issues 2002, *Newsweek* (2001 December-2002, February).

20. *See,* ibid., Fareed Zakaria, A plan for global security, pp. 16–17.

21. *See,* ibid., Alan Wolfe, It's all our fault, p. 48.

22. Presented data are generalizations from statistics covering the 2000 through 2005 period, based on the respective editions of *The Economist World in Figures,* The Economist in Association with Profile Books Ltd, London, UK. Analysis was based on Purchasing Power Parity Indices. Asia did not include Japan, Singapore, South Korea, Taiwan, and Hong Kong. Africa did not include South Africa.

23. A tale of two bellies (2002, August 24), p. 11 *The Economist,* and, in the same issue, Special report: Demography and the West, pp. 20–22

24. France, for example, lost its colony, Algeria, whereas EU easily comes to resource-related agreements with African, Pacific, or Caribbean (APC) countries. In 1957 Russia launched its Sputnik. 40 years later, through Aerospatiale, the European can launch their own satellites.

25. *Scientific American* (2013, May), p. 25

26. Special issue of *Newsweek,* The world in 2012 (2002, September 16), pp. 80–81.

27. *See,* David Cooper (1971), pp. 24–28, 54, 150–51. *The Death of the Family, Allen Lane,* The Penguin Press, London.

28. For example, we face a continuous need for change, as in the case of retailing, where success comes with change.

29. Peter Drucker (2001, November 3), pp. 3–22. Survey of the near future: The next society, *The Economist.*

30. *See* Chapters 1, 3, and 8, Managerial Perspectives. Also John Thanopoulos and with L. L. Schkade (2000, Summer/Fall), pp. 46–47. Towards global entrepreneurialism, *North Central Business Journal,* Volume I, Issue 7, and John Thanopoulos and with Charles Little (1998, Winter), p. 3. The brave new global enterprise, *Review of Business,* Volume 20 (Number 2).

31. *See* Chapter 9, Capstone.

32. A survey of the new media: Among the audience (2006, April 22), p. 3, *The Economist.*

33. A survey of the new media: Among the audience (2006, April 22), p. 3, *The Economist.*

Chapter 4

1. Chapter 2, section on Geopolitical Dynamics and the Role of Business.

2. Agora is the Greek ancient word of a marketplace, often the forum for political discussions.

3. For example, people or corporations can create their own blogs, websites, and so on.

4. Goodman (1999), p. 663.

5. Goodman (1999), p. 661.

6. Claire Gorden (2013, August 8). Japan unveils the Izumo, its largest warship since WWII, amid tension with China, *Time*.

7. Goodman (1999), p. 565.

8. Jonathan Alter (2006, June 19), p. 10. The new open-source politics, *Newsweek*.

9. Kathy Fogel (2006), p. 617. Oligarchic family control, social economic outcomes, and quality of government, *Journal of International Business Studies*, Volume 37, Issue 5.

10. Hong Kong handover: China stands up (1997, July 7). Special issue of *Newsweek*.

11. Ricky W. Griffin and Michael W. Pustay (1999), p. 293. *International Business: A Managerial Perspective*, Addison-Wesley Publishing Company, Inc., Reading, Massachusetts.

12. For those who are interested in the topic, the Economist Intelligence Unit produces specific reports on political risk.

13. Political risk services and related insurance needs can be supplied by organizations like the Overseas Private Investment Corporation (U.S.), www .opic.gov.

14. Oumlil Ben and C. P. Rao (2005, Fall), pp. 5–7. Special issue on globalization and its challenges to marketing, *Journal of Marketing Theory and Practice*, Vol. 13, Issue 4.

15. Goodman (1999), p. 488.

16. The case-law system originated in England in 1066 and is based on the principle *stare decisis et non quieta movere,* which translates as "staying with the tradition and not changing existing situations." For relevant sources about the different legal systems; Richard Shaffer, Beverley Earle, Filiberto Augusti (1990), pp. 3–62. *International Business Law and Its Environment*, West Publishing Company, St. Paul; Michael Litka (1988), pp. 3–9. *International Dimensions of the Legal Environment for Business*, PWS-Kent, Boston, Mass; Carolyn Hotchkiss (1994), pp. 49–95. International Law for Business, McGraw-Hill International Editions, NY.

17. Hotchkiss (1994), p. 73.

18. Like the International Union for Protection of Industrial Property (1883), known as the Paris Union.

19. Such efforts started as early as 1891 with the Madrid Agreement Concerning the International Registration of Trademarks. Other similar conventions include Pan American Convention, Paris Convention, and so forth.

20. Paul Magnuson (2005, March 7), p. 64. States' rights vs. free trade, *Business Week*.

21. *Shipping world and shipbuilder* (2003/2004, December/January), pp. 14–15.

22. Alkis Corres and John Thanopoulos (2005). *Maritime Theory & Entrepreneurialism*, Interbooks, Athens, Greece.

23. Litka (1988), p. 149.

24. For the reader interested in the economic arguments, we suggest any book in the field of international economics.

25. M. E. Porter (1990). *The Competitive Advantage of Nations*, New York Free Press, NY.

26. *Business Week* issue of February 8, 1999.

27. Chapter 7, section on entry methods in foreign markets.

28. The analysis of this section follows the standard approach of most texts on the world or political economy. Frederick P. Stutz and Anthony R. de Souza (1998), pp. 34–41. *The World Economy: Resources, Location, Trade and Development*, 3rd edition, Prentice-Hall, Upper Saddle River, New Jersey.

29. Frederick P. Stutz and Anthony R. de Souza (1998), p. 38.

30. Not those that are in the process of becoming for their user final goods or services.

31. It might be of interest to the reader to see how the issues of money and banks were handled in the antiquity; V. Doukakis (2012). *Money and Banking in Greek Antiquity*, Champaign, IL: Common Ground Publishing LLC.

32. This is the means of exchange for a great part of Europe (money, currency).

33. Naturally, a comparison between corporate revenues and country GNP presents major conceptual shortcomings. Data were retrieved from *Fortune* (European editions August 9, 2010, August 8, 2011, August 6, 2012, and July 22, 2013) and from the International Monetary Fund, "Report for selected countries and subjects." International Monetary Fund, retrieved June 2, 2012. It is understood that data may significantly vary given definitional and source discrepancies and comparability issues. For example, other GNP sources, like United Nations, the World Bank or the CIA Factbook, may vary between them more than 12% (for the same period, 2010–2011).

34. As a very simplistic verification of this contention, the reader may use as annual growth rate of the global GNP 4%, whereas he may use as the corporate growth rate of revenues, diminishing every 7 years, from 7%, to 6%, to 5%, and to 4%. Using the average data of note #125 (above from *Fortune*), the revenue growth of the largest global 500 corporations for 2009 through 2012 was 7.75%.

35. During the last 15 years this author, believing that a reversal of corporate to state responsibilities is *ante portas*, had many presentations dealing with the global enterprise, its new societal role, and entrepreneurialism. In a parallel way, *The Economist*, at the Special Report on "Companies and the

State, " February 22, 2014 issue, states: "The big question is whether it makes sense to tax corporate profits at all. A company is a legal entity; if it is taxed, it must pass the levy on" (page 6). Moreover, "Lobbying creates its own momentum. A company that sees its competitors doing it will follow suit and avoids losing out" (page 14). Nevertheless, in this author's opinion, even this targeted Special Report does not go far enough. For instance, in our entrepreneurial era volunteerism may create significant social value but it is not taxable and does not need to spend in vain lobbying efforts.

Chapter 5

1. *See* respective section at Chapter 2. Coined in 1899 by Rudolf Kjellen, geopolitics (then) described the geographical and resource base of a state which presumably determined its power potential. In the 1970s, Henry Kissinger used it as a synonym of balance-of-power politics and today its definition is according to the context in use, seeking to make "world politics" meaningful by providing a more comprehensive vision of the spatial dynamics around them. Geraroid O Tuathail, Simon Dalby, and Paul Routledge (Eds.). (2006), pp. 1–2. *The Geopolitics Reader*, 2nd edition, Routledge, London and New York.

2. *See* Graham Bateman and Victoria Egan (2000), pp. 489–491. *The Encyclopedia of World Geography*, Barnes and Nobles Books, New York; population figures are for 1994.

3. Details on the UN are provided by and are credited to its own website, www.un.org, accessed August 23, 2013.

4. *See* Chapter 2, section on "Civilization Clashes and Business Repercussions;" Chapter 3, section on "Entering the 21st century."

5. Goodman (1999), p. 604.

6. Details on the World Bank are provided by and are credited to its own website, www.worldbank.org, accessed August 23, 2013.

7. The role of these banks is pivotal for global business and country financing. It is worth noting that that the global debt crises maybe the result of funding oversupply, where the global investor "behaving" in a business manner undertakes similar risks; Angelos A. Antzoulatos and N. Seth (2003, Summer), pp. 19–36. Bank lending to LDCs: Lessons from the 1970s, *International Economic Journal*, Volume 17, Issue 2.

8. Details on the IMF are provided by and are credited to its own website, www.imf.org, accessed August 24, 2013.

9. Published since November 2002.

10. Details on the WTO are provided by and are credited to its own website, www.wto.org, accessed August 24, 2013.

11. Source Stanford University's http://gatt.stanford.edu GATT Digital Linrary: 1947–1994.

12. Details on the WTO are provided by and are credited to its own website, www.wto.org. As it happens with many of the UN agencies, individuals and business feel very far away from them and slowly develop major misunderstandings of UN operations. Critisms are not uncommon like being undemocratic, antigreen, oblivious to local development, and so forth. For counterarguments, please see its website.

13. WTO, World Trade Report 2006: Subsidies, trade and the WTO

14. Details on the European Union are provided by and are credited to its publications website, www.europa.eu.int.

15. Jeremy Rifkin (2005). *The European Dream: How Europe's Vision of the Future is Quietly Eclipsing the American Dream*, Polity Press, Cambridge, UK.

16. For an example, from the maritime industry, *see* Alkis J. Corres (2007). The role of ship owners unions in Greek shipping policies, chapter in *Maritime Transport: The Greek Paradigm*, Elsevier, London.

17. Owen Matthews (2006, August 21–28), pp. 30–31. Second thoughts, *Newsweek*.

18. Pascal Fontain (2004), p. 3. *Europe in 12 Lessons*, European Commission, Directorate General for Press and Communication Publications, Brussels.

19. Details on how the European Union works, are provided by and are credited to its publication *How the European Union Works: Your Guide to the EU Institutions* (2005, June), European Commission, Directorate-General for Press and Communication.

20. Alan Greenspan (2008), p. 468. *The Age of Turbulence: Adventures in a New World*, Penguin Books, New York.

21. Charles W. L. Hill (1998), pp. 246–247. *Global Business Today*, international edition, Irwin/ McGraw-Hill, Boston.

22. For example, allowing financial institutions unrestricted access to the Mexican markets by 2000.

23. Lowering of standards to lure investment is described as being inappropriate.

24. In 1991, on average, a work hour in Mexico was $2.32, $14.31 in the United States, and $14.71 in Canada.

25. Gary S. Becker (2001, January 8), p. 12. It's time for MAFTA to look further south, *Business Week*.

26. Details on ASEAN are provided by and are credited to its website, www.aseansec.org

27. Secretary-General of the United Nations, February 16, 2000; www.aseansec.org

28. *See* an interesting comment (box information) of Nobel laureate Gary S. Becker at the subsection on NAFTA.

29. Details on IMO are provided by and are credited to its website, www.imo. org. With a staff of around 300 people, IMO is one of the smallest of all United Nations agencies. 166 Member States participate in the IMO. For additional discussion on IMO and other maritime treaties, like SOLAS and MARPOL, that follow, *see* Alkis I. J. Corres and John Thanopoulos (2005). *Maritime Theory and Entrepreneurship in the Era of Quality*, (in Greek), Athens, Interbooks.

30. Geraroid O Tuathail, Simon Dalby, and Paul Routledge (Eds.). (2006), pp. 7–9, 39, 43, 136, 146, 188, 203, 265. *The Geopolitics Reader*, 2nd edition, Routledge, London and New York.

31. Jeremy Rifkin (2005).

32. Please revisit Chapters 1 and 2. There, too, the text implied that the reader should not see the objective of the analysis, culture, superficially.

33. In Chapter 4, *Towards a New Theory: The Era of Global Business*, the projections were made for 2033, 20 years from today. The analysis that follows is for 2040 and it is based on Woodall (2006, September).

34. Woodall (2006, September), p. 3.

35. Woodall (2006, September), p. 5, 10.

36. The Economist (2000), p. 22. *Pocket World in Figures*, 2001 edition, *The Economist* in association with Profiles Books, London.

37. The new titans: A survey of the world economy (2006, September 16), pp. 16 and 22. *The Economist.*

38. Michael Mandel (2006, September 25), pp. 55–62. What's really propping up the economy, *Business Week.*

39. Noam Chomsky (1994). *World Orders Old and New.*

40. Albert Jacquard (1991). *Voici le temps du monde fini*, Editons du Seuil, Paris.

41. In 2010 the author and 185 coauthors of his, his Fall 2009 students, prepared a limited electronic-only edition of a book entitled *The Global Manager: Self Actualization Perspectives*, Interbooks, Athens.

Chapter 6

1. Howard Lafay (1978, December), pp. 730–759. Ebla: Splendor of an unknown empire, *National Geographic*, Vol. 154, No. 6.

2. Frederick D. S. Choi, Carol Ann Frost, and Gary K. Meek (1999), p. 1. *International Accounting*, Prentice-Hall, Upper Saddle River, NJ.

3. Since 1920s, for example, the premier educational accreditation agency, the Association to Advance Collegiate Schools of Business (*see* www.aacsb.edu) was established.

8

4. Tom Morris (1997), p. 61. *If Aristotle Ran General Motors: The New Soul of Business*, Henty Holt and Company, New York.

5. *See* about this classification in Gerhard G. Mueller (1967). *International Accounting*, MacMillan, New York

6. G. Hoftsede (1980). *Culture Consequences: International Differences in Work-Related Values*, Sage Publications, Beverly Hills, California, and S. J. Gray's (1988, March), pp. 1–15, article. Towards a theory of cultural influence on the development of accounting systems internationally, *Abacus*.

7. The International Accounting Standards Committee (IASC) was founded in 1973 by accounting associations in Australia, Canada, France, Great Britain, Germany, Ireland, Japan, Mexico, the Netherlands, and the United States. From 2001 it became the International Accounting Standards Board (IASB).

8. Frederick D.S. Choi and Gerhard G. Mueller (1984), p. 74. *International Accounting*, Prentice-Hall, Inc.,

9. Article 4 of FASB's Mission Statement.

10. *See* their website at www.accountnet.nl/nivra (NivRA).

11. IASC was founded in 1973 from accounting organizations from Australia, Canada, France, Germany, Great Britain, Ireland, Japan, Mexico, the Netherlands, and the United States. It now has more than 100 members from more than 80 countries. IASC aims to introduce accounting procedures that are globally acceptable and works toward the improvement and standardization of accounting regulations, processes, practices, and reporting.

12. In order to further familiarize the reader with relevant literature, *see*: Ming-Jer Chen (2001). Inside Chinese Business: *A Guide for Managers Worldwide*, Harvard Business School Press, Boston, Mass. Ernst & Young, *Doing Business in China, Ernst and Young International*, New York. Yin Chen, P. Jubb, and A. Tran (1977). Problems of accounting reform in the People's Republic of China, *The International Journal of Accounting*, *32*(3).

13. Frederick D. S. Choi, Carol Ann Frost, and Gary K. Meek (1999), pp. 267 -271. *International Accounting*, Prentice-Hall, Upper Saddle River, NJ. Also, Per Thorell and Geoffrey Whittington (1994), p. 218. The harmonization of accounting within the European Union: Problems, perspectives and strategies, *The European Accounting Review*,

14. Arnord Schilder (1996, December). Research opportunities in auditing in the European Union, *Accounting Horizons*, 10.

15. EC Communication (1995, November 14). Accounting harmonization: A new strategy vis-a-vis international harmonization, *COM 95* (508).

16. Choi and Mueller (1984), pp. 216–230.

17. Special report on offshore financing (2013, February 16), p. 8. *The Economist*.

18. OECD is concerned about the companies' ability to manipulate their global tax obligations through transfer pricing. *See* about transfer pricing the OECD Center of Tax Policy at www.oecd.org.

19. For a summary of global taxation levels for corporations and their employees, *see* related issue in *Forbes magazine*. Example: Jack Anderson (2005, May 23), p. 28. The tax world gets flat and happy (the employee happiness index), *Forbes Global*.

20. $640 million in ten years! Gail Edmondson, David Fairlamb, and Nanette Byrnes (2004, January 26), pp. 17–19. The milk just keeps on spilling, *Business Week*.

21. This section was developed by Christos Tsoumas, Professor of Finance, University of Piraeus. It first appeared in John Thanopoulos (2007), pp. 137–138, *Global Business: Environment, Structure and Challenges*, Athens, Greece, Interbooks.

22. The term financial system is used to describe the collection of financial intermediaries and capital markets that are responsible for allocating resources and distribute risks in the economy.

23. Malcolm Edey and Ketil Hviding (1995). "An assessment of financial reform in OECD countries," *Organization for Economic Co-operation and Development*, Working Paper No 154; John Williamson and M. Mahar (1998, November). A survey of financial liberalization, *Princeton Essays in International Finance*, No. 211.

24. Andrei Shleifer and Robert W. Vishny (1997), pp. 737–783. A survey of corporate governance, *Journal of Finance*, 52.

25. In the so called Anglo-American model of corporate governance, ownership in corporations is dispersed, with arm's length relationships between shareholders and managers, whose interests are aligned with the interests of shareholders through stock market-based compensation. The primary objective in this model is the maximizing of the shareholder value, improving access of savers to investment opportunities, and firms' access to external funds. Corporate control is based mainly on hostile takeovers.

26. For statistics, *see* the website of the Bank for International Settlements, www.bis.org.

27. Found in Alan C. Shapiro (1996), p. 41. *Multinational Financial Management*, 5th international edition, Prentice-Hall, London.

28. For example, it is common for major banks to command assets over $2 trillion each. *See Fortune* (2013, July 22), pp. F–1 and F–2.

29. The opportunities for arbitrage, especially in developing nations, like Mexico, quite often start through programs of economic stabilization and reform. *See* Angelos A. Antzoulatos (2002), pp. 1013–1034. Arbitrage opportunities on the road to stabilization and reform, *Journal of International Money and Finance*, (21).

30. *See* texts in international financial management about adjusting cash flows, entering into forward contract, and exposure netting.
31. Classic ways to avoid this type of risk include the forward market hedge, the money market hedge, and shifting the currency exchange risk to the other party.
32. Other terms used by different authors for operating exposure include economic, competitive, or strategic exposure.
33. For more information on international finance and banking topics, visit the following websites:

Bank of England	bankofengland.co.uk
Bank for International Settlements	bis.org
International Monetary Fund	imf.org/external
UK Treasury	hm-treasury.gov.uk
U.S. Federal Reserve	federalreserve.gov
U.S. Securities and Exchange Commission	sec.gov
U.S. Treasury Department	ustreas.gov

34. Found in Alan C. Shapiro (1996), p. 603. *Multinational Financial Management*, 5th international edition, Prentice-Hall, London

Chapter 7

1. William E. Northdurft (1992), p. 2. *Going Global: How Europe Helps Small Firms to Export*, The Brookings Institution, Washington, DC.
2. Gerald Michaelson (2003), p. 94. *Sun Tzu for Success*, Adams Media Publication, Avon, MA.
3. In Chapter 9, where we define the major elements of success of corporation, there is a section on the creative enterprise. Innovation is central to creativity.
4. Any book of marketing may provide in-depth coverage of these topics. For example, *see* William G. Zikmund and Michael d' Amico (2001), pp. 281–283. *Marketing: Creating and Keeping Customers in an e-Commerce World* (7th ed.), South-Western College Publishing, Cincinnati, OH.
5. Gregory Beals (2001, June 18), pp. 42–48. The future of computers, *Newsweek*; Technology Quarterly (2006, March 11), pp. 14–16. *The economist*.
6. Oumlil Ben (2003, August 7–10). International alliances strategical decisions: An empirical study. *The 10th Recent Advances in Retailing and Services Science EIRASS Conference*, Portland, OR; and, P. Chakrpani (Ed.). (2005, February 23-27). Global strategic business decisions: A comparative study of domestic and international outsourcing, *ASBBS 12th Annual Conference*, Las Vegas, NV.
7. *See* Chapter 2, section on material culture.
8. Goodman (1999), p. 34.

9. Dean M. Peebles and John K. Ryans, Jr. (1984), p. 80. *Management of International Advertising: A Marketing Approach, Allyn and Bacon*, Inc., Boston.

10. Product design in the international marketing section, "consumer products" subsection.

11. Oumlil Ben and C. P. Rao (2005, Fall), pp. 5–7. Special issue on globalization and its challenges to marketing, *Journal of Marketing Theory and Practice*, Vol. 13, Issue 4.

12. William E. Northdurft (1992), p. 28. *Going Global: How Europe Helps Small Firms to Export*, The Brookings Institution, Washington D.C.

13. Data for this part have been taken from: The physical Internet: A survey of logistics (2006, June 17), *The Economist*.

14. Richard Templar (2005), p. 195. *The Rules of Management*, Financial Times Press, Upper Saddle River, NJ.

15. Wal-Mart, with over 6,600 worldwide stores and more than 300 billion dollar sales, is in a position to marshal even its own suppliers to follow its example, with significant impact on a global scale; Marc Gunther (2006, August 7), pp. 34-42. The green machine, *Fortune*. Nine years later from this 2006 depiction, Wal-Mart continues some of the same practices, has about 470 billion dollar sales and affects even the logistics flows of some of its suppliers, *Fortune*, July 22, 2013, p. F-1.

16. Technology Quarterly (2006, March 11), pp. 14–16. *The Economist*.

17. Like the U.S. National Trade Data Bank.

18. John D. Daniels, Lee H. Radebaugh, and Daniel P. Sullivan (2007), pp. 584–585. *International Business: Environments and Operations*, 11th edition, Pearson Prentice Hall, Upper Saddle River, NJ.

19. Raj Aggarwal, Business strategies for profitable sales to the poor: How free enterprise can fight poverty, Chapter 6 of S. Jain and S. Vahchani (Eds.). (2005), pp. 125–141. *Strategies for Serving the Poor Profitably: Can Free Enterprise Fight Poverty?* Oxford University Press, New York.

20. Goodman (1999), p. 161.

21. For example, *Fortune* publishes annually a list of the "most admired corporations," which in its opinion is "the definitive report card on corporate reputations." Is this list relevant for our company in Angola, Bermuda, or Cayman Islands, or in Austria, Belgium, or Canada? So attention on how the researcher selected its sample, what population it represents, and what was the purpose of this study. *Fortune* states that to "arrive at the top 50 Most Admired Companies overall, the Hay Group asked the 3,800 respondents to select the 10 companies they admired most, from a list made up from the companies that ranked in the top 25% in last year's survey." Does this suffice for our purposes or we need to be more careful in identifying the essence of most admired companies? *Fortune*, March 18, 2013, p. 33.

22. On purpose this section avoids specific in-depth technicalities and specialized business jargon which in class settings is confusing, easily forgotten, and rapidly changing. For a discussion of export, import, and direct investment strategies, *see* Chapters 13 and 14, of Daniels, Radebaugh, and Sullivan (2007).

23. *See* previous sections on distribution policy and logistics and on international business research.

24. Operational control must always follow FDI. Otherwise we refer to *portfolio investment*.

25. We have also nonexclusive licenses.

Chapter 8

1. Goodman (1999), p. 559.

2. Both places are at the south end of the Chinese peninsula.

3. "Japan special advertising section on global vision for the 21st Century: Japan's top managers speak out," *Forbes*, January 8, 2001, p. S5, S6, S9, S24, S31.

4. Jon Gertner [In Memoriam] (2006, May 29), p. 18. The people's economist.

5. Joseph W. Weiss (2003), pp. 213-315. *Business Ethics: A Stakeholder and Issues Management Approach*, 3rd edition, Thomson-South-Western, Mason, OH.

6. John Dunkelberg and Donald P. Robin (1998, November-December), pp. 77–82. The anatomy of fraudulent behavior, *Business Horizons*.

7. Kenichi Ohmae (1990). *The Borderless World: Power and Strategy in the Inter-linked Economy*, New York, Harper Business.

8. The very top, soared by stock options, was in 2000, 785 times the pay of the average worker. Top U.S. compensation for 2005 was for William McGuire of United Health estimated to a potential 1 billion dollars; Lee Raymond 405 million dollars (Exxon); Bob Nardelli (Home Depot) 250 million dollars; Hank McKinnell (Pfizer) 99 million dollars. In Europe and for 2005, top CEO compensation was to Lindsay Owen-Jones (L'Oreal, France) 32 million dollars; Daniel Vasella (Novartis, Switzerland) 19.9 million dollars. *Fortune*, July 10, 2006, pp. 47, 44, 55–56.

9. The three top executives for 2012 get more than $200 million each, though a decade ago Jack Welch got a larger golden parachute from GE at 417 million! Andrew Roberts (2013, June 16), pp. 26–28. Why fired CEOs go straight back to the bank, *Bloomberg Businessweek*.

10. Peter Coy and Elizabeth Dwoskin (2013, June 16), p. 34. A better way to get brains from abroad, *Bloomberg Businessweek*.

11. Kamal Fatehi (1996), pp. 160–161. *International Management: A Cross-Cultural and Functional Perspective*, Prentice-Hall, Upper Saddle, NJ.

12. PepsiCo, in 2005, had stock valuation and revenues, respectively, 108 and 33 billion dollars. Sources: Abrahm Lustgarten, Global 500, *Fortune,* July 25, 2006, p. F–4 and Regina Castro, et al., America's Power 50, *Fortune,* October 16, 2006, p. 55.

13. Abraham H. Maslow (1943), pp. 370–396. A theory of human motivation, *Psychological Review*, Volume 50; Abraham H. Maslow (1954). *Motivation and Personality*, Harper & Row, New York.

14. These five levels, according to other researchers, may not be always present. *See* Clayton P. Alderfer (1972). *Existence, Relatedness, and Growth*, Free Press, New York.

15. *See* statistics from Global 500, *Fortune,* July 22, 2013, p. F-10.

16. Economics discovers its feelings (2006, December 23), p. 33. *The Economist.*

17. Gerald Michaelson (2003), p. 50. *Sun Tzu for Success*, Adams Media Publication, Avon, MA.

18. Dr. Steven Ash of The University of Akron, originally developed this chapter subsection, appearing on the 1st edition of this book.

19. M.A. Huselid (1997), pp. 171–186. Technical and strategic human resource management effectiveness as determinants of firm performance. *Academy of Management Journal, 40*(1).

20. In Chapter 9, Capstone: Global Business Challenges, we summarize the five basic "core elements" of the corporation today. One of them refers to HR and another to technology.

21. B. Dineen, S. Ash, and R. Noe (2002), pp. 723–734. A web of applicant attraction: Person-organization fit in the context of web-based recruitment, *Journal of Applied Psychology, 87*(4).

22. Aldous Huxley (2007).

23. Boye Lafayette DeMente (1994), p. 171. *Japanese Etiquette and Ethics in Business*, 6th edition, NTC Business Books, Chicago, IL.

24. It started under the League of Nations, the previous of the UN country equivalent.

25. *See* also note number 21 in the previous chapter, section on Researching International Markets: Issues of Concern, where there is a comment on The World's Most Admired Companies, an annual list published by *Fortune.*

26. This chapter subsection was originally developed by Dr. Joseph W. Leonard of Miami University, appearing at the 1st edition of this book.

27. *See* for more details section on Entry methods in foreign markets , Chapter 7.

28. This is an investment strategist's advice and a variation of the now coined business word GLOCAL, which is a combination of the words GLObal and LOCAL. The essence of GLOCAL is not centered only on investment. It is to have a global business orientation, though the starting point is the company's local realities. Geoffrey Colvin (2006, December 25), pp. 84–86. What's ahead for 2007? *Fortune.*

29. William H. Davidow and Michael S. Malone (1993), pp. 5–6. *The Virtual Corporation: Structuring and Revitalizing the Corporation for the 21st Century,* Harper Business, New York. Since then many parallel concepts were proposed. For example, *see* the global e-corporation network structure at Helen Derensky (2014), pp. 273–274. , *International Management: Managing Across Borders and Cultures,* 8th edition, Pearson, Boston.

30. Bruce A. Pasternack and Albert J. Viscio (1998), p. 21. *The Centerless Corporation: A New Model for Transforming Your Organization for Growth and Prosperity,* Booz, Allen & Hamilton, New York.

31. Christopher Sauer, Philip W. Yetton, and Associates (1997). *Steps to the Future,* Jossey-Bass Publishers, San Francisco.

32. Michael N. O' Malley (2000). *Creating Commitment,* John Wiley and Sons, New York.

33. Thomas Kuczmarski, Arthur Middlebrooks, and Jeffrey Swaddling (2001). *Innovating the Corporation: Creating Value for Customers and Shareholders,* NTC Business Books, Chicago.

34. This chapter section was originally developed by Dr. Panagiotis Petratos, Professor at California State University at Stanislaus, appearing at the 1st edition of this book. It has been slightly modified for the purposes of the present edition.

35. E. Wainright Martin, Daniel W. DeHayes, Jeffrey A. Hoffer, and William C. Perkins (1994), p. 43, 46, and 50. *Managing Information Technology: What Managers Need to Know,* Macmillan Publishing Company, New York.

36. Yannis A. Pollalis (2003), pp. 469–492. Patterns of co-alignment in information-intensive organizations: Business performance through integration strategies, *International Journal of Information Management.*

37. Although both methods aim to cut costs through contracting work to third parties there is a slight distinction in their definitions. Outsourcing is the contracting of work to a third party which is typically an exoteric (does not belong to the corporation offering the contacting of work) smaller specialized company. On the other hand offshoring is the contracting of work to a third party which is typically a smaller specialized company which may belong to the corporation offering the contracting of work. Typically, international migration of U.S. computing work and services went to India and China.

38. Aspray William, Mayadas Frank, and Vardi Y. Moshe (Eds.). (2006). Globalization and Offshoring of Software, A Report of the ACM Job Migration Task Force, Association for Computing Machinery.

Chapter 9

1. The best advice I ever got (2005, March 21). *Fortune.*

2. Even in early 1970s there were clear trends toward the creation of business cultures and the ethical business. However, it might be interesting

to see that even in a philosophy-oriented book having the title *Ideas That Matter: A Personal Guide for the 21st Century,* the author A. C. Grayling avoids using terms like administration, business, commerce, corporation, enterprise, governance, labor, and production, whereas he does use words like business ethics, marketing, or human rights.

3. *Fortune,* March 6, 2006, p. 53. At that time GE has been voted 6 times the most admired American corporation.
4. Carol Matlack, et al. (2005, October 24), p. 58. Europe's hot growth companies, *Business Week.*
5. Bruce Nussbaum (2005, August 8–15), p. 60. Get creative! How to build innovative companies, *Business Week.*
6. Nussbaum (2005, August), p. 52.
7. Nussbaum (2005, August), p. 56.
8. Bruce A. Pasternack and Albert J. Viscio (1998). *The Centerless Corporation,* Booz, Allen and Hamilton, New York.
9. Matlack et al. (2005, October), pp. 56–72.
10. Kurt Badenhausen (2005, June 20), pp. 36–7. Brand-new world, *Forbes Global.*
11. Bruce Nussbaum (2005, July 4), pp. 52–62 The best product design of 2005: Winners, *Business Week.*
12. Gail Edmondson and Constance Faivre (2005, July 4), p. 19. Got 5,000 euros? Need a new car?, *Business Week.*
13. Deboral Orr (2005, April 25), pp. 18–23. Don't wrap the veggies, *Forbes Global.*
14. Nanette Byrnes (2005, October 10), pp. 45–46. Star search, *Business Week.*
15. Byrnes, N. (2005, October), p. 46.
16. John Kenneth Galbraith (1995), p. 54. *The World Economy Since the Wars: A Personal View,* Mandarin Paperbacks, London.
17. Nanette Byrnes (2005, October 10), p. 46. Star Search, *Business Week.*
18. Byrnes (2005, October), p. 49.
19. Jefferson Wells (2005), p. 52. Treating part-timers as Royalty, *Business Week.*
20. The traditional Maslow hierarchy has basic needs at the bottom of the pyramid, higher up are the security and social needs and even higher are the self-actualization needs. A satisfied need is not a motivator. We need to enhance personality traits for a mature well-balanced manager, if we want her to be motivated for growth, creativity, social responsibility, and results. For an opposite position, *see* Mimi Swartz (2006, March), pp. 148–154. Survival of the richest, *National Geographic.*
21. Adam Lashinky (2007, January 22), p. 49. Search and enjoy, *Fortune.* Other perks offered to every Google employee, regardless of rank, include: Annual ski trip with all expenses paid; onsite free doctors; brightly colored furniture;

media centers; TGIF parties; scoters; free onsite washers and dryers; free gourmet meals; famous-people lecture series; unlimited sick days; free flu shots; and many more. Swartz (2006, March), p. 46.

22. Ron Cowen (2007, March), p. 80. Bang: The cataclysmic death of stars, *National Geographic.*

23. The best advice I ever got, *Fortune,* March 21, 2005, p. 48.

24. Moon Ihlwan (2005, February 7), p. 24. A chilly reception for guest workers, *BusinessWeek.*

25. Justin Doebele (2003, September 15), pp. 43–45. The global home away from home, Forbes Global.

26. For example, in 1990 the Japanese, in average, were working over 2000 hours a year, whereas the Dutch under 1500. Fifteen years later the respective are under 1800 for the Japanese and under 1400 for the Dutch. *The Economist,* September 24, 2005, p. 124.

27. What is true (2000, October 2), p. 37. Special issue, supplement of *Forbes ASAP.*

28. *See The Technological Dimensions of International Competitiveness* (1988). National Academy of Engineering, Washington 1988.

29. Interview by Geoffrey Colvin (2006, April 17), p. 26. Question authority, *Fortune.*

30. Bill Gates (2006, April 17), p. 30. How I work, *Fortune.*

31. Death to folders (2005, September 17), p. 26. *The Economist,* Technology Quarterly.

32. Shih-Fen S Chen (2005, March), p. 233, Extending internationalization theory: A new perspective on international technology transfer and its generalization, *Journal of International Business Studies,* Volume 36, Issue 2.

33. Robert Barker (2005, July 4), p. 12. Tomorrow, world Domination, *BusinessWeek.*

34. Gary Dessler (2006), pp. 14–16. *A Framework for Human Resource Management,* 4th edition, Pearson-Prentice Hall, Upper Saddle River, NJ.

35. Rag Aggarwal (1999), pp. 83–104. Technology and globalization as mutual reinforcers in business: Reorienting strategic thinking for the new millennium, *Management International Review,* Volume 39/2.

36. *The Economist,* Technology Quarterly, December 2, 2006, pp. 13, 14, 27.

37. Allan Sloan and Michael Isikof (2008, January 28), p. 40. The Enron effect, *Newsweek.*

38. Corporate social responsibility (CSR) is a concept that refers to the processes and practices that a company employs during its efforts to be sensitive to the needs of all of its stakeholders. Ethical corporate behavior is the platform of CSR.

39. *See* Chapter 2, section on technology and philosophy.

40. An example of this observation are stock options and bonuses where near-term financial rewards may lead to violations of ethics (this maybe the case in strict Islamic environments and probably played in the Enron situation)

41. *See* Chapter 4 for discussion on politics and legal issues. The traditional capitalism view, for example, seeks to maximize profits (short- and long-term) and, therefore, poses a question of how that relates to ethics. The author's view that necessitates the development of a *New Economic Theory: The Enterprise in the Era of Global Business* is therefore stressed as imperative.

42. There exists a significant body of research addressing the conceptual and implementation sides of these issues, even case-specific analyses. For an example, *see* Kenneth Levitt and Edna Gilligan, "Corporate downsizing: An examination of the survivors," in the *2006 Proceedings*, of the annual meetings of the Association for Global Business.

43. Timothy J. Cusick (2006, Spring), p. 24. Management, labor, and the development of the human person: Insights from the compendium of the social doctrine of the church, *Review of Business*, Volume 27, Number 2.

Epilogue

1. An example is the GM-Renault-Nissan intention to associate, with potential to control 22% of the global car production.

2. Bahrain and Kuwait are typical examples of oil-producing countries with income that greatly benefited their people. Finland is a case in point for a country that excelled in business undertakings.

3. At the section of HR Challenges we referred to the generation that was born before War World II, the *silent generation* and then the *baby boomers*, and then the *baby busters*. When my Father, Nikos Thanopoulos, returned from the war he wrote in Greek two small books that will be republished later this year by Fedimos Publishing on "war impressions" and "tales for young people who think they are political leaders." I contrast his experiences and his era with how my students see theirs, their relationships, and their overall purpose in life. For years now my conclusion is that we must teach more philosophy, more ethics, more discipline, and more self actualization! Our technocratic offerings must be combined with more educational depth!

References

Abdi, M., & Aulakh, P. S. (2012). Do country-level institutional frameworks and interim governance arrangements substitute or complement in international business relationships? *Journal of International Business Studies 43*(5), 477–497.

Aggarwal, R. (1999). Technology and globalization as mutual reinforcers in business: Reorienting strategic thinking for the new millenium. *Management International Review 39*(2), 83–104.

Aggarwal, R. (2005). Business strategies for profitable sales to the poor: How free enterprise can fight poverty. In S. Jain & S. Vahchani (Eds.), *Strategies for serving the poor profitably: Can free enterprise fight poverty?* New York, NY: Oxford University Press.

Alderfer, C. P. (1972). *Existence, relatedness, and growth.* New York, NY: Free Press.

Alter, J. (2006, June). The new open-source politics. *Newsweek,* 10.

Anand, S. (2008). *Essentials of corporate governance.* Hoboken, NJ: John Wiley and Sons, Inc.

Anderson, J. (2005, May). The tax world gets flat and happy (The employee happiness index). *Forbes Global.*

Anglemyer et al. (1980). *A search of environmental ethics, an initial bibliography.* Washington, DC: Smisthonian Institution Press.

Antzoulatos, A. A. (2002). Arbitrage opportunities on the road to stabilization and reform. *Journal of International Money and Finance 21,* 1013–1034.

Antzoulatos, A. A., & Seth, N. (2003). Bank lending to LDCs: Lessons from the 1970s. *International Economic Journal 17*(2), 19–36.

Arpan, J., & Kwok, C. C. Y. (Eds.). (2001). *Internationalizing the business school: Global survey of institutions of higher learning in the year 2000.* The Academy of Global Business and the CIBER at the Darla Moore School of Business, University of South Carolina, Columbia, SC: AIB Foundation

Aulakh, P. S., Jiang, M. S., & Pan, Y. (2010). International technology licensing: Monopoly, rents, transaction costs and exclusive rights. *Journal of International Business Studies 41*(4), 587–605.

Autio, E., Pathak, S., & Wennberg, K. (2013). Consequences of cultural practices for entrepreneurial behaviors. *Journal of International Business Studies 44*(4), 334–362.

Badenhausen, K. (2005, June). Brand-new world. *Forbes Global,* 36–37.

Bargh, J. A. (2014, January). Our unconscious mind. *Scientific American,* 20–27.

Barker, R. (2005, July). Tomorrow, world domination. *Business Week,* 12.

Bateman, G., & Egan, V. (2000). *The encyclopedia of world geography.* New York, NY: Barnes and Nobles Books, 489–491.

Beals, G. (2001, June). The future of computers. *Newsweek,* 42–48.

Beauchamp, T. L., & Bowie, N. E. (1997). *Ethical theory in business* (5th ed). Upper Saddle River, NJ: Prentice-Hall.

Becker, G. S. (2001, January). It's time for NAFTA to look further south. *Business Week,* 12.

Belt, D. (2002, January). The world of Islam. *National Geographic,* 82.

Beugelsdijk, S., Hennart, J.-F., Slangen, A., & Smeets, R. (2010). Why and how FDI stocks are a biased measure of MNE affiliate activity. *Journal of International Business Studies 41*(9), 1444–1459.

Birkinshaw, J., Brannen, M.-Y., & Tung, R. L. (2011). From a distance and generalizable to up close and grounded: Reclaiming a place for qualitative methods in international business research. *Journal of International Business Studies 42*(5), 573–581.

Blackstone, W. T. (1979). The search of an environmental ethic. In T. Regan (Ed), *Matters of life and death.* New York, NY: Random House Inc.

Boeh, K. S., & Beamish, P. W. (2012). Travel time and liability of distance in foreign direct investment: Location choice and entry mode. *Journal of International Business Studies 43*(5), 525–535.

Boxell, J. (2006, November). Peers call for tax incentives to boost use of biofuels. *Financial Times,* 3.

Bresman, H., Birkinshaw, J., & Nobel, R. (2010). Knowledge transfer in international acquisitions. *Journal of International Business Studies 41*(1), 5–20.

Brock, R. H. (1978). *The anti-trust paradox: A policy at war with itself.* New York, NY: Basic Books.

Buffett, W., Branson, R., Whitman, M., Lafley, A. G., & 24 other luminaries. (2005, March). The best advice I ever got. *Fortune,* 39–51.

Byrnes et al. (2002, January). Accounting in crisis. *Business Week,* 50–54.

Byrnes, N. (2005, October). Star search. *Business Week,* 45–46.

Cantwell, J., Dunning, J. H., & Lundan, S. M. (2010). An evolutionary approach to understanding international business activity: The co-evolution of MNEs and the institutional environment. *Journal of International Business Studies 41*(4), 567–586.

Cappelli, P. (1999). *The new deal at work: Managing the market-driven workforce.* Boston, MA: Harvard Business School Press.

Castro et al. (2006, October). America's power 50. *Fortune,* 55.

Cavusgil, S. T., Knight, G., & Riesenberger, J. S. (2014). *International business: The new realities* (3rd ed.). Boston, MA: Pearson.

Chang, S.-J., Witteloostuijn, A., & Eden, L. (2010). From the Editors: Common method variance in international business research. *Journal of International Business Studies 41*(1), 178–184.

Chen, M. (2001). *Inside Chinese business: A guide for managers worldwide.* Boston, MA: Harvard Business School Press.

Chen, S. S. (2005). Extending internationalization theory: A new perspective on international technology transfer and its generalization. *Journal of International Business Studies 36*(2), 233.

Chen, Y., Jubb, P., & Tran, A. (1977). Problems of accounting reform in the people's Republic of China. *The International Journal of Accounting 32*(3).

Choi, F. D. S., Frost, C. A., & Meek, G. K. (1999). *International accounting.* Upper Saddle River, NJ: Prentice-Hall.

Choi, F. D. S., & Mueller, G. G. (1984). *International accounting.* Upper Saddle River, NJ: Prentice-Hall, Inc., 74.

Chomsky, N. (1994). *World orders old and new.* Columbia, UK: Columbia University Press.

Christmann, P., & Taylor, G. (2006). Firm self-regulation through international certifiable standards: Determinants of symbolic versus substantive interpretation. *Journal of International Business Studies 37*(6), 863–878.

Coggan, P. (2002, June). The tyranny of the benchmarks. *Financial Times,* 18.

Colvin, G. (2006, April). Question authority. *Fortune,* 26.

Colvin, G. (2006, December). What's ahead for 2007? *Fortune,* 84–86.

Companies and the State, Special Report of *The Economist,* February 22th, 2014, 6, 14.

Compton, W. D. (1988). The technological dimensions of international competitiveness: A report to the council of the National Academy of Engineering. Washington, DC: National Academy of Engineering.

Cooper, D. (1971). *The death of the family.* London, UK: Allen Lane, Penguin Press.

Corres, A. I., & Thanopoulos, J. (2005). *Maritime theory and entrepreneurship in the era of quality.* Athens (in Greek): Interbooks.

Corres, A. J. (2007). The role of ship owners unions in Greek shipping policies. In *Maritime transport: The Greek paradigm.* London, UK: Elsevier.

Cowen, R. (2007, March). Bang: The cataclysmic death of stars. *National Geographic,* 80.

Coy, P., & Dwoskin, E. (2013, June 16). A better way to get brains from abroad. *Bloomberg Businessweek,* 34.

Crooks. (Ed). (2006, November). Only 34% support building new nuclear plants, says poll. *Financial Times,* 1.

Cuervo-Gazurra, A. (2006). Who cares about corruption? *Journal of International Business Studies 37*(6), 807–822.

Cuervo-Gazurra, A. (2008). The effectiveness of laws against bribery abroad. *Journal of International Business Studies 39*(4), 634–651.

Cusick, T. J. (2006). Management, labor, and the development of the human person: Insights. from the compendium of the social doctrine of the Church. *Review of Business 27*(2), 24.

Czinkota, M. R., Ronkainen, I. A., & Moffet, M. H. (1996). *International business* (4th ed.). Fort Worth, TX: The Dryden Press.

Daniels, J. D., Radebaugh, L. H., & Sullivan, D. P. (2007). *International business: Environments and operations* (11th ed.). Upper Saddle River, NJ: Pearson Prentice-Hall.

Davidow, W. H., & Malone, M. S. (1993). *The virtual corporation: Restructuring and revitalizing the corporation for the 21st century.* New York, NY: Harper Business.

DeMente, B. L. (1994). *Japanese etiquette and ethics in business* (6th ed.). Chicago, IL: NTC Business Books, 171.

Derensky, H. (2014). *International management: Managing across borders and cultures* (8th ed.). Boston, MA: Pearson.

Desjardins, J. R. (2007). *Business ethics and the environment: Imagining a sustainable future.* Upper Saddle River, NJ: Pearson-Prentice Hall.

Dessler, G. (2006). *A framework for human resource management* (4th ed.). Upper Saddle River, NJ: Pearson-Prentice Hall, 14–16

Dineen, B., Ash, S., & Noe, R. (2002). A web of applicant attraction: Person-organization fit in the context of web-based recruitment. *Journal of Applied Psychology 87*(4), 723–734.

Doebele, J. (2003, September). The global home away from home. *Forbes Global,* 43–45.

Donaldson, T. (1966, September–October). Values in tension: Ethics away from home. *Harvard Business Review,* 48–62.

Doukakis, V. (2004). The industrial revolution that did not happen. Athens, Greek: Sakkoula Publishing.

Doukakis, V. (2013). *Money and banking in Greek antiquity.* Champaign, IL: Common Ground Publishing LLC.

Drucker, P. (2001, November). Survey of the near future: The next society. *The Economist,* 3–22.

Drucker, P. F. (1974). *Management: Tasks, responsibilities, practices.* New York, NY: Harper and Row.

Dunkelberg, J., & Robin, D. P. (1998, November–December). The anatomy of fraudulent behavior. *Business Horizons,* 77–82.

EC Communication. (1995, November 14). *Accounting harmonization: A new strategy vis-a-vis international harmonization* (COM 95 (508)).

Economics discovers its feelings. (2006, December). *The Economist,* 33.

Eden, L. (2010). Letter from the editor-in-chief: Scientists behaving badly. *Journal of International Business Studies 41*(4), 561–566.

Edey, M., & Hviding, K. (1995). *An assessment of financial reform in OECD countries* (OECD Economics Department Working Papers No. 154). OECD Publishing.

Edmondson, G., Fairlamb, D., & Byrnes, N. (2004, January). The milk just keeps on spilling. *Business Week,* 17–19.

Edmondson, G., & Faivre, C. (2005, July). Got 5,000 euros? Need a new car? *Business Week,* 19.

Elliott, D., Clemetson, L., Schell, O., Turnley, P., & Wehrfritz, G. (1997). *The Hong Kong handover: China stands up.* New York, NY: Newsweek.

Engardio, P. (2007, January). Beyond the green corporation. *Business Week,* 53.

Ernst & Young. (1994). *Doing business in China.* New York, NY: Ernst and Young International.

Famighetti, R., & Almanac, W. (Eds). (1999). *The world Almanac and book of facts 2000.* Mahwah, NJ: Primedia Reference Inc., World Almanac Books.

Fatehi, K. (1996). *International management: A cross-cultural and functional perspective.* Upper Saddle, NJ: Prentice-Hall.

Flavin, C. (1997, November). Culture of permanence. *Time.*

Fogel, K. (2006). Oligarchic family control, social economic outcomes, and quality of government. *Journal of International Business Studies 37*(5), 617.

Fontain, P. (2004). *Europe in 12 lessons.* Brussels: European Commission, Directorate General for Press and Communication Publications.

Freiburghouse, A. (Ed.). (2000, October). What is true? *Forbes.*

Galbraith, J. K. (1995). *The world economy since the wars: A personal view.* London, UK: Mandarin Paperbacks.

Garreau, J. (1981). *The nine nations of North America.* New York, NY: Avon.

Gates, B. (2006, April). How I work. *Fortune,* 30.

Gertner, J. (2006, May). [In Memoriam] The people's economist. *Fortune,* 18.

The ghostly flickers of a new down. (2006, November). *The Economist,* 65.

The global 500: The world's largest corporations. (2013, July). *Fortune,* F1–F22.

Goleman, D. (1995) *Emotional intelligence: Why it can matter more than IQ.* New York, NY: Batman Books.

Goodman, T. (1999). *The Forbes book of business quotations.* Cologne: Konemann.

Goodpaster, K. E., & Sayre, K. M. (Eds.) (1979). *Ethics and problems of the 21st century.* Notre Dame, IN: University of Notre Dame Press.

Gorden, C. (2013, August). Japan unveils the Izumo, its largest warship since WWII, amid tension with China. *Time.*

Gray, S. J. (1988, March). Towards a theory of cultural influence on the development of accounting systems internationally. *Abacus,* 1–15.

Grayling, A. C. (2010). *Ideas that matter: A personal guide for the 21st century.* Phoenix, London, UK: Weidenfeld & Nicolson.

The greening of America. (2007, January). *The Economist,* 9.

Greenspan, A. (2008). *The age of turbulence: Adventures in a new world.* New York, NY: Penguin Books.

Griffin, R. W., & Pustay, M. W. (1999). *International business: A managerial perspective.* Reading, MA: Addison-Wesley Publishing Company, Inc.

Grondova, M. (2000). *A cultural typology of economic development.* New York, NY: Basic Books.

Gunther, M. (2006, August). The green machine. *Fortune, 34–42.*

Hammer, M., & Champy, J. (1993). *Reengineering the corporation: A manifesto for business revolution.* New York, NY: Harper Business.

Harrison, L. E., & Huntington, S. P. (2000). *Culture matters: How values shape human progress.* New York, NY: Basic Books.

Hartman, L. P. (2002). *Perspectives in business ethics* (2nd ed.). New York, NY: McGraw-Hill Irwin.

Hawking, S. (2001). *The universe in a nutshell.* New York, NY: Bantam Press.

Hill, C. W. L. (1998). *Global business today* (international edition). Boston, MA: Irwin/McGraw-Hill.

Hoftsede, G. (1980). *Culture consequences: International differences in work-related values.* Beverly Hills, CA: Sage Publications.

Hotchkiss, C. (1994). *International law for business.* New York, NY: McGraw-Hill International Editions.

Huang, J. H. (1993). *Sun Tzu: The art of war (The New Translation).* New York, NY: Quill-William Morrow.

Huntington, S. (2001). *The clash of civilizations and the remaking of the world order* (4th ed.). Athens, Greece: Terzo Books.

Huselid, M. A. (1997). Technical and strategic human resource management effectiveness as determinants of firm performance. *Academy of Management Journal 40*(1), 171–186.

Huxley, A. (2007). *Brave new world.* Vintage Classics, London.

Ihlwan, M. (2005, February). A chilly reception for guest workers. *BusinessWeek,* 24.

Imbrahim, N. A., & Parsa, F. (2005). Corporate responsiveness orientation: Are here differences between U.S. and French managers? *Review of Business 26*(1), 28.

Jacoby, S. (1985). *Employing bureaucracy: Managers, unions, and the transformation of work in the American industry, 1900–1945.* New York, NY: Columbia University Press.

Jacquard, A. (1991). In du Seuil (Ed.), *Voici le temps du monde fini.* Paris.

Klein, N. (2007). *The shock doctrine: The rise of disaster capitalism.* London, UK: Allen Lane-Penguin Books.

Kroeber, A., & Kluckhorn, C. (1985). *A critical review of concepts and definitions.* New York, NY: Random House.

Kuczmarski, T., Middlebrooks, A., & Swaddling, J. (2001). *Innovating the corporation: Creating value for customers and shareholders.* Chicago, IL: NTC Business Books.

Kwok, C., & Solomon, T. (2006). The MNC as an agent of change for host-country institutions. *Journal of International Business Studies 37*(6), 767–785.

Lafay, H. (1978, December). Ebla: Splendor of an unknown empire. *National Geographic 154*(6), 730–759.

Lashinky, A. (2007, January). Search and enjoy. *Fortune, 49.*

Leung, K., Bhagat, R. S., Buchan, N. R., Erez, M., & Gibson, C. B. (2005). Culture and international business: Recent advances and their implications for future research. *Journal of International Business Studies 36*(4), 359.

Lexicon Webster Dictionary. (1977). (Encyclopedic ed.). English-Language Institute of America, Inc.

Litka, M. (1988). *International dimensions of the legal environment for business.* Boston, MA: PWS-Kent.

Liu, M. (2006, April). War of wills. *Newsweek, 20.*

London under attack. (2005, July). *The Economist,* 9, 26, 62.

Loomis, C. J. (2006, July). The global force called the gates foundation. *Fortune, 37.*

Luo, Y. (2006). Political behavior, social responsibility, and perceived corruption: A structuration perspective. *Journal of International Business Studies 37*(6),747–766.

Lustgarten, A. (2006, July). Global 500. *Fortune, F-4.*

Lyons, D. (2002, April). Full disclosure. *Forbes Global, 19.*

Magnuson, P. (2005, March). States' rights vs. free trade. *BusinessWeek.*

Mandel, M. (2006, September). What's really propping up the economy. *Business Week,* 55–62.

Martin, E. W., DeHayes, D. W., Hoffer, J. A., & Perkins, W. C. (1994). *Managing information technology: What managers need to know.* New York, NY:, Macmillan Publishing Company.

Maslow, A. H. (1943). A theory of human motivation. *Psychological Review 50,* 370–396.

Maslow, A. H. (1954). *Motivation and personality.* New York, NY: Harper & Row.

Matlack et al (2005, October). Europe's hot growth companies. *BusinessWeek,* 58.

Matlack, C., Kripalani, M., Fairlamp, D., Edmondson, G., & Reinhardt, A. (2004, April). Job exports: Europe's turn. *BusinessWeek,* 20–24.

Matthews, O. (2006, August). Second thoughts. *Newsweek,* 30–31.

Matthews, O. (2006, December). Who lost Turkey? *Newsweek,* 34–36.

McGregor, D. (1960). *The human side of enterprise.* New York, NY: McGraw-Hill Books Company, Inc.

McLuhan, M. M. (1967). *La galaxie Gutenberg face à l'ere electronique.* Paris, France: Mame.

McNamee, M., Borus, A., & Palmeri, C. (2002, April). Out of control at Andersen. *Business Week,* 78–79.

Meacham, J. (2013, February). A papal benediction. *Time, 42.*

Michaelson, G. (2003). *Sun Tzu for success.* Avon, MA: Adams Media Publication.

Molavi, A. (2007, January). Dubai: Sudden city. *National Geographic,* 94–113.

Morgan, B. D. (1996). *Going global.* OH: Summit Publishing Company.

Morris, T. (1997). *If Aristotle Ran General Motors: The new soul of business.* New York, NY: Henty Holt and Company.

Morrison, T., Conaway, W. A., & Borden, G. A. (1994). *Kiss, or, or shake hands: How to do business in 60 countries.* Holbrook, MA: Bob Adams.

Moshin, H., & Zurawicki, L. (2002). Corruption and foreign direct investment. *Journal of International Business Studies 33*(2), 291–307.

Mueller, G. G. (1967). *International accounting.* New York, NY: MacMillan.

Nachum, L., & Song, S. (2011). The MNE as a portfolio: Interdependencies in MNE growth trajectory. *Journal of International Business Studies 42*(3), 381–405.

Northdurft, W. E. (1992). *Going global: How Europe helps small firms to export.* Washington, DC: The Brookings Institution.

Nussbaum, B. (2002, January). Can you trust anybody anymore. *Business Week,* 39–40.

Nussbaum, B. (2005, August). Get creative! How to build innovative companies. *Business Week,* 60.

Nussbaum, B. (2005, July). The best product design of 2005: Winners. *Business Week,* 52–62.

O' Malley, M. N. (2000). *Creating commitment.* New York, NY: John Wiley and Sons.

O' Neil, T. (2007, February). Curse of the black gold: Hope and betrayal in the Niger Delta. *National Geographic,* 88–117.

Ohmae, K. (1990). *The borderless world: Power and strategy in the interlinked economy.* New York, NY: Harper Business.

Orr, D. (2005, April). Don't wrap the veggies. *Forbes Global,* 18–23.

Orwell, G. (2008). *1984.* London, UK: Penguin Books.

Oumlil, B. (2003, August). *International alliances strategical decisions: An empirical study.* The 10th Recent Advances in Retailing & Services Science EIRASS Conference, Portland, Oregon.

Oumlil, B. (2005, February). *Global strategic business decisions: A comparative study of domestic & international outsourcing.* In P. Chakrapani (ed.), ASBBS 12th Annual Conference, Las Vegas, NV.

Oumlil, B., & Rao, C. P. (2005). Special issue on globalization and its challenges to marketing. *Journal of Marketing Theory & Practice 13*(4), 5–7.

Our precious planet. (1997, November). *Time,* 82.

Pasternack, B. A., & Viscio, A. J. (1998). *The centerless corporation: A new model for transforming your organization for growth and prosperity.* New York, NY: Simon and Schuster.

Peebles, D. M., & Ryans, Jr. J. K. (1984). *Management of international advertising: A marketing approach* (p. 80). Boston, MA: Allyn and Bacon, Inc.

Peterson, M. F., Arregle, J.-L., & Martin, X. (2012). Multilevel models in international business research. *Journal of International Business Studies 43*(5), 451–457.

The physical Internet: A survey of logistics. (2006, June). *The Economist.*

Pollalis, Y. A. (2003). Patterns of co-alignment in information-intensive organizations: business performance through integration strategies. *International Journal of Information Management 23,* 469–492.

Porter, M. E. (1990). *The competitive advantage of nations.* New York, NY: Free Press.

Quammen, D. (2005, September). Views of the continent. *National Geographic 208*(3), 2–35.

Rand, A. (1964). *The virtue of selfishness.* New York, NY: New American Library.

Reeb, D., Sakakibara, M., & Mahmood, I. P. (2012). From the editors: Endogeneity in international business research. *Journal of International Business Studies 43*(3), 211–218.

Reich, R. B. (2007). *Supercapitalism: The transformation of business, democracy and everyday life.* New York, NY: Random House.

Renault, N., & General Motors. (2006, July). Sayonara, general moteurs. *The Economist,* 57–58.

Rifkin, J. (2005). *The European dream: How Europe' vision of the future is quietly eclipsing the American dream.* Cambridge, UK: Polity Press.

Roberts, A. (2013, June). Why fired CEOs go straight back to the bank. *Bloomberg Businessweek,* 26–28.

Rodriguez, P., Siegel, D. S., Hillman, A., & Eden, L. (2006). Three levels of the multinational enterprise: Politics, corruption, and corporate social responsibility. *Journal of International Business Studies 43*(6), 733–746.

Rugman, A. M., & Verbeke, A. (2004). A perspective of regional and global strategies of multinational enterprises. *Journal of International Business Studies 35*(1), 3–18.

Santangelo, G. D., & Meyer, K. E. (2011). Increases and decreases of MNE commitment in emerging economies. *Journal of International Business Studies 42*(7), 894–909.

Sauer, C., Yetton, P. Y., & Associates. (1997). *Steps to the future.* San Francisco, CA: Jossey-Bass Publishers.

Schilder, A. (1996, December). Research opportunities in auditing in the European Union. *Accounting Horizons 10.*

Scientific American. (2011). *Questions about the multiverse: What lies beyond the cosmic horizon of 42 billion light-years.* Scientific American.

Shaffer, R., Earle, B., & Augusti, F. (1990). *International business law and its environment.* St. Paul, MN: West Publishing Company.

Shapiro, A. C. (1996). *Multinational financial management* (5th International ed.). London, UK: Prentice Hall.

Shipping world and shipbuilder. (2003/2004, December/January).

Shleifer, A., & Vishny, R. W. (1997). A survey of corporate governance. *Journal of Finance 52,* 737–783.

The short arm of the law. (2002, March). *The Economist,* 67.

Skelly, J. (1995, March–April). The caux round table: Principles for business, the rise of international ethics. *Business Ethics,* 2–5(supplement).

Sloan, A., & Isikof, M. (2008, January). The Enron effect. *Newsweek,* 40.

Special report on offshore financing. (2013, February). *The Economist,* 8.

Special report: Demography and the west. (2002, August). *The Economist,* 20–22.

Stone, R. (2006, April). The long shadow of Chernobyl. *National Geographic,* 38, 43.

Stutz, F. P., & de Souza, A. R. (1998). *The world economy: Resources, location, trade and development* (3rd ed.) (pp. 34–41). Upper Saddle River, NJ: Prentice -Hall.

A Survey of the new media: Among the audience. (2006, April). *The Economist,* 3.

Swartz, M. (2006, March). Survival of the richest. *National Geographic,* 148–154.

A tale of two bellies. (2002, August). *The Economist,* 11.

Technology quarterly. (2005, September). *The Economist,* 26.

Technology quarterly. (2006, December). *The Economist,* 13–27.

Technology quarterly. (2006, March). *The Economist,* 14–16.

Templar, R. (2005). *The rules of management.* Upper Saddle River, NJ: Financial Times Press.

Thanopoulos, J. (2007). *Global business: Environment, structure and challenges.* Athens, Greece: Interbooks.

Thanopoulos, J., co-authored with 185 of his Fall 2009 students. (2010). *The global manager: Self actualization perspectives* (1st electronic ed.). Athens, (in Greek): Interbooks.

Thanopoulos, J., & Schkade, L. L. (2000). Towards global entrepreneurialism. *North Central Business Journal 1*(7).

Thanopoulos, J., & Little, C. (1998). The brave new global enterprise. *Review of Business 20*(2).

Thanopoulos, N. (2014, second printing; first 1946). *Tales for young people who think they are political leaders* (in Greek). Athens, Greece, Fedimos Publishing

Thanopoulos, N. (2014, second printing; first 1946). *War impressions* (in Greek). Athens, Greece, Fedimos Publishing.

The Economist. (2000). *Pocket world in figures* (2001 ed.). London, UK: The Economist in association with Profiles Books, 22.

Theil, S. (2005, August). The next petroleum. *Newsweek*, 42–48.

Thiroux, J. (1998). *Ethics: Theory and practice* (6th ed.). Upper Saddle River, NJ: Prentice-Hall.

Thomas, E., & McGuire, S. (2005, July). Terror at rush hour. *Newsweek*, 14–22.

Thorell, P., & Whittington, G. (1994). The harmonization of accounting within the European Union: Problems, perspectives and strategies. *The European Accounting Review 3*(2), 215–240.

Tuathail, G. O., Dalby, S., & Routledge, P. (Eds.). (2006). *The geopolitics reader* (2nd ed.). London, UK: Routledge.

The Urantia book. (1955). Chicago, IL: The Urantia Foundation.

Wallace, S. (2007, January). Last of the Amazon. *National Geographic*, 40–71.

Warner, J., Engardio, P., & Peterson, T. (1999, February). The Atlantic century. *Business Week*.

Weber et al. (2002, January). Can Andersen survive. *Business Week*, 46–47.

Webster, D. (2002, January). China's unknown Gobi Alashan. *National Geographic,* 56.

Weiss, J. W. (2003). *Business ethics: A stakeholder and issues management approach* (3rd ed.) (pp. 213–315). Mason, OH: Thomson-South-Western.

Weitzel, U., & Berns, S. (2006). Cross-border takeovers, corruption, and related aspects of government. *Journal of International Business Studies 37*(6), 786–806.

Wells, J. (2005, October). Treating part-timers as royalty. *Business Week,* 52.

Westney, D. E., & Maanen, J. (2001). The causal ethnography of the executive suite. *Journal of International Business Studies 42*(5), 602–607.

A white-hot elephant. (2006, November). *The Economist,* 67.

Who are the champions? (2007, February). *The Economist,* 3.

William, A., Frank, M., & Moshe, V. Y. (Eds.). (2006). Globalization and offshoring of software. A Report of the ACM Job Migration Task Force, Association for Computing Machinery.

Williamson, J., & Mahar, M. (1998, November). *A survey of financial liberalization* (No. 211). Princeton, NJ: International Finance Section.

Wise, T. A. (1966, July). The very private world of Peat, Marwick, Mitchell. *Fortune,* 89.

Wolfe, A. (2001). It's all our fault. *Newsweek*, 48.

Woodall, P. (2006, September). The new Titans: A survey of the world economy. *The Economist*.

The world in 2012. (2002, September). *Newsweek*, 80–81.

Zakaria, F. (2001, December). A plan for global security. *Newsweek*, 16–17.

Zakaria, F. (2006, March). India rising. *Newsweek,* 31.

Zellner, W., & Anderson, S. F. (2002, January). A hero-and a smoking-gun letter. *BusinessWeek*, 42.

Zikmund, W. G., & d' Amico, M. (2001). *Marketing: Creating and keeping customers in an e-commerce world* (7th ed.) (pp. 281–283). Cincinnati, OH: South-Western College Publishing.

Index

SOLAS. *See* Safety of Life at Sea
Spot rate, 70
SRC. *See* Self-reference criterion
Statements of Financial Accounting
    Standards (SFAS), 100
Sun Tzu, 13, 116, 138, 145

Taniguchi, Ichiro, 138
Technology shapes philosophy
    death of family, 46
    emergence of global enterprise, 47
    media society, 47–48
    world of aging people, 46
Templar, Richard, 127
Thanopoulos, John, 185
Traditional economies, 66
Transfer risk, 54
Translation, 109
Treaty of Maastricht, 81
Turner, Ted, 171
A 28-Member Union, 83–84
21st Century, philosophical tenants,
    40–41
    agreements, 44
    civilization clashes, 43
    economic issues, 44
    farewell to isolation, 43
    global security, 43–44
    technology shapes philosophy,
        44–48
    unions of countries, 44
Typology of corporate cultures,
    142–143

UN Commission on Trade and
    Development (UNCTAD), 77
Uncontrollable variables, 49

UNCTAD. *See* UN Commission on
    Trade and Development
UNIDO. *See* UN Industrial
    Development Organization
Uniform accounting approach, 98
Uniformity *vs.* flexibility, 99
UN Industrial Development
    Organization (UNIDO), 77
United States, accounting standards,
    100–101
UNU. *See* UN University
UN University (UNU), 77
Urantia, 6

Vernon, Raymond, 61

Warranties, 119
WCL. *See* World Confederation of
    Labor
Wealth of Nations (Smith, Adam),
    61
Welch, Jack, 164, 167
Wennberg, Karl, 20
Wise, T. A., 9
Wolff, Michael, 34, 172
Woodall, Pam, 92
World Bank, 77–78
World Confederation of Labor
    (WCL), 151
World Trade Center, 54
World Trade Organization (WTO),
    77, 79–80
World War II, 3, 42, 74
WTO. *See* World Trade
    Organization

Zhang, 68

OTHER TITLES IN THE INTERNATIONAL BUSINESS COLLECTION

Tamer Cavusgil, Georgia State, Michael Czinkota, Georgetown, and Gary Knight, Florida State University, Editors

- *Successful Cross-Cultural Management: A Guide for International Managers* by Parissa Haghirian
- *Inside Washington: Government Resources for International Business, Sixth Edition* by William Delphos
- *Practical Solutions to Global Business Negotiations* by Claude Cellich and Subhash Jain
- *Trade Promotion Strategies: Best Practices* by Claude Cellich and Michel Borgeon
- *As I Was Saying...Observations on International Business and Trade Policy, Exports, Education, and the Future* by Michael Czinkota
- *China: Doing Business in the Middle Kingdom* by Stuart Strother
- *Essential Concepts of Cross-Cultural Management: Building on What We All Share* by Lawrence A. Beer
- *As the World Turns...Observations on International Business and Policy, Going International and Transition* by Michael Czinkota
- *Assessing and Mitigating Business Risks in India* by Balbir Bhasin
- *The Emerging Markets of the Middle East: Strategies for Entry and Growth* by Tim Rogmans
- *Doing Business in China Getting Ready for the Asian Century* by Jane Menzies, Mona Chung, and Stuart Orr
- *Burma: Business and Investment Opportunities in Emerging Myanmar* by Balbir B. Bhasin

Announcing the Business Expert Press Digital Library

Concise E-books Business Students Need for Classroom and Research

This book can also be purchased in an e-book collection by your library as
- a one-time purchase,
- that is owned forever,
- allows for simultaneous readers,
- has no restrictions on printing, and
- can be downloaded as PDFs from within the library community.

Our digital library collections are a great solution to beat the rising cost of textbooks. E-books can be loaded into their course management systems or onto students' e-book readers.

The **Business Expert Press** digital libraries are very affordable, with no obligation to buy in future years. For more information, please visit **www.businessexpertpress.com/librarians**. To set up a trial in the United States, please email **sales@businessexpertpress.com**.

www.ingramcontent.com/pod-product-compliance
Lightning Source LLC
Chambersburg PA
CBHW071641200326
41519CB00012BA/2355